THE VIRTUE OF WAR

RECLAIMING THE CLASSIC
CHRISTIAN TRADITIONS
EAST & WEST

Fr. Alexander F.C. Webster
Dr. Darrell Cole

"An important and timely contribution to one of the most important ecumenical debates of the early twenty-first century."

GEORGE WEIGEL
Senior Fellow & Director of the Catholic Studies Project
Ethics and Public Policy Center
Washington, D.C.

"While appeals to the idea of just war have been frequent in recent public debate over the use of armed force, little attention has been given to the way the Orthodox Christian tradition casts the conception of justifiable war or to how the legacy of Reinhold Niebuhr has been used in some Protestant circles to oppose just war thinking. This book usefully broadens the shape of reflection about just war and its implications by addressing both these critical matters and setting them in relation to Roman Catholic and Reformation Protestant just war thought, producing a genuinely comprehensive study of Christian tradition on the justification and limitation of war."

DR. JAMES TURNER JOHNSON
Professor of Religion
Rutgers University
New Brunswick, NJ

"In *The Virtue of War: Reclaiming the Classic Christian Traditions East and West* the authors deal with the intractable issues of peace and war from within the Christian Traditions of both Eastern and Western Christian thought. Webster and Cole make a strong case for their convictions that war by Christians can be virtuous and justifiable. They will probably not convince all their readers, but the evidence they offer together with their interpretations provide the reader a vigorous and rigorous argument that will certainly contribute to the ongoing debate."

V.REV. STANLEY S. HARAKAS
Archbishop Iakovos Professor of Orthodox Theology Emeritus
Holy Cross Greek Orthodox School of Theology
Brookline, MA

THE VIRTUE OF WAR
Reclaiming The Classic Christian Traditions East And West

Regina Orthodox Press Inc.
PO Box 5288
Salisbury MA 01952
USA

800 636 2470
Non-USA 978 462 7645

www.reginaorthodoxpress.com

ISBN 1-928653-17-0

ABOUT THE AUTHORS

Fr. Alexander F. C. Webster holds a B.A. degree in history (*Summa cum Laude* and *Phi Beta Kappa*) from the University of Pennsylvania, a Master of Arts in history and education from Columbia University, a Master of Theological Studies from Harvard University Divinity School, a Graduate Certificate in International Security Studies from the University of Pittsburgh, and a Ph.D. in religion / social ethics from the University of Pittsburgh. He serves concurrently as parish priest of St. Mary Orthodox Church in Falls Church, Virginia; as Associate Professorial Lecturer in the University Honors Program of The George Washington University; and as a Chaplain (Lieutenant Colonel) in the Virginia Army National Guard. His current assignment is Division Chaplain, 29th Infantry Division (Light), headquartered at Fort Belvoir, Virginia. His previous books include *The Pacifist Option: The Moral Argument Against War in Eastern Orthodox Theology* (Rowman & Littlefield, 1999); *The Price of Prophecy: Orthodox Churches on Peace, Freedom, and Security* (Ethics and Public Policy Center and William B. Eerdmans, 1995); and *The Romanian Legionary Movement: An Orthodox Christian Assessment of Anti-Semitism* (Carl Beck Papers, No. 503; University of Pittsburgh, 1986).

Dr. Darrell Cole holds a B.A. degree in philosophy from Lynchburg College, a Master of Arts in philosophy from Ohio University, a Master of Religion in ethics from Yale Divinity School, a Master of Theology from Duke Divinity School, and a Ph.D. in religion from the University of Virginia. He has previously taught at the College of William and Mary and is currently Assistant Professor of Religion at Drew University in Madison, New Jersey. He is the author of *When God Says War Is Right* (Waterbrook, 2002).

The Virtue of War: Reclaiming the Classic Christian Traditions East and West

Our way of life here in the West is currently under assault, and Western Civilization itself hangs in the balance. The war against Islamic terrorism, which began officially on September 11, 2001 ("Nine-Eleven"), has already led to two unfinished military campaigns in the Middle East: one in Afghanistan and the other in Iraq. In these dangerous times, more than ever, Christians need to look for guidance in the classic Christian traditions on war—both Eastern and Western. But Christians also need to reclaim the great moral teachings on war and peace from the contemporary revisionists who would have Christians believe it is necessary to choose a "lesser evil" for a good cause or as a way of being "responsible" citizens of a nation-state.

Professors Webster and Cole boldly accept those challenges in this book. They explore in detail the great moral teachings found in Holy Scripture, the ancient and Byzantine Church Fathers, canon law, manuals of penance, lives of the saints, liturgical texts, visual icons, the medieval Scholastics, the great Reformers, and even among modern theologians and literary authors. And they present a powerful, genuinely ecumenical, meticulously documented, incontrovertible case on behalf of the moral teachings known to Eastern Orthodox, Roman Catholic, and Protestant Christians as the just or justifiable war traditions. Together these classic traditions provide consistent, sound reasoning for why *some* wars are virtuous enterprises and ought to be pursued as a *good* (not an "evil"), and why other wars are vicious enterprises that ought to be rejected as evil. These traditions also enable Christians to determine when certain acts in a just or justifiable war are incompatible with virtue or holy living, and thus can never be allowed in a war to which Christians may give assent.

The classic Christian traditions—East and West—sound a clarion call for virtue in war. Wisdom, justice, courage, self-control, mercy, and patience should—and can—be displayed prominently in wars that are justifiable or just. The virtuous have nothing to be ashamed of when they act virtuously. And that includes contemporary soldiers who fight virtuously in a just or justifiable war, and all those on the home front who support them.

This book provides a firm biblical, theological, and historical foundation for that confidence.

TABLE OF CONTENTS

PREFACE

A collaborative work such as the present volume poses a number of intellectual challenges: different, and possibly conflicting, religious identities, scholarly priorities, and writing styles, to name a few. However, we are convinced that these potential differences pale in significance before what we share in common as Christian theologians and observers of the current geopolitical situation. The supreme urgency of the war against terrorism and the dire necessity of reclaiming the great moral traditions on war and peace from the revisionists in both the Eastern and Western Christian communities who have highjacked them have brought us together for this project.

We would like to think it was providential, not merely a happy coincidence, that our parallel thinking on justifiable war as a virtue tradition led to our initial encounter at the College of William & Mary in the autumn of 2001, where one of us was teaching as a visiting professor and the other had a son enrolled as a freshman. It was also no accident that Frank Schaeffer proposed this project in April 2003, when Fr. Alexander called to commend him for his op-ed on the Orthodox Peace Fellowship in the *Washington Post*. The Lord does, indeed, work in mysterious ways, even in the world of book publishing.

Collaborative works tend to have more shortcomings than virtues, and we wish to acknowledge the former up front, as it were. Although we have read and contributed to each other's work in these pages and, consequently, own the contents of the entire book, the chapters remain primarily the product of one or the other of us. Thus Fr. Alexander is the author of Chapters 1, 3, 4, and 5, as well as the first half of Chapter 2. Professor Cole is the author of Chapters 6, 7, 8, and 9, as well as the second half of Chapter 2. Not only have we decided to leave our respective writing styles and endnote citations virtually intact; we have also allowed some relatively minor substantive differences to stand. For example, the key virtue in the

Eastern Orthodox justifiable war trajectory is justice, while charity (love) is the defining virtue of the Western Christian just war tradition. We have even retained our preferred labels for the parallel traditions: just war (West) and justifiable war (East).

It should also become quickly apparent that our respective methodologies differ somewhat. The "Orthodox" chapters are organized in terms of the six components of the Orthodox moral tradition in general: Holy Scripture, the Church fathers, canon law, lives of the saints, liturgical texts and visual icons, and modern theologians and literary authors. The "Western" (that is, Roman Catholic and Protestant) chapters are devoted in sequence to six historic figures in Western Christianity: the Latin Church fathers St. Ambrose of Milan and St. Augustine; the medieval Roman Catholic theologian St. Thomas Aquinas; and three Protestant theologians from the Reformation era, Martin Luther, John Calvin, and Hugo Grotius. The concluding chapter applies the (primarily Western) penitential tradition to the practice of just war in general and, in particular, to the most recent military operations of the United States in Afghanistan and Iraq.

These divergences may seem a little unsettling at times, or leave the impression of two books sandwiched together. But we are confident that the common teaching that at least some wars are not only just or justifiable, but also virtuous and good—instead of "evil"—moral actions, will become equally apparent as the reader moves from East to West in the pages of this book. Despite our sometimes divergent theologies, methodologies, and emphases, what unites us in respecting the virtue of war is, at once, surprising and reassuring. Christianity may be divided along historical East-West lines, but the deepest moral chasm separates those who affirm our classic common heritage of virtue in war and those who insist, incomprehensibly against the textual evidence and against history itself, that no war may be more than a "necessary" or "lesser" evil.

No scholarly endeavor is pursued alone, especially a collaborative effort like this book, and so we wish to express our gratitude to those persons and institutions who have provided invaluable assistance.

In particular, Fr. Alexander thanks Ashgate Publishing Limited in England and *St. Vladimir's Theological Quarterly* (for permission to expand previous versions of the specifically Orthodox content of this book); Gelman Library at The George Washington University; the parishioners of St. Mary Orthodox Church in Falls Church, Virginia (for not complaining too often while their pastor vanished for a day or two every now and then to research and write his chapters); the officers and enlisted soldiers of the U.S. Army and the Army National Guard, with whom he has served in uniform and whose dedicated service to God and country epitomize the virtuous warrior; and last, but certainly not least, his wife Kathleen, a living exemplar of the more pacific virtues of patience and forbearance.

Professor Cole thanks James F. Childress, G. Scott Davis, Stanley Hauerwas, Charles T. Mathewes, and Eugene F. Rogers (for helpful comments on earlier versions of the material that appear in Chapters 6, 7, and 8) and the Drew University Library (and in particular Suzanne Selinger, the Theological Librarian).

As is usually the case, any errors or shortcomings in this book are entirely the fault of the authors, for which we ask forgiveness and a lenient penance.

Fr. Alexander F.C. Webster, Ph.D.
Woodbridge, Virginia

Professor Darrell Cole, Ph.D.
Madison, New Jersey

October 18, 2003

CHAPTER 1

Civilization and Its (Terrorist) Discontents

To say that the perennial, intractable political conflicts in the Middle East have attained biblical proportions may sound trite. And yet it is true. Places and personal names familiar to any devout Christian or Jew—Jerusalem and Damascus, the Tigris and Euphrates, Abraham and Nebuchadnezzar—pepper the news and seem to be on everyone's mind in the heretofore distant, safe, immune North American continent. Since the atrocities now commonly referred to as "Nine-Eleven," those conflicts in the Levant have become, for Americans no less than others on this planet, truly global, which means they may equal or even exceed the merely "biblical" in magnitude.

A Defining Moment

The terrorist attacks via civilian airliners in New York City, Washington, D.C., and southwest Pennsylvania on September 11, 2001, ("Nine-Eleven") constitute arguably a defining moment for the entire nation of America. That date has been indelibly etched into the consciousness of the present generation much as the assassination of President John F. Kennedy on November 22, 1963, and the Japanese attack on Pearl Harbor on December 7, 1941, affected previous generations for the remainder of their lives. For those of us who are citizens of the United States, "Nine-Eleven" has certainly assumed biblical proportions.

When the Apostle Paul proclaims to the Church in Galatia, "I have been crucified with Christ" (Galatians 2:20, RSV), it is quite obvious he is speaking spiritually. "It is no longer I who live," he continues, "but Christ who lives in me." This is a deeply mystical union, but one in which the Apostle's identity as a personal subject endures. In the morning hours of Tuesday, September 11, 2001,

1

America was crucified with Christ. This was no inward, spiritual event alone. It was a rapid series of atrocities in the realm of flesh and blood, of steel and stone, of the very physical and tangible—a sundering of the sinews of civilization. On that bright, sunny, still summery morning, hidden, sinister agents of darkness stormed heaven itself through their suicidal descent to the earth. Having seized their innocent human cargoes, they forfeited their own humanity. Having sought to obliterate others, they found only the oblivion of the damned.

On "Nine-Eleven," Christ was crucified with America, in the persons of the multitudes who perished. Words fail us here. Human language reaches its limits. The lives of some 3,000 human beings were instantly snuffed out in fiery collisions or crumbling monoliths.

Some 3,000 human beings: the number is too big to fathom. A small town in America? Half of an ancient Roman legion of troops? The multitudes who heard the Sermon on the Mount in Israel? Some 3,000 human beings: still, despite the extraordinarily poignant media coverage and innumerable memorials, mostly anonymous souls to most Americans, who have probably forgotten what few of the many names we heard and commemorated in our hearts in the immediate aftermath of the atrocities.

On the third day following "Nine-Eleven," President George W. Bush invoked those names in an eloquent sermon at the Washington Cathedral:

> They are the names of men and women who began their day at a desk or in an airport, busy with life. They are the names of people who faced death, and in their last moments called home to say, be brave, and I love you.
>
> They are the names of passengers who defied their murderers, and prevented the murder of others on the ground. They are the names of men and women who wore the uniform of the United States, and died at their posts.

> They are the names of rescuers, the ones whom death found running up the stairs and into the fires to help others. We will read all these names. We will linger over them, and learn their stories, and many Americans will weep.[1]

Americans did, indeed, weep in unison for our cities in distress, like T. S. Elliot, the Englishman whose poem "The Wasteland" in 1922 presaged our current plight:

> What is that sound high in the air
> Murmur of maternal lamentation
> Who are those hooded hordes swarming
> Over endless plains, stumbling in cracked earth
> Ringed by the flat horizon only
> What is the city over the mountains
> Cracks and reforms and bursts in the violet air
> Falling towers
> Jerusalem   Athens   Alexandria
> Vienna   London
> Unreal[2]

We did more than weep, however. On September 11, 2001, America was shocked beyond belief. By Friday of that week, America was saddened beyond endurance. By Sunday, America was angry beyond measure. The terrorists had awakened the sleeping giant once again. Slow to anger, but irascible and ruthless when disturbed, America has not always demonstrated proper restraint in the pursuit of international justice in time of war. America has not always been on the side of the angels. But America has become truly great, because our people are fundamentally decent. And this was an assault on Americans, whether civilian or military at the Pentagon, who were merely carrying out their routine daily activities, sinners before God but innocent of any charge that might have warranted such a terrorist enormity. Dr. Martin Luther King, Jr., was fond of saying that all innocent suffering is somehow redemptive. The sufferings and deaths of the victims of "Nine-Eleven" added nothing,

3

of course, to the unique, salvific sacrifice of Christ. Yet, through their sad demise and the inspirational examples of heroism by victims and rescuers alike on that fateful occasion, especially in contrast to the horror of the circumstances and the abounding hate of its perpetrators, the sacrifice of Christ at the hands of His self-proclaimed enemies was made palpable yet again.

For one, unhappily brief, Camelot season, Americans were treated to a miracle of national unity. In that very abnormal time, out of the depths of our national pain and sorrow, the fundamental virtue of the American citizenry began to shine through the dust clouds over downtown Manhattan and the charred, gaping wound in the Pentagon. As the noble, relentless rescuers continued to dig, like careful archaeologists, through rubble and debris, we heard over and over again the stirring sound of bagpipes piercing the air for stricken firemen and police officers—as well as haunting choruses of "Amazing Grace" and mournful melodies of many religions *in memoriam* for *thousands* of others. There was also the reverberation of refrains of "God Bless America" and spontaneous, off-key renditions of the "Star Spangled Banner." Patriotism was no longer unfashionable. The "Stars & Stripes" was everywhere to be seen, proudly and defiantly unfurled in front of homes, hanging from highway overpasses, displayed on store and car windows. A common national purpose and fellowship bonded the American people, almost like Christmastime, when people are friendlier, more courteous, and even deferential to one another. But as the Christmas season each year gives way too soon to the normal nastiness of the New Year, so Americans soon let go of the embrace of the spirit of "Nine-Eleven," and it was the usual politics and cultural conflict as the order of the day. Our national redemption, as it were, by the innocent suffering on that fateful day proved short-lived, merely a season. And yet we stand in the shadow of the collective cross of "Nine-Eleven," even as the once majestic Twin Towers once stood in the shadow of the cross and cupola of little St. Nicholas Greek Orthodox Church half a block away.

"Nine-Eleven" has secured a place alongside other recent events with unique global significance. Among the glorious turning points in modern history are the two moments that marked the demise of Soviet communism: the dismantling of the Berlin Wall beginning in November 1989 and erstwhile Communist *apparatchik* Boris Yeltsin atop a tank amidst the anti-Soviet rebels on August 21, 1991. On the darker side, the atomic bombings of Hiroshima and Nagasaki on August 6 and 9, 1945, ushered in the nuclear era with its constant threat of the mass annihilation of civilian populations. The toll in human life on "Nine-Eleven" hardly approaches the tens of thousands in the Japanese cities; but, like those abominations, the atrocities committed by the Islamic terrorists signaled a new era of barbarism and possibly limitless casualties among innocent civilians. The potent symbolism of "Nine-Eleven," particularly the audacious assault on the architectural icons of contemporary commerce and military might (as well as political power, if the aborted terrorist mission of the highjacked United Airlines flight 93 was intended for the White House or the Capitol building), also hearkens back to an ancient turning point. In A.D. 410, the barbarian Vandals sacked Rome, sending a shockwave throughout the Roman Empire, including northern Africa. There, St. Augustine of Hippo was inspired by that unprecedented blow to the *imperium* to write his magnum opus, *The City of God*, as a spiritual encouragement to Christians suddenly aware of their vulnerability to hostile forces and Rome's temporal fragility.

That leads us to the present predicament of Western civilization in general and of America in particular. "Nine-Eleven" brought to these shores the deadly threat of international Islamic terrorism, which has already plagued the Middle East and much of the Eastern Hemisphere for more than a decade. It is almost as if this latest global scourge took the baton from Soviet communism, which,

5

in turn, displaced European fascism as the most lethal ideological assault on the civilized people and institutions of the West.

Terrorism is obviously the infliction of terror on intended victims. Since the "reign of terror" during the French Revolution, when thousands of aristocrats and anyone opposed or merely thought to be opposed to the *nouveau regime* had to endure the guillotine in the name of *liberté, egalité, fraternité* (in other words, revolutionary ideological purity), terror has been the preferred method of those who are otherwise unable to assert their will on peoples and states through a more conventional exercise of armed force. The common goal of such terrorists, whether solitary snipers and bomb-throwers or organized rogue groups, is to generate a paralyzing fear in their intended targets. Michael Walzer of the Institute for Advanced Studies at Princeton University provides a concise description in his classic 1977 study, *Just and Unjust War*:

> The systematic terrorizing of whole populations is a strategy of both conventional and guerilla war, and of established governments as well as radical movements. Its purpose is to destroy the morale of a nation or a class, to undercut its solidarity; its method is the random murder of innocent people. Randomness is the crucial feature of terrorist activity. If one wishes fear to spread and intensify over time, it is not desirable to kill specific people identified in some particular way with a regime, a party, or a policy. Death must come by chance to individual Frenchmen, or Germans, or Irish Protestants, or Jews, simply because they are Frenchmen or Germans, Protestants or Jews, until they feel themselves fatally exposed and demand that their governments negotiate for their safety.[3]

In their peculiar extremism, the current crop of international Islamic terrorists—such as the al-Qaeda organization responsible for "Nine-Eleven"—exceed even the radical fanaticism depicted by Walzer with their manifest disinterest in negotiation with any government or individual. We are confronted by an evil so base as to

6

defy description; an evil that cannot be swayed by logic or kindness or good intentions; an evil that, as President Timothy Sullivan of the College of William & Mary said to a gathering of shocked and anxious students on the night of "Nine-Eleven," "delights in the doubts of the righteous." This is a uniquely anarchic, nihilistic form of terrorism that seeks no settlement with the hated Americans and Western civilization, no redress of grievances or solution to a problem. Al-Qaeda and other like-minded Islamic extremist groups wish only to destroy "the Great Satan," to annihilate our citizens— one by one, or by the thousands if possible, but all of us in the end— unless we eradicate all offensive elements in our own civilization and adopt wholesale their narrow version of Islam and Islamic "civilization." Al-Qaeda, its minions, and the various and sundry Muslim-dominated or -influenced states (most notably Saddam Hussein's Iraq) that provide aid and comfort to the Islamic terrorist organizations intend to kill as many Western civilians as possible and to terrorize the rest[4] to keep us in a perpetual state of anxiety over the next surprise assault. Thereby they endeavor to destabilize the U.S. government, the governments of historic allies such as the United Kingdom, and perhaps the entire world community, if the "suicide" truck bombing (that is, more properly, homicide bombing) of the building housing the United Nations representatives in Baghdad on August 19, 2003, provides any clue.

Terrorism or "Crescade"?

How widespread is this new global threat of international Islamic terrorism, and how typical is it of Islam as a world religion? Simply to raise the latter question is to incur the risk of a hasty dismissal by the ecumenical and scholarly communities, while having to suffer all sorts of unpleasant epithets, such as "intolerant" or even "bigoted." Nonetheless, the post-"Nine-Eleven" world is so unstable, with Western civilization itself hanging in the balance, that we would be academically and morally derelict to avoid the question.

Since "Nine-Eleven", Americans have been subjected to a barrage of assurances that Islam is a religion of "peace and tolerance."[5] That this veritable mantra has been uttered by President George W. Bush, countless scholars of religion (both Muslim and non-Muslim) and political pundits, Hollywood celebrities such as Oprah Winfrey, and numerous ordinary citizens may seem to lend it an aura of authenticity. But Orthodox Christians certainly know better than most the potential danger that millions of Muslim believers may pose to Christians and Jews in this country and throughout the world.

It is not merely the obvious extremists like al-Qaeda and its ilk who ought to be of concern to us. Experts in comparative religion such as Charles A. Kimball caution us against vicious stereotypes. The vast majority of Muslims in the world were presumably outraged by the indiscriminate violence perpetrated on September 11, 2001, against New York City and the Pentagon by the al-Qaeda terrorists, who ignored the proscriptions in the Qur'an against suicide and violence upon innocent human life.[6] Islam, like other world religions, is hardly monolithic: there are "denominations" in the Western sense ranging from the mainstream Sunnis to the mystical Sufis, factions within each of those communities, and a kaleidoscopic variety of cultural manifestations, as the anthropologist Clifford Geertz has demonstrated, in such diverse ethno-political settings as Morocco and Indonesia.[7] Obviously, not all Muslims are fundamentalists, nor are all Muslim fundamentalists extremists. The Muslim extremism expressed so brazenly by al-Qaeda's public statement on October 9, 2001, is not typical of Islam: "those youths who did what they did and destroyed America with their airplanes did a good deed … The Americans must know that by invading the land of Afghanistan they have opened a new page of enmity and struggle between us and the forces of the unbelievers."[8] And yet the extremists who share Osama bin Laden and al-Qaeda's twisted Islamic antipathy toward the West still form a sizable contingent. As political columnist Diana West observes sardonically: "The experts tell us militant Islamic fundamentalists, or 'Islamists,' represent a narrow, if murderous, fringe. They number no more than 10, maybe 15, percent of all Muslims. That works out to somewhere between 100 million and 150 million people. Which is a lot of murderous fringe."[9]

Although it may be politically incorrect to say so, the history of Islam since its inception in the seventh century has been one long story of conquest and reconquest. It began with an incredibly swift sweep through the Arabian Desert and peninsula led by the prophet Muhammad himself—uniquely a warrior among the founders of world religions. After the founder's death, Islam engulfed in rapid succession Antioch and Syria, the Holy Land, Egypt, the whole of North Africa, Spain and southern France all the way to the gates of Paris, and eventually Asia Minor, Constantinople and the dwindling Byzantine Empire, the Balkans, and Eastern Europe all the way to the gates of Vienna—not to mention the eastward thrust through Persia, the Caucasus region, and the rest of Asia all the way to the Indonesian archipelago. The term "conquest" is not an exaggeration. No less reliable a classical Muslim source than Ahmad bin Yahya al-Baladhuri attests to this phenomenon in his ninth-century compilation, *Kitab Futuh al-Buldan* ("Book of Conquests of the Lands").[10]

In almost every instance this new faith was spread largely through intimidation and coercion and usually through military means, especially through what is familiar to us as "holy" war—a trend that continued through the last century to the present moment. Muslim scholars such as Hilmi M. Zawati may continue to insist that "Muslim jurists did not justify wars for such worldly purposes as territorial expansion, imposing their religion on unbelievers, or supporting a particular social regime."[11] But John Kelsay, a non-Muslim scholar sympathetic toward Islam, is compelled by the evidence to concede that for "classical, especially Sunni, scholars,

9

the norm was offensive war, at the command and by the direction of the caliph" (in Baghdad) "as a useful means of extending the territory of Islam and thus a tool in the quest for peace"[12] (albeit a *Pax Islamica*). Even more damning is the assessment of Bassam Tibi, a Muslim scholar in the field of international relations:

> [The] Western distinction between just and unjust wars linked to specific grounds for war is unknown in Islam. Any war against unbelievers, whatever its immediate ground, is morally justified. Only in this sense can one distinguish just and unjust wars in Islamic tradition. When Muslims wage war for the dissemination of Islam, it is a just war. ... When non-Muslims attack Muslims, it is an unjust war. The usual Western interpretation of *jihad* as a "just war" in the Western sense is, therefore, a misreading of this Islamic concept.[13]

In another essay, Tibi frames the issue in its peculiarly religious geopolitical context. Islam from its inception has propounded a

> worldview based on the distinction between the abode of Islam (dar al-Islam), the "home of peace" (dar al-Salam) (Qur'an, Jon. 10.25), and the non-Muslim world, the "house of war" (dar al-harb). ... The establishment of the new Islamic polity at Medina and the spread of the new religion were accomplished by waging war. The sword became the symbolic image of Islam in the West.[14]

In the 1996 book-length version of his seminal essay, "Clash of Civilizations?" Samuel Huntington of Harvard University brings the story up to date:

> Wherever one looks along the perimeter of Islam, Muslims have problems living peaceably with their neighbors. The question naturally rises as to whether this pattern of late-twentieth-century conflict between Muslim and non-Muslim groups is equally true of relations between groups from other civilizations. In fact, it is not. Muslims make up about one-fifth of the world's population

but in the 1990s they have been far more involved in intergroup violence than the people of any other civilization. The evidence is overwhelming.[15]

Orthodox Christians, in particular, are well acquainted with this legacy of religious intolerance, the popular claims to the contrary notwithstanding. We need only read *The Bridge on the Drina*, a gripping, historically accurate novel written in 1945 by Nobel-laureate Ivo Andric (a Bosnian Serb, no less) to learn how the Ottoman Turks stole young Orthodox boys from their mothers' arms and turned them into Muslim Jannisaries to guard the Sultan, or how they punished rebellious Serbs and other subjugated Christians in the Balkans by sadistic impalement.[16] Or we may consider the unequivocal judgment of the great Church father, St. Gregory Palamas, who refuted the claims of his Turkish captors in 14th-century Thessalonika that their prophet was the fulfillment of the messianic hope revealed in Matthew 24:27:

> It is true that Mohammed started from the east and came to the west, as the sun travels from the east to west. Nevertheless, he came with war, knives, pillaging, forced enslavement, murders, and acts that are not from the good God, but instigated by the chief manslayer, the devil ... Though Mohammed may employ violence and offer pleasures, he cannot secure the approval of the world.[17]

Lest anyone object that even this consistent historical record fails to abide by the original teachings and intent of Islam, let us turn to the Qur'an itself. What we find in that foundational religious text is a moral code of war that echoes elements of the Old Testament *harem* or "ban"—total "holy" war against the perceived enemy, including women and children—but bears little, if any, semblance to the New Testament. To be sure, the Qur'anic concept of *jihad* is not the simplistic, war-mongering militarism that has seized the popular imagination in the West. Nor is it synonymous with the

11

indiscriminate, unlimited violence advocated by Osama bin Laden and his ilk. Literally "struggle" or "effort," the Arabic *jihad* refers primarily to the struggle within the heart of the Muslim believer to conform his will to that of Allah, and only secondarily to the use of military force "to extend the boundaries of the territory of Islam, and thus to extend the influence of Islamic values."[18] Another Arabic term, *qital* (usually translated as "fighting" or "warfare"), often expresses the military, physically violent dimension of the concept of *jihad*. In an early *sura*, or chapter, the Qur'an itself acknowledges that such strife and violence may be disagreeable to Muslims: "Fighting (*qital*) is obligatory for you, much as you dislike it. But you may hate a thing although it is good for you …" (*Sura* 2:216).[19] All the more, then, would Christians and Jews in America find *jihad,* much less *qital,* as it appears in the Qur'an quite appalling.

A sampling of passages from various s*uras* should illustrate the qualities of *jihad* as holy war according to the quadripartite typology of what Protestant theologian Edward LeRoy Long, Jr., has labeled the "war ethic of the crusade," as distinguished from the "justifiable war" tradition. Long detected four peculiar characteristics: (1) religious motivation as the sole, or at least primary, justification for military action; (2) "extrinsic religious rewards" (such as a plenary forgiveness of sins or admission to Paradise as a martyr) for the soldier's work; (3) an erosion of restraints against hostility toward the enemy (including noncombatants such as women and children); and (4) an absolutist spirit that tends to justify all means, however extreme or otherwise immoral, to achieve objectives.[20]

First, there are verses in the Qur'an that stress a **supreme religious motivation** for war or violence:

- "Fight against them [i.e., unbelievers] until idolatry is no more and God's religion reigns supreme." (*Sura* 2:193; cf. 8:39)

- "The true believers fight for the cause of God, but the infidels fight for the devil. Fight then against the friends of Satan." (*Sura* 4:76)

- "Fight against such of those to whom the Scriptures were given [i.e., Christians and Jews] as believe in neither God nor the Last Day, who do not forbid what God and His apostle have forbidden, and do not embrace the true Faith, until they pay tribute out of hand and are utterly subdued." (*Sura* 9:29)

Second, there are verses that promise **religious rewards**:

- "God has purchased from the faithful their lives and worldly goods, and in return has promised them the Garden [i.e., Paradise]. They will fight for the cause of God, they will slay and be slain." (*Sura* 9:111)

- "Prophet, We have made lawful for you the wives to whom you have granted dowries and the slave-girls whom God has given you as booty [i.e., spoils of war]." (*Sura* 35:50)

- "As for those who are slain in the cause of God, He will not allow their works to perish. He will vouchsafe them guidance and ennoble their state; He will admit them to the Paradise He has made known to them." (*Sura* 47:6)

Third, there are verses that speak of Islam's enemies with **unrestrained hostility**:

- "Those that make war against God and His apostle and spread disorder in the land shall be slain or crucified or have their hands and feet cut off on alternate sides, or be banished from the land. They shall be held up to shame in this world and sternly punished

13

in the hereafter." (*Sura* 5:34)

- "Prophet, make war on the unbelievers and the hypocrites and deal rigorously with them. Hell shall be their home: an evil fate." (*Sura* 9:73)

- "We have indulged them [unbelievers] and their fathers, so that they have lived too long. Can they not see how We invade their land and diminish its borders?" (*Sura* 21:44)

Finally, there are verses that exhort Muhammad and Muslims to employ all **expedient means:**

- "Muster against them [i.e., unbelievers] all the men and cavalry at your command, so that you may strike terror into the enemy of God and your enemy ... All that you give in the cause of God shall be repaid to you." (*Sura* 8:60, 61)

- "When the sacred months are over slay the idolaters wherever you find them. Arrest them, besiege them, and lie in ambush everywhere you find them. If they repent and take to prayer and render the alms levy, allow them to go their way." (*Sura* 9:5)

- "When you meet the unbelievers in the battlefield strike off their heads and, when you have laid them low, bind your captives firmly. Then grant them their freedom or take a ransom from them, until War shall lay down her burdens." (*Sura* 47:4)

Although these Qur'anic verses are offered without full and proper consideration of their contexts or chronological sequence (a task beyond the scope of this book), their moral significance is still quite clear. Devout Muslims claim, rather boldly, that the Qur'an contains, in the original Arabic, the literal—hence infallible—words

14

of Allah as revealed to Muhammad by the Archangel Gabriel. Thus the full, brutal impact of this direct revelation (even in the supposedly unworthy, corrupting language of English) can be neither denied nor deconstructed. In the aggregate, the selected verses provide sufficient evidence to conclude that Islam is a religion that was conceived and born in violence. Even the Muslim scholar Majid Khadduri would agree with our thesis that *jihad* is equivalent to the Western concept of the crusade.[21]

Long ago, at the Peace of Westphalia in 1648, Western Christianity abandoned its religiously motivated holy wars or crusades, and Orthodox Christianity never embraced them in theory or practice (with a few deviant exceptions).[22] In stark contrast, the entire history of Islam has been, to coin a term, one long "crescade" against unbelievers—Christians and Jews as well as pagans. The term is shorthand for crusade for the crescent moon, the perennial symbol of Islam. Orthodox Christians and the Western world in general remain in a state of perpetual peril in our encounter with Islam. It would be in our own best interest to maintain a constant vigilance toward Islam in general and to steel our resolve to defend Western civilization from the more militant, violent extremists who populate the ranks of international Islamic terrorist organizations spearheaded by al-Qaeda.

Fighting Back

Fortunately, the war on the West launched by the latter has been joined by what President George W. Bush famously calls the "coalition of the willing." In a gradual, measured, efficient build-up of military forces in the region, coupled with skilled politicking of the U.S. Congress and deft international diplomacy, the Bush administration forcefully removed the Taliban regime in Afghanistan in autumn 2001 and subsequently toppled Saddam Hussein and his Ba'athist Party in Iraq in April 2003. Notwithstanding the political wrangling and moral controversies that each of those military

15

operations generated in the American public square, both ventures may be deemed stunning military successes, at least in terms of the conduct of the hostilities in the short-run.[23]

In both operations, particularly the three-week American *blitzkrieg* leading to the fall of Baghdad, to put a twist on one of Winston Churchill's memorable remarks after the Battle of Britain in World War II, never has so much been accomplished so ethically by so few in so short a time. If the systematic destruction of the ruthless Taliban, with the concurrent decimation of al-Qaeda's main camps and operations in the cities and mountain ranges of Afghanistan, defied the historical odds and silenced the many Cassandras in the major media, the veritable race across the desert and complete dismantling of Saddam's terror-regime and its vaunted Republican Guard in a scant three weeks was truly breathtaking. Although the toll in civilian casualties in each case will probably remain a bone of contention between supporters and critics of the president's policies—a reasonable, impartial estimate of the deaths in Afghanistan would range between 1,000 and 2,000[24]—what's perfectly clear to the vast majority of Americans is the categorical difference between the United States and its allies, on one hand, and the Islamic terrorists and their sponsoring governments, on the other hand, in their policies toward civilians as potential targets. The terrorists exult in harming civilians by any means available—from crude, so-called suicide bombings to sophisticated weapons of mass destruction, which certainly include the possibility of biological and chemical agents and, in the ultimate, though still hypothetical, nightmarish scenario, nuclear devices. The "coalition of the willing" strains to halt and even preempt such atrocities without responding in kind by adamantly refusing to target civilians and minimizing such unintended casualties, especially through extraordinary risk-taking and vulnerability on the part of the soldiers and marines on the ground.

Despite the inherent disproportionality entailed in combat

16

between those who valiantly attempt to abide by classic moral standards and those who cast off all moral restraints, the decisive military victory in Iraq demonstrated that moral principle and military success may go hand-in-hand. In a speech aboard the USS Abraham Lincoln, an aircraft carrier off the coast of California on May 1, 2003, President Bush painted a hopeful picture indeed:

> In the images of fallen statues we have witnessed the arrival of a new era. For a hundred of years of war, culminating in the nuclear age, military technology was designed and deployed to inflict casualties on an ever-growing scale.
>
> In defeating Nazi Germany and Imperial Japan, Allied forces destroyed entire cities, while enemy leaders who started the conflict were safe until the final days. Military power was used to end a regime by breaking a nation.
>
> Today we have the greater power to free a nation by breaking a dangerous and aggressive regime.
>
> With new tactics and precision weapons, we can achieve military objectives without directing violence against civilians.
>
> No device of man can remove the tragedy from war, yet it is a great advance when the guilty have far more to fear from war than the innocent.[25]

Out of the ashes of "Nine-Eleven" a new way of warfare has, like the proverbial phoenix, ascended and raised the armed forces of this nation and the United Kingdom to an unprecedented standard of moral virtue. First in Afghanistan and then in Iraq, those armed forces (and the contingents of other nations in minor supporting roles) have pursued justice with relentless determination and unflagging zeal—not in a spirit of anger, or revenge, or bloodlust, but rather with all deliberate speed, and even temperament, and

17

sharpened focus on doing the *right* thing for the *right* reasons and in the *right* way.

To be sure, the victorious military operations in Afghanistan and Iraq represent successful battles or campaigns in a protracted war against terrorism, as President Bush and Prime Minister Tony Blair of the United Kingdom have repeatedly reminded their respective national constituencies and the United Nations. Neither al-Qaeda nor the last vestiges of Saddam Hussein's radical *Feddayin* have, at this writing, been eradicated as terrorist threats to the Western powers and Western civilization. Other Islamic terrorist organizations such as Hamas and Islamic Jihad continue to thrive despite the best efforts of the state of Israel to neutralize them. The tentacles of international terrorism continue to reach every part of the globe, including the Central American nation of Honduras, which has joined the "coalition of the willing" in response to international terrorists within its own borders by sending a small military contingent to Iraq as part of the "stabilization force" following the toppling of Saddam Hussein's regime. The next phase and venue of the war against terrorism is anyone's guess; perhaps it will involve Iran or Syria, although we should hope that both of these Muslim states will renounce and cut all ties to extremist Islamic terrorist groups, thereby removing any grounds for military intervention by the anti-terrorist coalition. Meanwhile, the seemingly interminable conflict between the state of Israel and the Palestinians continues to boil over with disturbing regularity. The post-"Nine-Eleven" world is extremely volatile everywhere, and America can no longer sit on the sidelines feigning neutrality, or insisting on its irrelevance to us, or protesting our national transcendence of such unseemly foreign entanglements. We are in this fight whether we like it or not: the terrorists of "Nine-Eleven" saw to that.

So what ought to be our national response as a self-described moral or righteous people?

18

We need not have any moral qualms about the war against international Islamic terrorism. Unlike the wars in the last century against fascism and communism, we have made quantum leaps in technology with precision-guided munitions and in moral understanding with a resolute commitment to the principle of noncombatant immunity from direct attack. This time our cause *is* unquestionably just. This time our intentions *can be* unquestionably noble. As the vanguard of Western civilization, we Americans and our allies in the "coalition of the willing" are duty-bound to lead the counterassault against the evil scourge of anarchic, nihilistic terrorism, to exact a heavy toll from its perpetrators, protectors, and state-sponsors—by military means, if necessary; over a period of years and decades, if necessary; on a scale, if necessary, such as the world has never seen.

In the coming battles and campaigns of the war that commenced in earnest on Tuesday, September 11, 2001, we shall, each of us, hear the clarion call to duty. Some, who wear the uniform of the armed forces, will take the fight to the lairs of the enemy. Others will support the war effort by making economic and personal sacrifices. Still others will offer their prayers and moral support, for they who keep the home fires burning also serve. But make no mistake about it: we are all involved, whether we relish the prospect or not. We Americans have been crucified as a people, but we have already begun to rise again, stronger and more righteous than ever. "Our help is in the name of the Lord," says the psalmist (Psalms 124:8). But the virtues of prudence, courage, justice, and charity demand that we continually prepare to resort to force of arms in accordance with the highest moral teachings of historic Christendom, both East and West.

It is to those rich, longstanding traditions that we now turn to discover what guidance they may provide American political and military leaders—and our entire citizenry—concerning the virtue of war.

19

CHAPTER 2

Divided Christendom

It is fashionable in American intellectual circles to refer with favor to our current era as "post-Christian." In particular, "Christendom" as the rule or dominance of one or another kind of Christianity in the public square and popular culture is clearly a thing of the past. And good riddance to it, as far as our secular intelligentsia is concerned.

But not so fast! Contemporary American society may be at the mercy of the militant purveyors of the misleading concept of "strict separation" of church and state. Religious communities may be on the defensive, fighting to preserve their doctrinal standards, communal ethos, and institutional integrity from hostile political interference, particularly judicial activism. Anti-Christian bigotry may be the last "respectable" prejudice among intellectuals. But the spiritual and moral vitality of the more traditional Christian and Jewish communities—the so-called conservative churches and observant synagogues—may not be doubted. Western civilization may no longer be hospitable to an official "Christendom," but seriously devout Christians—both Eastern and Western—may still exert a significant, powerful influence on the wider society and public policymakers when they act in concert.

In this chapter, we shall provide brief sketches of the Eastern Orthodox and Western Christian communities in the United States to set the stage for detailed presentations of their respective moral traditions on the virtue of war. What are these communities and who actually belongs to them? How do they reason morally and attempt to provide a public moral witness? What are the chief characteristics of their moral positions on the issues of war and peace? As we take these questions in turn, it shall become increasingly evident that, at least on the war question, traditional Christianity in America is not so divided after all.

I. Sailing from Byzantium

Religion has shaped American culture since the earliest colonial settlements. In the 1830's, Alexis de Tocqueville could still admire the vibrant religious communities that furnished the backbone of this New World society.[1] Even as late as the halcyon decade of the 1950's, President Dwight Eisenhower opined that every American ought to have a religious faith, although the specific divine object of that faith didn't matter to him. From established state churches to the ethos of the "unknown god," from Pilgrims and Puritans to ecumenists and sectarians, the American experiment in religious freedom has captivated the world. These shores continue to attract immigrants who wish to practice their religions unhindered by princes or prelates—and more and newer religious communities who seek to influence the moral, cultural, and political direction of American society. It's a safe bet that the historic troika of participants in the American religious experiment—whom Will Herberg of Drew University identified in the 1950's rather simply as "Protestant, Catholic, and Jew"—will soon be joined by a new partner among those religious groups currently struggling to occupy the last vacant corner of the public square. The rapidly growing Muslim community, whose numbers in the United States range from two to three million, has made a serious bid of late, even before the ironically enhanced public consciousness of Islam following "Nine-Eleven."

Enter the Orthodox

Although Eastern Orthodox Christians number some 250 million worldwide, the Orthodox community in the United States is quite small—only about four million souls, and even that number may be inflated. Further, Orthodox Americans are distributed among a dozen or so fragmented, mostly ethnic jurisdictions, each of which seems reluctant to occupy the fourth corner of the public square as a dialogue partner alongside the Protestant, Roman Catholic, and Jewish communities.

This public shyness is, in part, the result of popular misperceptions of the Orthodox in America. Roman Catholics tend to regard them as some kind of exotic Catholic community, confusing the ancient Orthodox Churches with Eastern Rite Catholics in union with Rome. Protestants often presume that the several Orthodox jurisdictions are "denominations" like themselves—somehow "Protestant," as if that term were synonymous with non-Roman Catholic. Even less informed Americans may ask their Orthodox neighbors if they believe in Christ, or exclaim with genuine confusion, "You don't look Jewish!"

Much of the blame for this uncertain identity in the public mind must be laid at the doorstep of the Orthodox Churches themselves. The several jurisdictions have, for the most part, cast their lot with the same "mainline" Protestant organizations—especially the National Council Churches—that many astute observers of the ecumenical scene believe time has passed by. The ethical pronouncements of the NCC routinely echo the political ideology of the religious left in America, and the national Democratic Party in particular. Lacking a useful political-ethical compass of their own, Orthodox Americans have thus far failed to articulate what Fr. Richard John Neuhaus has aptly termed "a public ethic ... informed by religiously grounded values" through which they might contribute substantively to the American experiment in religious freedom and democratic culture.[2] In 1994 Eastern Orthodox Christians celebrated the bicentennial of the first permanent Russian Orthodox church community in Alaska. A national shrine in St. Augustine, Florida, commemorates the arrival in 1768 of the first Greek Orthodox colonists on what is now the territory of the United States. And yet, despite this longstanding presence in North America, the collective moral contribution of the Orthodox Churches to the American ethos and the general culture has been negligible. In fact, Fr. Neuhaus observed in *The Naked Public Square* that the influence of the Orthodox "upon the general culture" in the United States "escapes detection."[3] For serious-minded, socially conscious Orthodox, that pointed observation contains a painful truth.

Byzantine Legacies

The pain is especially acute in light of the self-understanding of Eastern Orthodox Christians as precisely that—the practitioners of the original *orthodox* Christianity.[4] "Orthodox" is a loan word from the ancient Greek language. It's a conflation of two words: *orthos*, an adjective meaning "correct," and either *dokein*, "to think," or *doxa*, "glory" (as in worship). Both meanings of the second term are applicable: Orthodox Christians everywhere and in every era share the same "correct thinking" about doctrinal and moral matters and the same "correct worship" of the God who has revealed Himself as Father, Son, and Holy Spirit. Whether situated in the Eastern Mediterranean or Eastern Europe, or in more recent émigré settlements in Western Europe, North and South America, and Australasia, the Orthodox Churches regard one another as equal heirs of the biblical, patristic, canonical, hagiographical, liturgical, iconographic, and spiritual patrimony derived directly from the ancient, undivided Christian Church of the first millennium after the life, death, and resurrection of Jesus Christ. That patrimony is most easily distinguished from all of the contemporary "Western" Christian communities—whether Roman Catholic or Protestant—by strict adherence to the original Nicene Creed forged at the first two (of seven) Ecumenical Councils of the universal Church (Nicea in A.D. 325 and Constantinople in A.D. 381). That is to say, the Orthodox categorically reject the infamous interpolation (officially

23

added in the West by the pope in Rome early in the 11th century) known as the "*filioque*" from the Latin conjunction that would have the Holy Spirit proceed from the Father *and the Son*, instead of from the Father alone, as the original Greek text proclaimed.

The truly formative period of Orthodox Christianity, when the strands of living tradition stemming from the Bible coalesced in a unique doctrinal and spiritual tradition, was the once glorious Byzantine, or East Roman, Empire—of which the Orthodox Churches of Greece, Russia, Ukraine, Romania, Serbia, Bulgaria, Albania, Georgia, the Middle East, and the Americas are the direct descendents. Byzantium may seem an unlikely port of call for Americans, religious or otherwise, in search of a contemporary public philosophy. The adjective "byzantine" commonly connotes something complex, devious, or scheming, owing to the intrigues of the Byzantine imperial court. But Americans unschooled in this neglected corner of Western civilization need not conjure up images of "I, Claudius" in pseudo-Christian drag.

The Byzantine Empire centered in Constantinople (modern Istanbul in Turkey) lasted more than a millennium—from 330, when the Emperor Constantine moved the primary capital of the Roman Empire from "old" Rome to the "New Rome" on the Bosphoros, until its conquest by the Ottoman Turks in 1453. But there was far more to Byzantium than mere longevity. That culture has retained its original majesty for Orthodox Christians in Greece, as well as much of Eastern Europe and the Middle East, who proudly and tenaciously perpetuate the rich spiritual, social, political, and cultural heritage of Byzantium even amidst the modern ruins of their societies. As we might expect, however, this has not happened in North America.

And yet the two-thousand-year Eastern Orthodox experience, particularly the Byzantine millennium, offers untapped spiritual, social, political, and cultural resources that may make important contributions to the unique American experiment. At the same time, involvement by Orthodox Christians in the American public square, including the often nasty business of political governance, may help them to forge a unified and unmistakable identity—not merely as another "denomination" among many, or a "diaspora" of ethnics pining for the "old country," but rather *the* venerable, ancient, undivided, unchanged Christian Church called by God the Holy Trinity to bear witness, to baptize, and to make disciples of the unique people called American.

In that spirit, let's examine several Byzantine concepts that appear particularly promising for a public moral witness by Orthodox Americans.

First, in its heyday the Byzantine Empire was not so much a Greek entity as a multinational "commonwealth" of diverse peoples united in one imperial society. Although the Greek language continued to inspire philosophers and theologians, Latin remained the language of government, and indigenous tongues proliferated throughout the empire, including the written Slavonic language created at the end of the ninth century by Greek missionaries to Moravia. The Byzantine experience of "commonwealth" not only resonates well with the contemporary American phenomenon of social and cultural "pluralism." The triumphs and tragedies of this Byzantine experience in unity-and-diversity may help our fellow Americans as they struggle with the paradoxes of pluralism—such as those generated by the current debates over internal "multiculturalism" and U.S. foreign policy, particularly the use of military might in historic Orthodox homelands or against Islamic states.

Second, the Byzantine political-ethical ideal envisioned a genuine "symphony" of church and state, which, regrettably, was rarely practiced. The Orthodox Byzantine emperors, more often than the Orthodox Church hierarchy, exploited this harmonious arrangement to their own advantage. But the hackneyed term "caesaropapism" oversimplifies the political complexities of both theory and praxis.[5] In any event, the ideal of cooperation between the *imperium* and the *sacerdotium* resonates well with the "accommodationist"—as opposed to "strict separationist"—approach to contemporary issues of church and state or religion and society in America. The Byzantine "symphonic" model may provide an unexpected but firm historical grounding for those public policymakers who look with some favor upon the contributions of religion to the American public square.

Third, if the principle of political "symphony" was honored in the breach, the Byzantine concepts of the virtuous community and voluntary philanthropy were consistently practiced. In his classic study *Byzantine Philanthropy and Social Welfare*, Fr. Demetrios Constantelos chronicled the remarkable achievements of both church and state in caring for orphans, strangers, the elderly, the sick, and the imprisoned. Those charitable efforts were rooted in a vision of a *virtuous* society composed of virtuous individual persons. Byzantium at its best thus prefigured the contemporary American values of social compassion, voluntarism, and justice tempered by mercy.

Beyond Byzantium / Beyond America

Even in the best of all possible worlds, which Byzantium, notwithstanding its underappreciated genius, certainly was not, such distinctive Eastern prisms for refocusing the current public policy debates would hardly suffice to reshape the American ethos. Several nagging questions require cogent responses if Orthodox Americans hope to bring their spiritual and moral legacy into the American public square. How politically or ethically normative and relevant is the oriental Byzantine imperial model of government? How religiously homogeneous were Byzantium and the modern Orthodox pre-Communist nation-states in Eastern Europe, and to what extent, if any, were the rights and dignity of religious minorities respected? What moral and cultural leverage may a distinct religious minority like the Eastern Orthodox realistically hope to exert in American society?

If the Orthodox community expects to engage American society and culture in a genuine social ethical dialogue, Orthodox leaders will have to navigate these uncharted waters very carefully. A dialogue implies risk—an openness to the possibility of being changed by the other. Orthodox Americans should anticipate that their "living Tradition," as so many Orthodox theologians are wont to say, will undergo a positive metamorphosis in its American context, even as it may suffer some corruption. The American ethos, particularly its traditions of liberal democracy and "no Establishment" of religion, may have a salutary effect on the social ethical thinking of an Old World religious community seeking its way in the New World. But it will be necessary for Orthodox Americans to avoid both the Scylla of sectarian arrogance and the Charybdis of cultural conformity.

Byzantine civilization, however romantic Orthodox might remember it with fondness, cannot be simply "transplanted" to America. Nor is Washington, D.C., capable of becoming a Byzantium on the Potomac. If they hope to seize the moment and become full dialogue partners with the other religious communities, Orthodox Christians will have to recognize a two-fold challenge. First, they must articulate clearly what constitutes the Orthodox Byzantine legacy, or what the Romanian historian Nicolae Iorga described so felicitously in French in 1935 as "Byzance après Byzance."[6] Second, they must interpret that tradition to other Americans in fulfillment of the Great Commission to witness to all nations. That means the Orthodox will have to transcend elements of this historic legacy—to go "beyond Byzantium," as it were.

On the other hand, there is no gainsaying the moral disarray in so much of contemporary American culture. The same society that has maximized individual liberty, equal opportunity for all, and the pursuit of happiness suffers from radical individualism,

27

reductionist egalitarianism, and rampant materialism. If Greek Orthodox Metropolitan Maximos Aghiourghoussis of Pittsburgh has correctly defined a religious heresy as "a truth pushed too far," then these American vices are American virtues pushed to extremes. Yet what may be said about society at large in this regard applies also, regrettably, to the life of the Orthodox community in the United States.

Virtually any Orthodox priest can testify to the corrosive effects of these modern American faults on the lives of individuals and communities. Many of the faithful prefer to abide by Orthodox teachings that suit their convenience: period. Too many clergy and laymen have been captivated by the demands of the counterculture for governmental validation of "rights." Too many parishioners are too busy pursuing their own material happiness to deepen their spirituality, or to share from their abundance with their less fortunate neighbors.

The great Protestant theologian H. Richard Niebuhr defined one model of the Christian encounter with culture as the Augustinian approach: "Christ the transformer culture."[7] This aptly describes Eastern Orthodoxy at its best. Even as they transcend the distinctive Byzantine legacy that they have inherited, Orthodox Americans must transform or, better yet, "transfigure" the America in which they live. For if their contribution to the American ethos is to have any enduring value, they will have to articulate a vision that goes "beyond America."

Such a vision would indeed constitute a quantum leap in the Orthodox manner of witnessing to America. The first phase of the Orthodox presence in this country, as in the initial stages of Irish Catholic immigration after the potato famine in the 19th century, may be characterized—in Washington, D.C., attorney Dean Popps' apt phrase—as "bricks and mortar," the construction of churches and social halls. The second phase, "black ties and fluff," has focused on attaining recognition by the political and religious elites as the "fourth major faith" alongside the Protestant, Catholic, and Jewish communities. The third phase may have begun with those Orthodox clergy and laity who have grasped a simple but elusive truth: that the best way to stake a claim to the hearts and minds (and souls) of Americans is to establish a coherent, intellectually credible, politically savvy but non-partisan presence in the arenas where the arguments that eventually determine our politics are formed and shaped. This includes attention to the halls of government; but it also means a presence in the broadcast media, on the op-ed pages of the major newspapers, in opinion journals, and in the academy. What this third phase requires is nothing less than a full-fledged "public theology."

Two-Tiered Morality

Orthodox moral tradition, like its Roman Catholic counterpart, is eminently configured for this purpose. Since the patristic era, Orthodoxy has proffered what might be termed a "two-tiered morality."

There is first an ethic inherent in the created order, a common-denominator ethic for humanity based on natural law. The idea of a "natural law" itself is, of course, one of the contentious issues that divide contemporary philosophers, theologians, and public policymakers. We may hardly expect to resolve this question in the present volume.

But a few salient characteristics of the natural law may be posited with profit. This "inborn moral law," as Orthodox moral theologian Fr. Stanley Harakas has dubbed it, is universal, unchanging, and perceivable by the effort of unaided reason.[8] The classic example cited by the Church fathers is the Decalogue in the Old Testament, especially the last six commandments. These are material norms that specify what humans *ought to do* or ought not to do. Though, from an Orthodox perspective, merely a preparatory step in God's economy of salvation, this **civilizing ethic**, or natural

29

law ethic, may serve as a suitable "grammar" for Orthodox Christians who wish to have a direct, immediate impact on American public policy, while they pursue the long-range objective of "enhancing" the American ethos.

The higher **transfigurative morality** reflects mankind's greatest potential and fulfillment. Revealed by the incarnate Son of God Himself, this "evangelical ethic," in the words of Fr. Harakas, inspires religiously motivated conformity by believers to divine law. The Sermon on the Mount, for example, and particularly the Beatitudes, completes or perfects the natural law ethic by positing formal norms governing virtuous behavior—that is, how humans *ought to be*, such as merciful, humble, and pure in heart. This evangelical ethic obviously shapes the personal morality of Orthodox Christians and the communal ethos of that special community called Church. The transfigurative morality of the gospel of Jesus Christ as interpreted by the Church fathers, expressed in the liturgical life of the community, codified in the canons of the Church, and lived by the saints may motivate and frame the general moral concerns of those Orthodox Christians who wish to influence American public policy.

But this revealed morality may not be imported wholesale into the public square of the larger American society, which does not necessarily share the Orthodox faith in divine revelation. In the interest of genuine religious liberty, the Orthodox faithful may not expect secular Americans, or those whose own faith is grounded in other theological premises, to behave in accordance with what the Orthodox take to be divine revelation. If Orthodox Americans hope to be, as the great German sociologist Max Weber would have it, ethically "responsible" to the larger society as well as true to their own moral vision, they will stand on the common ground of the virtues and norms that once shaped our common moral life in this country. A genuinely public theology requires that Orthodox operate in the public square in ways that permit their arguments to be engaged by their fellow Americans.

They need not, however, do so with an air of resignation. A serious effort to summon America to heed the "civilizing ethic" would, if successful, still represent a marked advance over our current circumstances of moral fragmentation.

Orthodox Justifiable War in Outline

If the Orthodox East never produced a full-blown just war theory as did the Roman Catholic West, Orthodoxy certainly developed a realistic justifiable war tradition firmly grounded in natural law and the ancient Christian virtue tradition.[9] Eastern Orthodox teaching on the morality of some wars forms one of only two dynamic "trajectories" through the entire multi-millennial history of the Church, beginning with the experience of ancient Israel as recorded in the Old Testament. The other trajectory is absolute pacifism, which a previous volume has explored in detail.[10] To be sure, the Orthodox justifiable war tradition reflects the lower "civilizing ethic" rather than the higher "transfigurative morality" exemplified by the absolute pacifist trajectory. But it is precisely the synthesis of idealism and realism, of vision and power, of mysticism and justice in the Orthodox justifiable war tradition that might speak forcefully to the role of the United States in the contemporary world.

The justifiable war trajectory may be traced in the six types of textual sources that the Orthodox moral tradition comprises: Holy Scripture (that is, the complete Bible of the Church in the fourth century, including the *Septuagint* Greek version of the Old Testament—which remains normative for the Orthodox—and, of course, the New Testament); the writings of the Church fathers from the first century through the entire Byzantine era that ended in 1453 with the conquest of Constantinople by the Ottoman Turks; canon law; hagiographic literature and the associated icons of the saints as narrative theology "in color and form"; devotional literature, which

31

includes liturgical and hymnographic texts and a special type of spiritual writing focusing on ascetical or mystical themes; and the works of modern theologians and literary authors. In the next two chapters, we shall provide a few decisive examples of how each of these components allows for an Orthodox moral perspective on the conduct of some wars as, at least, a "lesser good."[11] That's the moral category known in the West as *jus in bello*: literally, "right in war," or, more loosely translated, the right (morally virtuous and hence good) conduct of war.

The decision to resort to military force in the first place—that is, the moral criteria known in the West as *jus ad bellum* (literally, "right to war")—is not as systematically developed in the Christian East as it is in the Christian West. But there are three conditions that clearly emerge from the various components of Orthodox moral tradition.

First, a *proper political ethos* is the Orthodox equivalent of "legitimate authority" in the Western just war tradition since St. Ambrose of Milan (d. 397).[12] The erstwhile role of the Byzantine emperor, or the *imperium* in general, as the sole political authority legitimated through divine election and capable of summoning the Orthodox faithful to war may, arguably, be assumed in the post-imperial modern era by formal equivalents such as the people's national representatives in the U.S. Congress or international organizations like the United Nations and the North Atlantic Treaty Organization (NATO). However, a given government and society may be deemed worthy of defense by military means only to the extent that the government and society abide by the norms of the natural law ethic, foster justice for the entire populace (or commonwealth), and have positive relations with the Orthodox community in their midst. This obtains whether the latter constitutes the majority of the citizens (as in Russia, Ukraine, Romania, Greece, Serbia, Bulgaria, Georgia, and Macedonia) or merely another religious minority (as in the United States). Conversely, any serious expression of political hostility toward Eastern Orthodox Christianity would constitute a violation of proper political ethos and relieve Orthodox Christians from the moral duty to defend their homeland from external aggression.

Second, *defense of the People of God* is the Orthodox equivalent of "just cause" in the Western just war tradition. The cause of any justifiable war in which Orthodox Christians may engage has its ultimate grounding in the promise of the Lord Himself that "the gates of hell shall not prevail against" the Church founded on the faith of St. Peter (Matthew 16:18). Of course, gates are stationary, so the implication of the passage—usually missed by those who cite it in such circumstances—is that the Church ought to be on the offensive against hell, Satan, and evil, not merely hanging on for dear life in a defensive posture. In either mode, offense or defense—both of which may be required in justifiable war—military combat invariably involves the shedding of human blood, maiming, and massive destruction of lives and property. It would be, *prima facie*, an obviously evil event unless the decision to resort to war by legitimate and competent authorities entailed an intrinsically good cause—such as the defense of otherwise defenseless persons and the preservation of the Church from destruction by those inspired by the demonic forces within the "gates of hell"—and the use of military force, including violence, was carefully calibrated to achieve a victorious end with a maximum of speed and efficiency and a minimum of physical harm to both combatants and noncombatants. Such force would, in this prospective action, constitute a good and proportionate means to a good end.

Although the ancient Church struggled to survive the regimes of hostile, often brutally oppressive pagan Caesars, the Byzantine Church knew relative peace within the Empire. Thus the moral tradition as it developed during that era and the successor Orthodox monarchies in Russia and the Balkans did not envision a reversion to barbarism and anti-Orthodox hostility by the political or social elites.

33

As just another institution in such a seemingly symphonic religio-cultural society, the Church was no more worthy of armed defense than any other human institution or cultural entity. To defend the Byzantine Empire from external aggressors such as the Zoroastrian Persians, Muslim Arabs and Turks, or pagan Slavs was to defend the Church as the People of God within the boundaries of the Empire. But the Church, in the Orthodox view, claims a unique nature as nothing less than the divine-human Body of Christ on earth. As such it may not suffer desecration by those who would clearly dishonor it and thereby blaspheme with impunity against God Almighty. Moreover, the Church as the People of God must survive to fulfill the divine commission to witness on behalf of Christ to the ends of the earth. Granted on the individual level, a person ought to suffer injustice in imitation of Christ's voluntary Passion and supreme Sacrifice. But Orthodox moral tradition obligates each Orthodox Christian to defend the collective entity of the whole People of God—which is, mystically to be sure, greater than the mere sum of its individual parts—from any and all forms of injustice and unrighteousness, particularly the violence that is endemic to foreign invasion or domestic oppression by those hostile to the free exercise of Orthodox Christian faith. In such extreme circumstances an essentially defensive war on behalf of the continued existence of the Church, even in a secular or otherwise non-Orthodox society, may become morally imperative. That condition would appear to be fully met, for example, in the current war against international Islamic terrorism.

Third, a *proper spiritual intent* is the Orthodox equivalent of "right intent" in the Western just war tradition dating back to St. Ambrose of Milan. Lest the contemplated military action be tainted and even undermined by vengefulness, self-righteousness, or a desire for conquest, Orthodox Christian moral tradition, like its Western Christian counterpart, insists that enemies of the *imperium* or modern nation be viewed also as persons created in the image and likeness of

God who, therefore, must never be reduced to the status of impersonal, expedient means to ends, however virtuous the ends. The ultimate goals of forgiveness and rehabilitation of the "enemy" must govern the decision to resort to force and the conduct of any military action. Though resonant of the language of the "transfigurative morality" of the gospel, this spiritual intent also bespeaks a more basic moral pragmatism characteristic of the "civilizing ethic" of the natural law. As the Allied victors in the First World War discovered to their shock and regret, an unforgiving treatment of vanquished enemies may lead in the next generation to a Frankenstein monster (Hitler's Germany) hell-bent on revenge and conquest. A proper spiritual intent, according to the Orthodox moral tradition of *jus ad bellum*, entails a sincere, focused, and consistent pursuit of justice—for the "enemy" no less than the People of God and one's fellow citizens.

That leads to a final consideration in this primer on the Orthodox moral trajectory of justifiable war. If **mercy** is the virtue that the Orthodox absolute pacifist endeavors to maximize by refraining from all violence against human beings, the corresponding virtue that has priority for the Orthodox just warrior is **justice**. Whereas the pacifist seeks to emulate Jesus Christ as the Good Shepherd who allowed Himself to be slain unjustly by and for sinners, the just warrior perceives a higher duty: to defend the relatively innocent from unjust aggression. If the Orthodox pacifist can never do anything that he deems evil even for a reasonably just end, the Orthodox warrior cannot preserve his personal holiness by allowing evil to triumph through his own inaction. In the chapters that follow on the Orthodox version of *jus in bello*, we shall see how the virtue of justice is the primary characteristic of the conduct of justifiable war, as well as the decision to go to war in the first place. Justice is, or ought to be, from beginning to end, *the* virtue of war.

II. Traditional Catholics and Protestants

Who are the traditional Catholics and Protestants? What exactly makes them traditional? Trying to identify traditional Western Christians with particular communions is a fruitless task. For our purposes we may say that traditional Catholics and Protestants are those members of their respective communions who rely on their traditional teachings to guide them in matters of faith and morals. Traditional Catholics and Protestants do not merely give lip service to the old adage that Christians ought to read Scripture with their forefathers; they actually allow their forefathers some trumping power when traditional teaching conflicts with the prevailing whims of contemporary liberal culture. Put differently, traditional Western Christians take their forebears so seriously that they are actually willing to follow their forebears when it means possible (when not certain) ostracism by the liberal culture that they inhabit. Traditional Western Christians believe that truth is found in Holy Writ and that Holy Writ is best understood with the help of those who came before. Traditional Catholics will look to the likes of a St. Ambrose, St. Augustine, or St. Thomas Aquinas (and, of course, the Magisterium). Traditional Protestants will look to the likes of a Luther or a Calvin, and, more often than not, to the early fathers and Aquinas.[13] Traditional Western Christians consider their forebears reliable guides for understanding what it means to be a virtuous Christian wherever and whenever that Christian may live.

Traditional Catholics and Protestants, who have much more in common with each other (and with the Orthodox) than with the more "liberal" members of their respective churches, often find themselves in conflict with modern liberal politics. This conflict is not between traditional Christians and liberalism per se, but between traditional Christianity, which demands that its adherents bring their religious convictions with them to the public realm of discussion, and a certain kind of liberalism, which demands that everyone who would be a discussant in the public realm leave their religious convictions at home. This conflict is especially acute when it comes to warfare, because liberalism itself was born partly as a result of a war-weary Europe letting go of the attempt at complete religious hegemony. But this is jumping ahead; let us begin by exploring this conflict between traditional Western Christianity and liberalism.

Traditional Christians and Liberal Political Order

A common feature among many liberal writers is the assumption that religious convictions should be restricted in the public realm. The severity of the restriction varies, but the restriction is always present to some degree. Why is the restriction always present? The answer, at least in part, is fear. Liberal scholars by and large fear the consequences of unrestricted religious convictions in the public realm. The liberal story behind this kind of thinking is a narrative of how the avoidance of religious wars begot liberal ascendancy. In short, our liberal, pluralistic democratic society was created in order to free the public realm from religious convictions. While the historical point is partly indisputable, some questions need to be asked. First, was the solution to the religious wars (banishment of religious convictions from the public realm) the right one? And even if it was the right solution, is it now time for a reversal? In the words of Michael Sandel, "is it possible that, in the United States today, we have learned that lesson too well?"[14] For the Christendom-informed citizen, there can be no doubting the answer.

What do we mean by a Christendom-informed position? Let us state first what we do not mean. We most certainly do not mean a theocratic position where the church rules the state. Too often the term "Christendom" is thought merely to refer to the opposite of Enlightenment liberalism's model for church/state relations where the two are put into separate air-tight compartments. The Christendom-informed position, as we want to defend it, does not call for the collapse of church and state. What we will defend, however, is a

37

theologically-informed politics that has as its goal the duty to open up politics to the authority of God. This theology says, to be brief, that the life, death, and resurrection of Christ are indispensable for the Christian's impetus to become involved in the political order. Politics do not set the tone for how theologians read the Gospel, but rather, the Gospel sets the tone for how the church witnesses to the state. In summation, what the Gospel calls for is a kind of people shaped by the theological virtues of faith, hope, and especially charity. These are the people who constitute the Church's missionary presence to the governing authorities, and more importantly, to the society at large.

The Christendom-informed political theology views the liberal state as it views any other political regime: as a work of divine providence and not the mere results of human endeavor. All earthly governing authority is instituted by God for the restraint of evil. The church's main business will always be with society and with providing the means for the salvation of all; this is the church's mission. The duty of the church, therefore, is not to flex political muscle in order to restrain evil, but to provide a voice of guidance or dissent when that muscle is not properly flexed by the state. Nevertheless, the very purpose of the church's missionary presence is to seek a Christian community that includes all of society, and although this will never be accomplished on this side of history, it is the church's missionary duty to make the attempt. The most important duty is a witness to the divine transcendent good, a good that the church has a duty to persuade—not coerce—others to acknowledge. The church, in other words, does not have a duty to make a Christian political order, but it does have a duty to witness to the kingdom of God. This is the very core of Christendom-thinking: to demonstrate the working of the kingdom within the world. Christ's triumph in the resurrection, which redeemed every sphere of existence, begets both the missionary presence of a distinctive community and the governing authority's response to that missionary presence. As Oliver O'Donovan has remarked, this "may lead either to martyrdom, or to mutual service."[15]

Notice how this is not another radical communitarian call for the abolishment of the liberal state. The liberal tradition is not to be overturned (even if such a thing were possible), but the church must see that the state recognizes the victory of Christ in the Advent. What does this mean practically for the Christian citizen of the United States? First and most important is a witness that points to the heresy of the First Amendment to the U.S. Constitution when that Amendment is read as a doctrine of the separation of church and state to such an extent that the state denies that it should offer assistance to the church's mission. The Christian must repudiate a reading of the First Amendment that claims the state has no responsibility to recognize God's self-disclosure in history.

What does the Christian expect the state to do? At a minimum, Christians ought to be able to expect the State to be welcoming of their particular theological points of view, and not seek to keep Christians from thinking and voting like Christians. At a maximum, to borrow from John Courtney Murray, Christianity and other traditional religious groups of the West should enjoy positive (empowering) liberty, while other religious groups should be tolerated to the degree that they still enjoy negative liberty—no one will harm them, but they will not be empowered. If Christians cannot at least be allowed to seek the former, then the Augustinian alternative must be considered. This alternative says that the Christian must not look for virtue and the good life in earthly political authority, which is always more or less vicious, but only in the heavenly city to be reached when this life ends. In short, the Christian withdraws from the public realm and leaves it in the hands of the vicious. The Augustinian Christian becomes involved in state affairs only when called upon, but in a liberal society such as ours, one that harbors a great fear of theological reflection in the public realm, this seems very unlikely.

Let us consider briefly a few liberal thinkers who have touched on the role of religious convictions in a liberal society. This will allow us to make the Christendom-informed position clearer in the light of opposition and in light of how it deals with similar problems. It will become clear that the traditional Christians considers the current liberal, plural, democratic society as a society that has, indeed, "learned the lesson too well" and seeks a corrective. Also, it will show why Christians must consider the Augustinian withdrawal as an option if the picture the liberals paint cannot be altered. In other words, if the liberal restrictions on religious convictions cannot be corrected, then the Christian may find it necessary for her or his very identity to withdraw from the public realm until some such time that her or his distinctive Christian convictions may play a part in the public realm.[16] What this means in warfare is that, for traditional Christians, the pacifist option is always a real one.

John Rawls, perhaps the most respected American liberal philosopher of the 20th century, was compelled to place restrictions on how a religious person may act in the public realm. In *Political Liberalism*,[17] he argues that citizens holding comprehensive doctrines (read: religious convictions) cannot vote using their comprehensive doctrines, for people should vote using "public" reasons only. Again, the question of loyalty arises for Christians who may well ask why anyone would want to support a state that required its citizens to suspend obligations crucial to their identity when they make political decisions. Traditional Christians, for example, find the virtue of charity indispensable as a reason for action. When Christians act in order to secure earthly goods such as peace and order, they do so out of charity, out of a certain relationship with God and all that relationship entails for human relationships; they do not do so in order to be good liberal citizens. The appeals to Biblical faith by the abolitionists of the antebellum South, for example, were not attempts to make their fellow citizens better political liberals; they were attempts to make all citizens see what God intended us to be. If Christians cannot act as Christian in the public realm, then why should they act in the public realm at all?

It would be unfair and inaccurate to paint all liberal writers with the same brush. Indeed, some liberal writers wish to make a place for religious convictions in the public square. Robert Audi is one such scholar. Nevertheless, in *Religion in the Public Square*,[18] Audi claims that one has a *prima facia* duty not to advocate or support a law or public policy that restricts human conduct unless one is sufficiently motivated by adequate secular reasons (in which "adequate" means one would still act so if all non-secular reasons were eliminated). Again, let's apply this to the abolitionists of the antebellum South, who sought to restrict activities that they knew (theologically) to be unjust. Audi would find it acceptable for abolitionists to act as they did; it was even acceptable to make biblical appeals, but only if they would have done the same thing if their religious views were eliminated. Clearly there is something wrong here. The abolitionists' motivations and the very content of their actions were theologically orientated in such a way that it does not make sense to ask if they would act the same way even if their religious views were eliminated. The content of their convictions, no doubt, may seem admirable and even identical to the liberal's, but the abolitionists were not motivated by liberal concerns per se, nor did they act liberally per se. They were motivated by theological concerns born from a Scriptural/traditional authority on the equality of human beings under God, and they acted theologically in that they saw themselves as being faithful to the cross of Christ. In this respect, the abolitionists were sterling examples of how the Christendom-informed citizen acts politically.

There are those who, although they are not afraid of an effective missionary presence in the U.S., nevertheless would find the mission misguided. In *The First Liberty*,[19] William Lee Miller exemplifies this kind of thinking when he acknowledges that even though we are now a "nation endlessly deliberating about first principles, and even about how to state the condition of our deliberation," this need not mean "shallowness, conflict, chaos." The metaphysical underpinnings of the American republic cannot be formulated as an "official, closed, final statement," for the argument among various formulations is "itself of the essence of the society, and valuable by its lights." Miller, in concluding, uses an ironic approval of Murray's claim that we are "locked in argument," and that we must continue to be so if Truth and Liberty are not to destroy one another.

The implication of Miller's view, that the U.S. is a nation defined by its "locked argument," adds credence to Alasdair MacIntyre's claim that the liberal tradition is constituted by that very process of continual argument.[20] But the Christian cannot condone a system that is so locked in argument that it prohibits the state from recognizing God's self-disclosure in history. Thus, Miller's use of Murray's claim is ironic, because Murray wished, to some degree, to break the lock. Murray argued that traditional religious groups of the West should enjoy positive (empowering) liberty, while others should be tolerated. Under these conditions, Murray and those who think like him will certainly have good reasons for demonstrating what Miller believes the state ought to cultivate: civic loyalty and affection toward the state. But why should they feel great affection for a state that does not provide positive liberties (again, beyond gratitude for bare-bones peace and order). More than this, what if the State thinks it a positive duty to see that Christians are not able to hold public positions based on theological assumptions in conflict with the accepted liberalism of the State? If they cannot enjoy positive liberties or even the ability to proclaim their views in public, will they not take something like an Augustinian approach and view the state as certainly worthy of defense for the peace and order it provides but look for virtue and objects of affection elsewhere?

If there comes a time when Christians are penalized for declaring their theological opinions in the public realm, then there may be time for Christians to take Alasdair MacIntyre's advice and retreat into the monasteries. One could argue that Christians should not wait in monasteries for the dark ages to end but go into the marketplace to ask questions and make deals with unbelievers. But who is going out and what kind of questions will be asked? What kind of answers will the church be able to give? What kind of deals should be made? This job calls for a certain kind of Church, and that is where MacIntyre's "monastery religion" can help. As Duncan Forrester points out, MacIntyre shares with Karl Rahner and Leonardo Boff the belief that the minority Church, the Church at the margins, has the ability to be what the Church is supposed to be.[21] The Church on the margins, as an "experiment in fellowship, in living together in love and truth" and as a "forum of moral discourse," is the kind of Church that will know how to engage others in the marketplace. The Church at the margins—in the monasteries MacIntyre might say—can be distinctive enough to ask the right kind of questions and give the right kind of answers. Traditional Catholics and Protestants (and, in the eyes of these Catholics and Protestants, the Orthodox too)[22] now constitute the body of Christ at the margins of society. The church at the margins may be the only morally and spiritually viable body of people to survive the liberal hegemony of contemporary Western culture. For the church at the margins can exist as a body of people who say (to borrow from H. Richard Niebuhr) that Christ will transform culture instead of aiding culture in transforming Christ.

Liberal-Humanism and Warfare

The use of force in the liberal-humanist's eyes is always something unreasoned and not purposeful. Let's be clear about this. Scholars as diverse as Jeffrey Stout and John Rawls can agree on one point concerning the birth of liberalism itself: that it was, in part, a reaction against the brutal and fratricidal religious warfare of the late middle ages.[23] By "liberal-humanists" we follow Michael Howard in meaning a subset of liberalism that includes "all those thinkers who believe the world to be profoundly other than it should be, and who have faith in the power of human reason and human action so to change it that the inner potential of all human beings can be more fully realized."[24] What liberal humanism would like to change most of all is the human propensity to make war. Liberal humanism shares with liberalism in general the notion that moral progress is

43

measured, to a large degree, by the amount of agreement achieved on abstract moral principles that will serve to lessen conflict among individuals and, more importantly, groups of people. Virtually all forms of liberalism insist on abstract principles, for the goal is agreement among many different kinds of peoples. The goal is best achieved by formulating moral principles applicable to anyone, anywhere, at anytime, *regardless of religious beliefs*. Thus religious belief and tradition are obstacles (historically, the main obstacles[25]) we must try to hurdle in formulating universal principles. Tradition-free morality, in short, is the best way to describe this sort of principles-based morality. Everyone should be able to agree on such principles, and when they do, social harmony will be achieved, which would, indeed, be progress of a kind. Absence of conflict is the goal, while universal moral principles are the tools.

The World Council of Churches produced a document in 1958 on the prevention of war ("Christians and the Prevention of War in the Atomic Age") that is a perfect example of liberal-humanist thinking of war, and is, in addition, a low mark of Protestant political thinking in the 20th century. The document is a prime example of the liberal Protestant movement to "outlaw" war. According to the WCC, the only principle of legitimate war seems to be proportion; that is, calculating the consequences. A discussion of the kind of actions in war that may be absolutely forbidden is sadly, but unsurprisingly, absent. Because the abolition of war is the goal, there is little reason to limit the conduct of any particular war. The Council even rejects the notion of a "just" war, since the term never should have meant the justification of war but the allowance of a lesser of two evils.

There is one useful thing found in the WCC's document, and that is its honesty. The WCC realizes the logic of the "lesser evil" scheme in morality and what it does to the notion of a just war in ways scarcely to be found in similar positions. When we say that we will allow evil act X in order to avoid greater evil act Y, then X is hardly a "just" act. It is a permissible act in the moral world of the WCC and the like-minded moralists who allow evil for supposedly good ends, but it is certainly not a just act—not a positively good act. All acts of force are evil acts in the lesser evil scheme. Thus, on this view, strictly and honestly speaking, there can be no "just" wars.

The use of force is something hateful to the WCC, as it is to liberal-humanism in general. Put differently, the WCC shares the liberal-humanist mindset when it comes to the use of force (as it does on so much else as well). However, one need not be a liberal-humanist in all matters in order to share liberal-humanist ideas about war. Roman Catholic theologian Charles Curran is a good example of what we are talking about here. Curran, who can in little else be described as a liberal-humanist, worries that Christian ethicists such as Paul Ramsey do not take seriously enough the fact that war must be an *ultima ratio*. Thus, similar to the liberal-humanist ethos, he fears that people like Ramsey think war a reasonable form of human activity; for if we consider war reasonable, then we might be more likely to fight one and less likely to be reluctant to fight one. Curran finds the horrors of war to be the most important point, ethically speaking, about them: "There should be a horror of going to war and a striving for peace on the part of all men that contributes to a real reluctance for any nation to embrace war."[26] For Curran, the taking of a human life "should be very upsetting to the moral sensitivities of human beings who realize the precarious gift that is life."

On one level, of course, Curran is on the right track. War is not to be entered into lightly, especially modern war with its propensity for disproportionate measures in combat. Nor is it a bad thing to want our nations to refrain from going to war at the drop of a hat as, say, the Italian city-states were wont to do in the 16th century. On another level, however, Curran is on the wrong track. There is no reason to assume that simply because we believe that war can be a purposeful and reasoned activity that we will not have enough reluctance to go to war. In fact, just warriors will be very reluctant to fight wars that are not reasoned sufficiently and fail to show what good purposes may be achieved. Just warriors regret that they live in a world where they have to kill human beings in order to restrain evil; that is to say, they regret the Fall. But it is more "upsetting" for just warriors to watch others being abused and killed unjustly when they could put an end to that injustice.

Liberal-humanists view all war as inherently bestial. The odd but inevitable corollary to viewing war as something bestial is that one tends to view those who start it as beasts—something less than human—and thus deserving of no moral consideration in war. This tendency has been the moral and practical shaper of Western policy decisions including our present nuclear policy, born in the aggressor-defender doctrine, which excuses any sort of response to an unjust aggressor, and, consequently, does not do justice to the aggressor who is, after all, still our neighbor. Americans, shaped by the liberal-humanist view of war, typically consider the aggressor as so in the wrong—and so offensive to our ideals about proper political action—that anything at all may be done to destroy him utterly. This leads Americans to treat the aggressors not as unjust neighbors but as beasts. Is it too far fetched to suggest that the fervor we show in prosecuting aggressors shows that we view all war as inherently evil and its initiation an unnecessary evil at that? The perfectionist goal of banishing all war, something much more at home in Radical Reformation thinking than in traditional, orthodox (and Orthodox) Christianity, as the only reason for justifying war (a staple of liberal-humanist thinking) precludes limits on war-making once it begins. For if we really could end all war by this particular war, what difference will it make in the long run how we win it? A little bit (or even a whole lot) of evil in what is, after all, an already inherently evil business, should not make much difference when the result will be the permanent elimination of this kind of evil. One result of this kind of thinking is the elimination of a preventive war, for such a war requires us to take the first step of force, and hence we become the aggressor.

Just wars must be limited wars. Wars for the goal of unconditional surrender or in devotion to some ideal (and all otherwise just wars that devastate population centers) all overstep the limit. As Paul Ramsey once put it: "Men have to control their arms, not arms the men."[27] Americans, regretfully, tend to think that the loss of any life "can be justified only in terms of infinite goals made to appear ultimate and permanent."[28] Thus we lack the self-discipline required for making war limited. The West's nuclear arms policy is the result of this kind of attitude. Actual winnable fighting requires a morally possible war; yet because the West has, since the 1950's, shifted its defense posture to an over-reliance on nuclear arms, it is no longer capable of fighting a moral large-scale war; the West can no longer "win" in any conceivable sense. The West has effectively said that it would rather annihilate most of the world than fight another large-scale conventional war. Is this the way sane people react to possible large-scale conflicts? Clearly not.

Love and War—The Christian Just War Tradition

Flannery O'Connor once remarked that how a man reacts in a violent situation reveals a lot about his character. We can amend and expand O'Connor's remark to cover peoples. How peoples react to war says a lot about them. To the pagan ancients—Homer, Plato, Aristotle, Cicero—warfare is chiefly the place where one displayed courage and showed love and loyalty to the family, city, republic, or empire. Thus, how the pagan ancients reacted to war says a lot about them: they greatly valued the virtues of courage and piety. The Christian just war tradition—East and West, too—says a lot about Christians. For the Christian just war tradition is a body of thought built on three things: charity, justice, and the church. Charity—love of God and neighbor—compels Christians to seek justice for their neighbors. The just war tradition provides the Church with the means to determine how justice is to be sought and the grounds for penalizing those who stray too far from its prohibitions.

Many who read the early Church fathers, medieval theologians, or even the great Reformation leaders, are struck by the vast difference between the approaches to human morality found in pre-modern and modern theologians. When we pick up a modern book of moral theology or philosophy, we are usually presented with an ethical system meant to solve all the dilemmas we might run into when a critical stage is reached in our lives. This means that modern moral theology and philosophy is preoccupied with helping us out of dilemmas instead of helping us avoid dilemmas in the first place. But when we read St. Ambrose, St. Augustine, St. Thomas, Luther, or Calvin, we notice that the goal for these theologians is holiness. The idea is not to create an ethical system to answer all our problems, but to create a sort of person who will know how to act in a given situation and have the power to do so. This difference in moral approaches can be seen in how modern ethicists usually handle the moral problems of war. Modern accounts of morality in warfare center largely upon problems *in* war: those critical stage problems that concern decisions, for example, of saturation bombing or hostage-taking. But if we take the ancients as our guide, then, as Alasdair MacIntyre once suggested, we must realize that the preoccupation with such problems is a symptom of earlier moral failings.[29] The ancients would advise that we should seek a way to avoid the extreme situations in the first place. How we go about doing this will tell us a lot about ourselves. Put more strongly, how we handle the moral problems of war displays our fundamental moral capacity.

Accounts of war that concentrate on critical-stage problems often rely upon rules for making decisions. These rules more often than not are culled from what are generally known as the just war criteria. This situation has bequeathed us a rule-driven theory of morality in warfare that, unfortunately, tends to pay little attention to how war is actually fought and who does the fighting. Right acts in warfare, like right acts in most complex activities, are hard to capture in a set of rules formulated to be accessible to anyone, anywhere, and at

48

anytime. This form of critical-stage ethics is simply another form of the modern propensity for what Edmund Pincoffs calls "quandary ethics." Quandary ethics, as Pincoffs shows, is "a newcomer."[30] Pre-modern philosophers (including Aquinas) were concerned not with how to get out of traps but how to avoid falling into them in the first place. Pincoffs employs a helpful analogy with medicine, with character development likened to preventive medicine and the modern emphasis on rule-responsibleness likened to curative medicine. The analogy, though imperfect, is imperfect in a way that emphasizes the value of character development over rule-responsibleness: only a person of good character is liable to be able to find a way out of a quandary. In just war doctrine, we might say that only a person of good character will know when to react with violence toward injustice and how to use force once violent action is underway.

We believe that a close examination of the classic Christian approach to warfare found in the Church fathers, St. Thomas Aquinas, and the great Reformers will reveal resources necessary for reformulating modern just war approaches that are overly dependent upon rules and lack an account of how anyone can obey those rules, or why they should want to do so in the first place. We will argue that a return to the ancients will show why a tradition of the virtues is desirable for a coherent moral approach to war to which Christians can subscribe. It also explains how we can go about forming Christian just soldiers and what they will look like after they have been formed. For example, an account of the virtues will deal with moral dilemmas in a way quite different from rule-driven accounts and will even show us how to avoid such dilemmas. The virtuous soldier acts in view of who he is and does not make critical "decisions" in the way described by critical-stage moralists. Thus, critical-stage problems can often be forestalled because the very character of the virtuous combatant prevents, in the first place, the sort of actions that, in their chain of consequences, inevitably issue in such dilemmas.

49

For the Christian, however, it is not enough to formulate an account of how the natural moral virtues help us in just war approaches, for it is the theological virtue of charity that enables the just Christian soldier to act in reference to his ultimate end: happiness with God. For the Christian, then, any just war theory that does not include attention to charity will have to find some other way to ground the agent's acts of force in that agent's way of life such that the acts of force are constitutive of leading a life that brings the agent closer to God. In other words, the classical Christian account of virtuous soldiering shows us that acts of force actually bring the soldier closer to God, that acts of force can be consonant with holy Christian living, and any alternative approach will have to show the same; namely, that acts of force are divine-like, constitutive of holy life, and bring the agent closer to God.

The Western just war tradition as a distinctly Christian project began with St. Ambrose of Milan. St. Augustine, a pupil of Ambrose, inherited and expanded upon the major themes of Ambrose's approach to the moral problems of war and, thus, bequeathed to all of Western Christianity a distinctive theological just war project. This project was greatly enhanced by St. Thomas Aquinas, retained by the great Reformers Luther and Calvin, and was prepared for the modern world of international lawyers by the Calvinist theologian/philosopher Grotius. In fact, Grotius represents the end of the classical account. He is the last writer of importance to Christendom thinking on just war before the Enlightenment project removes theological thinking on war from the public realm in the West. Grotius's position is theologically based (a point lost on some observers) but not in the same way as Aquinas's. Grotius, a Dutch Calvinist, inherits the natural law and virtue accounts given from the Roman Catholic West and creates an international law account of war that spells out what Aquinas only implies: a *jus in bello* where justice means adherence to international law as the minimum moral requirement. Therefore, Grotius provides the West—both Protestant and Catholic—with a conception of acting justly in war for justice and with the restraint of law providing the impetus. Thus, no account of classical Christian-informed just warfare can be complete without Grotius. The purpose of sketching the classical Western Christian just war tradition is that the reader will have an understanding of why many modern Christian approaches to war are incoherent and why adherence to the thought of the ancients on the just war can help clear up the muddiness of modern Christian thought on war.

The Just War Criteria

The Western Christian just war tradition, simply because it is a tradition, is a body of Christian thought on the morality of war that is always, to some degree, in flux. What counts as virtuous action can change from place to place and from time to time. Nevertheless, there are criteria that have stood the test of time. The *jus ad bellum*, the criteria that enable Christians to decide when a proposed war is a just war, are the very definition of the practice of just war as a just war. In other words, there can be no talk of a just war if these criteria cannot be met. There are five *jus ad bellum* criteria: (1) proper authority, (2) just cause, (3) right intention, (4) war as the only reasonable means to right the wrong, and (5) reasonable hope for success. Proper authority means a legitimate head of state. Just causes include, especially, self-defense or defense of a weaker neighbor. Right intention means securing the common good. The fourth criterion is a call for caution and patience; it is also a call to count the probable costs and to weigh the expected good with the expected (but unintended) suffering. It is *not* a call for "last resort," a criterion unknown to the original framers of the just war tradition, introduced in modern times, and abused by the pacifist-influenced who are always looking for an excuse not to fight, regardless of prudence. The fifth criterion is a call for prudence; it asks if we can achieve what we hope to achieve by use of force. The *jus in bello* are the criteria that enable Christians to distinguish virtuous from vicious acts in war. These criteria are what are most in flux in the

51

tradition, for what counts as virtuous behavior on the field of battle is partly dependent on culture. Put differently, virtue in war depends somewhat on when and where you are fighting. However, there are two broad strictures on proper combat action: first, one may never intend to harm noncombatants (though who counts as a "noncombatant" can change); and second, one must form battle plans where the expected good (the military objective) outweighs the expected but unintended evil (collateral damage).

Stanley Hauerwas, as staunch Protestant pacifist and critic of liberalism, once observed that modern theologians, under the influence of the Enlightenment project of morality, tend to use the just war criteria as a theory applicable to anyone, anywhere, and at any time.[31] What this error ignores is that the just war doctrine as a Christian practice is unintelligible and unworkable outside of a Christian theological framework. Because modern theologians have not realized this, their use of the just war criteria lack the necessary embodied practices that make application of the criteria possible in a concrete situation. For what modern accounts of just war lack is an account of virtue in warcraft as a practice, a practice informed by a community of believers in the risen Christ and Lord. This lack of virtue in practice, and the grounding of theory in a body of people that sees it is put into practice, puts modern accounts in the unenviable position of defending what relevance they have for actual warfare. The lack of the virtue of charity—the failure to place Christian participation in war within the virtue of charity—divorces Christians from the real good (not a necessary evil) that can be achieved by just acts in a just war. Moreover, their dependence on a tradition of liberal-humanism betrays an incoherence that does not allow their projects to succeed on their own terms.

Many who read St. Ambrose and the other major figures who contributed to the Christian just war tradition may wish to dismiss the tradition as a work of "Constantinianism" or of "Christendom:" a dead political order that no one desires to see resurrected. Unfortunately, we too often think we have a grasp on Constantinianism and everything that tradition entails, when in reality we possess but a vague notion that more often than not views Christendom merely as the opposite of modern liberalism's prescription for the separation of church and state. Christendom, we must repeat, does not, in fact, call for the mixing of church and state, at least in the modern sense of the term "state." What it does recognize is the inseparable relationship between church and the common good. The duty this relationship gives for the church's influence on the governing authorities of a particular society is what gives the modern reader the false impression of Christendom as a theocracy. In truth, Christendom calls for a Christian witness to the governing authorities, and the just war tradition is but one way this witness is embodied in practice. With the just war tradition the church offers a witness that the governing authorities and society as a whole cannot ignore. When the governing authorities respond positively, they better resemble what they are ordained by God to be: a sign of His kingdom on earth.

CHAPTER 3

Orthodox Jus in Bello I:

Scripture, Fathers, and Canons

Holy Scripture

Orthodox Christians, like other Christians, as well as observant Jews and Muslims who respect the Bible, cannot avoid the disturbing presence of "holy wars" in the Old Testament. Whether intended as a sacrifice of non-Hebrews to ensure Yahweh's aid in battle or to purify the Hebrew community by eradicating injustice and evil beyond the Jewish community, the "ban" (*harem* in Hebrew) enjoined Israel to kill all human beings—irrespective of age, sex, or noncombatant status—in its numerous wars of conquest and survival in Canaan.[1] Such military campaigns of extermination appear, ironically, as "Yahweh's wars" in the original Hebrew text. For example, Numbers 21:14 refers to "the Book of the Wars of the Lord," while King Saul asks the young David in 1 Samuel 18:17 to "be valiant for me and fight the Lord's battles."[2] We can only wince when we read the divine command relayed through Moses that epitomizes the "ban" in Deuteronomy 20:10–18:

> When you draw near to a city to fight against it, offer terms of peace to it. And if its answer to you is peace and it opens to you, then all the people who are found in it shall do forced labor for you and shall serve you. But if it makes no peace with you, but makes war against you, then you shall besiege it; and when the LORD your God gives it into your hand you shall put all its males to the sword, but the women and the little ones, the cattle, and everything else in the city, all its spoil, you shall take as booty for yourselves; and you shall enjoy the spoil of your enemies, which the LORD your God has given you. Thus you shall do to all the cities which are very far from you, which are

not cities of the nations here. But in the cities of these peoples that the LORD your God gives you for inheritance, you shall save alive nothing that breathes, but you shall utterly destroy them, the Hittites and the Amorites, the Canaanites and the Perizzites, the Hivites and the Jebusites, as the LORD your God has commanded; that they may not teach you to do according to all their abominable practices which they have done in the service of their gods, and so to sin against the LORD your God.

But the Old Testament, especially the "official" Orthodox *Septuagint* version that extends the revelatory history of Israel to the first century B.C. (and possibly even the first century A.D.), is a rich tapestry of religious and moral traditions. Careful, critical, methodical exegesis can unravel from the original strands of the "ban" limitations on the means and targets of violence. This progressive moral tightening suggests a dynamic trajectory through ancient Israel's history. According to this "salvation history," God leads His people from the primitive barbarism of captivity in Egypt to the more complex ethical civilization in the Maccabean period (second and first centuries B.C.) and on to the perfect holiness revealed by Jesus Christ in the New Testament gospels.

What Jewish scholar Susan Niditch identifies as the "bardic" tradition in the Hebrew texts contains "the outlines of a just war code especially pertaining to *jus in bello*, a code of conduct shared by fighters on the same side and by enemies."[3] In Judges 8:18–21, for example, Gideon reveals to the two kings of Midian whom he has captured that he would have allowed them to live if they had not killed two of his brothers. The issues here concern virtue rather than mere revenge—specifically fairness, reciprocity, and mutual honor in war, together with loyalty to family. The two Midian kings even exhort Gideon himself to slay them as a man of "valor" when his eldest son hesitates. Similarly heroic in style is the familiar encounter between young David and the giant Philistine named

55

Goliath in 1 Samuel 17, as well as other passages such as the truce following the death of Asahel in 2 Samuel 2:18–28 and the valiant deeds of David's "mighty men" in 2 Samuel 23:8–39. Niditch observes astutely: "these war portrayals reflect an idealization of combat, its victors, and its motivations. In this way, war is glorified and made palatable, a game of sorts, a fair game, for the best man wins."[4]

Another progressive strand is the ethical reworking of the older narrative in the books of 2 Samuel, 1 Kings, and 2 Kings by the editor who produced the books of 1 & 2 Chronicles. Though the latter still retains some of the unsavory features of the Israelites' militaristic exploits and the wretched excesses of the "ban," the chronicler aspires to a more idealistic depiction of a decent, ethical, righteous leadership for Israel. In 1 Chronicles 22:7–10, a poignant explanation is offered as to why, in the earlier text found in 2 Samuel 7:1–29, God did not allow David to build the temple in Jerusalem: he had shed too much blood in his wars. In 2 Chronicles 28:9–11, an obligation is imposed on the northern Kingdom of Israel to handle the prisoners-of-war—whom they had taken from the sister Kingdom of Judah—with respect and generosity of spirit, even returning them to their kin. (An earlier text in 2 Kings 6:22–33 goes even further, when the prophet Elisha demands that the non-Jewish Aramaean prisoners be feted as guests and sent home without harm.)

The later texts found in 1–3 Maccabees (written originally in Greek and hence excluded from the Jewish Bible but not the Christian *Septuagint*) round out this progressive Old Testament trajectory. These books perpetuate the emphasis on justifiable defensive war (rather than the older wars of conquest) sounded so distinctly in the post-exilic fourth-century-B.C. Hebrew book of Nehemiah. In the earlier text, Nehemiah encourages the Jews attempting to rebuild the walls of Jerusalem to overcome their fears of the local Gentile tribes opposed to their divine project: "Do not be afraid of them. Remember the Lord, who is great and terrible, and fight for your brethren, your sons, your daughters, your wives, and your homes" (Nehemiah 4:14). The book of 1 Maccabees (*ca.* 140 B.C.) contains seven episodes that place additional limits on the conduct of war by Israel: 1 Maccabees 2:29–48 allows the Jews to engage in righteous self-defense, even on the Sabbath; 1 Maccabees 5:28, 35, and 51 relate the killing of every male enemy, but not their women; 1 Maccabees 5:55–62 enunciates a proto-principle of "legitimate authority" by making it clear that only the Hasmonean dynasty is called by God to lead Israel in battle; 1 Maccabees 5:67 depicts the personal defeat of some brave Jewish priests who fight unwisely and without proper divine sanction; and 1 Maccabees 13:43–48 reveals how Simon the high priest and commander of the Jews (d. 134 B.C.) spared and exiled all of the survivors of the siege of Gamara ("Gaza" in Greek).

Perhaps the most dramatic instance of war as a moral good in the Maccabean era occurs in 2 Maccabees 15:11–16. Confronting a powerful army of the Seleucid King Demetrios I Soter led by the treacherous Nicanor, Judas Maccabeus (d. 160 B.C.), the most celebrated hero of the Hasmonean dynasty founded by his father Mattathias, tells his fellow Jews a dream, "a sort of vision" (2 Maccabees 15:11), to inspire them in the coming battle:

> What he saw was this: Onias, who had been high priest, a noble and good man, of modest bearing and gentle manner, one who spoke fittingly and had been trained from childhood in all that belongs to excellence, was praying with outstretched hands, for the whole body of the Jews. Then likewise a man appeared, distinguished by his gray hair and dignity, and of marvelous majesty and authority. And Onias spoke, saying, "This is a man who loves the brethren and prays much for the people and the holy city, Jeremiah, the prophet of God." Jeremiah stretched out his right hand and gave to Judas a golden sword, and as he gave it he addressed him thus: "Take this holy sword, a gift from God, with which you will strike down your adversaries. (2 Maccabees 2:12–16)

In a scene reminiscent of Shakespeare's depiction of the English at Agincourt after King Henry V's soliloquy on St. Crispin's day, the narrative then describes the effect of this amazing story on the Jewish warriors:

> Encouraged by the words of Judas, so noble and so effective in arousing valor and awaking manliness in the souls of the young, they determined not to carry on a campaign but to attack bravely, and to decide the matter, by fighting hand to hand with all courage, because the city and the sanctuary and the temple were in danger (2 Maccabees 12:17).

Although many prominent Old Testament personages served as courageous, if not always consistently virtuous, warriors—including Moses himself, as well as Joshua and the judges Gideon and Samson, to name a few—David ultimately became the exemplar of the just warrior in ancient Israel and the early Church. It was the young shepherd boy David, of course, who slew the giant Goliath of the Philistines with a slingshot (1 Samuel 17:31–58), one of the greatest feats in military history, if only for its sheer audacity, element of surprise, and economy of force. However, the same David, later as king, shamelessly abuses his role as commander-in-chief of Israel when, consumed with lust for Bathsheba, he positions her husband, Uriah the Hittite, one of his captains, "in the forefront of the hardest fighting" and orders Joab the commander to "draw back from him, that he may be struck down, and die" (2 Samuel 11:15). And yet David's reputation did not suffer in the long run, because he was fundamentally a just man. When the prophet Nathan rebukes him for his sin through the clever parable of the ewe lamb, David repents immediately, telling Nathan, "I have sinned against the Lord" (2 Samuel 12:13).

It is no wonder, therefore, that the prophet Isaiah (or "Second Isaiah," according to most modern biblical scholars) quotes the

Lord's promise of an everlasting covenant with Israel based on his "steadfast, sure love for David," whom the Lord had made "a witness to the peoples, a leader and commander for the peoples [*archonta kai prostassonta ethnesin* in the *Septuagint*]" (Isaiah 55:3, 4). The key to (Second) Isaiah's esteem for David lies in the latter's love of justice, both divine and human, the defining virtue of the just warrior. The prophet models his "servant songs" during the Babylonian Captivity in the mid-sixth century B.C. on the righteous and just kingship of David, the earthly prototype of the messiah yet to come. Thus the exemplary virtue of David undergirds, for example, the messianic revelation of the Lord in the first servant song in Isaiah 42:1–4:

> Behold my servant, whom I uphold,
>> my chosen, in whom my soul delights;
> I have put my Spirit upon him,
>> he will bring forth justice to the nations.
> He will not cry or lift up his voice,
>> or make it heard in the street;
>> a bruised reed he will not break,
>> and a dimly burning wick he will not quench;
>> he will faithfully bring forth justice.
> He will not fail or be discouraged
>> till he has established justice in the earth;
>> and the coastlands wait for his law.

Among the early Church fathers, St. Ambrose of Milan (d. 397) in the Latin West was particularly enamored of David as the just warrior par excellence. As Professor Darrell Cole has observed in a previous volume, for St. Ambrose,

> David was "brave in battle, patient in adversity, peaceful in Jerusalem, and merciful in victory" (*On Duties* 1:114). To Ambrose, there appeared to be no virtue lacking in Israel's shepherd-king. David considered not his own advantage but the advantage of the people. He "never waged war unless driven to

it. Thus prudence was combined in him with fortitude in battle."
And David "never entered on a war without seeking counsel of
the Lord" (1.177). In common with other Old Testament
figures, David possessed "fortitude, which both in warfare and at
home is conspicuous in greatness of mind and distinguishes
itself in the strength of the body" (1.115).[5]

Turning to the New Testament, we find the justifiable war
trajectory much more difficult to detect amidst a plethora of texts
that clearly reflect an absolute pacifist perspective.[6] It might be
prudent to resist the temptation to mimic the popular use of a number
of passages that may be viewed as too vague or incidental to
accommodate theories of the nature of war or the soldier's
profession. The use of military imagery is common in the epistles of
St. Paul, but caution is advised lest we read too much into such
literary conceits. References to the "weapons of righteousness" (2
Corinthians 6:7; 10:5) or to fighting the "good fight of faith" (1
Timothy 6:12) clearly designate the spiritual and not worldly variety.
Other passages such as 1 Thessalonians 5:8 and Ephesians 6:10–17
employ predominantly defensive armor—helmet, breastplate, shield,
etc.—as metaphors for exhorting the Christians either to withstand
the onslaughts of the devil or to continue in love and hope of
salvation. And yet the appearance of such military images, whether
as similes or metaphors, may not be dismissed so quickly. For
example, Jesus's parable about the king preparing for war
(Luke14:31–33) is a simile that may not reveal anything about
Jesus's moral judgment of war. But absolute pacifists must still
explain why the Lord would resort to such a militaristic image if He
categorically disapproved of all war and violence on moral or
spiritual grounds.

Jesus Himself appears to sanction the use of swords by His
disciples in two rather perplexing passages, but again prudence
dictates caution. In Matthew 10:34, Jesus's words seem plain
enough: "I have not come to bring peace, but a sword." But the

presence of the word "division" in lieu of "sword" in the parallel passage in Luke 12:51 suggests that both versions were intended as metaphors: instead of an endorsement of violent warfare, the statement probably alludes to the adverse consequences that the disciples will experience from the world as a result of their faith and love.[7] The other gospel text is even more problematic. The two swords that Jesus deems sufficient in Luke 22:35–38 are undoubtedly symbolic of a deeper truth—but what is that truth? Although the two swords may represent approval of the use of force by the disciples in self-defense,[8] the sheer inadequacy of two swords for proper resistance by a band of disciples leaves this interpretation without firm support. And yet absolute pacifists and others who find the work of soldiers somehow intrinsically evil are unable to provide a better interpretation.

A similarly nagging uncertainty obtains in several passages in which centurions or other Roman military officers enjoy a major or minor role.   The hostile actions of soldiers toward Christ or Christians are quite in evidence in Matthew 27:27, Mark 15:16, Luke 23:36, John 19:2–3, and Acts of the Apostles 12:2, 6, 18–19. Far more favorable impressions arise from the believing centurion in Matthew 8:5–13 and Luke 7:1–10, Cornelius the centurion (Acts 10:1–48), the centurion at the Cross (Matthew 27:54 and parallels), and several centurions and a tribune who display a modicum of kindness to St. Paul under arrest (Acts 21:31–40; 22:25–26; 27:1–32).   In light of the odious role of the Roman soldiers in the crucifixion detail and in the subsequent persecution of Christians, it may appear strange that *any* positive military persons occasionally populate the New Testament. But those passages do not necessarily, in the aggregate, amount to a general assessment of the Roman military profession; what emerges from the vignettes is the individual, personal character of the soldiers in question. The most that we may assert with confidence, based on the generally favorable images of soldiers in the Acts of the Apostles, is that its author—who also wrote the final version of the Gospel of St. Luke—may have directed his evangelistic efforts in particular toward the pagan Roman government and its military.[9] Conversely, we may also reasonably conclude that the New Testament writers did not reject the Roman soldiers in their midst as so hopeless, or their work as so heinous, as to be precluded by virtue of their profession from salvation *qua* soldiers.

Four New Testament passages that may have profound relevance to the question of military service are Romans 13:1–7, Titus 3:1, 1 Timothy 2:1–2, and 1 Peter 2:13–17. All of these parallel texts have been pressed into service on behalf of Christian collaboration with existing socio-political orders, but it is safe to assert that these texts were never intended by St. Paul or St. Peter to provide blanket approval of governing authorities as abominable as German Nazis, Soviet Communists, oppressive Muslim regimes, or the worst of the pagan Caesars. The most that we may conclude with some measure of confidence regarding the oft-quoted passage in Romans is that St. Paul does view the Roman government as directly, albeit unwittingly, serving the Lord's divine purposes at least on occasion—it "does not bear the sword in vain" (Romans 13:4)—but only when the Roman authorities act in accordance with God's judgment on good men and evil men. In this connection, it is worth mentioning a parallel instruction of the early second-century patristic text, *Martyrdom of Polycarp* 10.2: "Christians ought to render honor to rulers except when it does themselves harm." Another Church father, St. Irenaios of Lyons, issued a similar injunction in his late-second-century text, *Against Heresies* 5.24.2. St. Paul thus regards even the pagan Roman state as worthy of the obedience and cooperation of Christians in certain specified circumstances for the sake of "conscience"—a crucial qualification. And if the Apostle Paul intends by his use of the term "sword" either capital punishment or military might (or both) as moral goods, then it is also conceivable, though unlikely, that he condones military service by Christians for that state. In any case, if we may presume that St. Paul wrote his epistle to the Romans *ca.* A.D. 55—that is, well before the Neronian persecution when the Apostle himself perished together with St. Peter—then even St. Paul's conditional optimism about the potential good of the Roman government and military may have vanished.

Each of the three parallel passages to Romans 13:1–7 may have a similar genesis in a particular crisis confronting the early Christians. In each of these texts, to be sure, the Roman state, including the pagan emperor, fares rather well, but neither St. Paul nor St. Peter declares unequivocally that Rome is *ipso facto* ordained by God and worthy of unqualified obedience and military service by Christians. The implied antinomy between Church and empire allows for no more than a nuanced recognition of the potential value of the pagan empire and the military profession.

However, two Pauline passages do offer at least an apparent sanction of military service. The analogies in 2 Timothy 2:3-6 to the priorities of the conventional soldier, victorious athlete, and hard-working farmer may constitute little more than a device for stressing the similar sense of priorities expected of Christians. St. Paul declares, "No soldier on service gets entangled in civilian pursuits, since his aim is to satisfy the one who enlisted him" (2 Timothy 2:4). Similarly, the Apostle's invocation of soldiers, vinedressers, and goatherds in 1 Corinthians 9:7 may be merely expedient to his argument for financial support from the brethren. St. Paul asks, "Who serves as a soldier at his own expense?" But once again, not so fast! In each passage neither of the two other social roles— athletes and farmers in one case and vinedressers and goatherds in the other—pose any moral challenge to Christians. If there is nothing intrinsically objectionable in their professions, why should we assume that St. Paul has any qualms about the morality of the soldiers to whom he compares the diligent disciples of Christ? The context of the verse in 2 Timothy even suggests that St. Paul has a positive attitude toward the profession of arms. The preceding verse that introduces his analogy to the professionally responsible soldier reads as follows: "Share in suffering as a good soldier of Christ Jesus" (2 Timothy 2:3). In his homily on 1 Corinthians 9, St. John Chrysostom presumes such a positive attitude by the Apostle:

> And not this only doth he establish by his illustrations, but he shows also what kind of man a priest ought to be. For he ought to possess both the courage of a soldier and the diligence of a husbandman and the carefulness of a shepherd, and after these, to seek nothing more than necessaries.[10]

Once again, the burden of proof rests not with those biblical exegetes, including the Church fathers, who detect in these passages a positive regard for the soldiers who carry out their work justly, but rather with those who would dismiss such biblical references to soldiers as materially irrelevant to the moral worldview St. Paul and the New Testament.

Similarly, the reply of St. John the Baptizer to the soldiers who come to him for advice (Luke 3:14) need not imply an acceptance of their profession, especially if, as seems probable, they were Gentiles for whom the Jewish law was not binding. But, again, not so fast! In the narrative, first "the multitudes that came out to be baptized by him" (John 3:7) ask St. John what they ought to do, then tax collectors who wish to be baptized ask him what they ought to do, and finally "[s]oldiers also asked him, 'And we, what shall we do?'" (Luke 3:14). The context is clearly the condition for St. John's "baptism of repentance for the forgiveness of sins" (Luke 3:3). So when the prophet replies to the soldiers, "Rob no one by violence or by false accusation, and be content with your wages" (Luke 3:14), the implication is profound: St. John would have those soldiers avoid certain grievous, sinful abuses of their power as military men without abandoning their chosen profession. Through baptism, their personal sins would be forgiven, but their profession of arms—even in the service of the oppressive Roman Empire—was not *ipso facto* in need of such forgiveness or rejection. St. Cyril of Alexandria in the fifth century is one Church father who approached this passage with such equanimity. Given the context of St. John's preaching to sinners who had to repent to be forgiven by the Lord, St. Cyril observed that "as a skillful physician applies to each malady a suitable and fitting remedy, so also the Baptist gave to each mode of life useful and becoming counsel ... and very wisely tells the soldiers to oppress no one, but be content with their wages."[11] St. Augustine of Hippo in the Latin West went even further in drawing a positive conclusion about the military from what is *not* said in the passage:

> For if the Christian religion condemned wars of every kind, the command given in the gospel to soldiers asking counsel as to salvation would rather be to cast away their arms, and withdraw themselves wholly from military service; whereas ... the command to be content with their wages manifestly impl[ies] no prohibition to continue in the service.[12]

In short, if the profession of arms were intrinsically evil or sinful like prostitution, the "oldest profession," St. John the Baptizer would not, it is safe to assume, have been so sanguine in his reply to the soldiers seeking baptism. It is also quite reasonable to assume that he would have, instead, exhorted the soldiers to find another line of work, as he would have so advised any harlot who came to him for baptism. He did, after all, demonstrate a particular disdain for sexual immorality when he publicly denounced Herodias for harlotry by implication for marrying her dead husband's brother (Matthew 14:4; compare to Leviticus 20:21). As Professor Darrell Cole asks in a previous volume, "Can you imagine John giving advice to prostitutes about how to prostitute more justly? Yet he did advise soldiers on how to soldier more justly? What's going on here?"[13]

Patristic Writings

The only Church father of the ancient Church to achieve celebrity status as an original thinker on issues of war and peace among contemporary Western religious and secular scholars is St. Augustine of Hippo (d. *ca.* A.D. 430). The contribution of this North African bishop was indeed profound and need only be summarized here from a distinctively teleological Eastern Orthodox perspective.[14]

St. Augustine's fundamental ethic may be characterized as a "teleology of theocentric love."[15] Intentionality is the decisive standard for ethical judgment according to the Latin father, and he redefines the classical category of virtue (*arete*, or "excellence," in Greek) in a peculiarly Christian manner as the perfect love of God, the supreme good. He effects the transition from this teleology to his justification of some wars in his discussions on what modern jurists might term justifiable homicide in his magnum opus *The City of God*, a lesser treatise *Against Faustus*, and in several key letters. St. Augustine defines justice and injustice in relation to the propriety of means to ends. Thus, in the wars conducted by Moses according to the Old Testament, the prophet's obedience to God's providential commands determined their relative goodness.[16] The salient point here, and throughout his *ouvre*, is the relativity of justice (hence Paul Ramsey's astute preference for the neo-Augustinian term "justifiable war" in lieu of the more familiar "just war"). Human motives are usually quite mixed, and each person is both a "saint" and a "sinner" (*simul sanctus et peccator,* in his felicitous Latin phrase). In no way does the great Latin bishop exult in the misery of war or soft-pedal its omnipresence in human history as the vanquished hope of peace on earth and a consequence of sin. The "wise man," he avers, "if he remembers that he is a human being ... will rather lament the fact that he is faced with the necessity of waging just wars; for if they were not just, he would not have to engage in them, and consequently there would be no wars for a wise man. For it is the injustice of the opposing side that lays on the wise man the duty of waging wars."[17] But victory in war providentially still goes to the "juster" side, and St. Augustine does not shrink from assigning the moral description of "good" to that result: "Now when the victory goes to those who were fighting for the juster cause, can anyone doubt that the victory is a matter for rejoicing and the resulting peace is something to be desired? Those things are goods and undoubtedly they are gifts of God."[18]

Another crucial element in St. Augustine's teleological approach to the morality of war is his differentiation of "the interior disposition of the heart" from "the act which appears exteriorly."[19] A Christian as an individual person has no right to kill even in self-defense, for killing another person betrays a sinful interior attachment to one's own transitory life that excludes loving the enemy for the sake of God.[20] However, as a soldier of the community—which, by St. Augustine's time, was preeminently the Christianized Roman Empire—a Christian may kill. Such an outward act in obedience to divinely ordained political authority absolves the soldier of guilt and can be instrumental in assisting the enemy, in an act of other-regarding love, to "yield to their own welfare"![21] The only possible evil in a justifiable war is the sinful love of violence, cruelty, power, etc., that may still characterize the internal disposition of the individual soldier who fulfills, exteriorly, the mandate of "righteous retribution" to "correct or punish" the sins of the wicked against the community while pursuing an ordered, or just, peace as "the desired end of war."[22] Conversely, as long as the Christian soldier engages in combat and even killing of enemy soldiers on proper authority and without internal rancor, he does not contravene the teleology of theocentric love but actually fulfills it by seeking and attaining retributive justice, a lesser virtue (in the Aristotelian ethical tradition) in service of the ultimate Christian virtue of love.[23]

As influential as St. Augustine has proved in the Western world, his impact on Eastern Orthodoxy has been minimal.

Orthodoxy relies more heavily on the patristic patrimony of the Greek and Middle Eastern fathers, and so it is to them that we now turn.

Only two Church fathers before Emperor Constantine the Great's Edict of Milan in 313 regarded Christian participation in the Roman military as a morally acceptable occupation. St. Clement of Rome, third in succession to the Apostle Peter as bishop of the imperial capital, acknowledged in his first epistle (in Greek) to the Church of Corinth around A.D. 96 the providential source and role of the Roman Empire and offered fervent prayer to God on its behalf. This is the context of his explicit admiration for "the discipline, readiness, and obedience" of "those who serve under generals" as a literal reference to the Roman army and not a mere metaphor for Christians and their bishops. The next sentence in the same passage makes this still clearer. Quoting a phrase from 1 Corinthians 15:23 in the New Testament, St. Clement compared the diversification of functions in both Church and military: "But 'each in his own rank' carries out the orders of the emperor and of the generals."[24] Such overt language is more than a rhetorical device and suggests that St. Clement, notwithstanding the recent persecution of the Church under Emperor Domitian, must have been quite enamored of the efficiency, unity, and perhaps personal virtue of the very military that had been turned loose on the faithful.

Clement of Alexandria's few casual remarks are less ambiguous. From his vantage in Roman Egypt toward the end of the second century, he clearly accepted the active involvement of Christians in military life as a meritorious enterprise. In *Christ the Teacher* (*Paidagogos* in Greek), he proposed the soldier, the sailor, and the ruler as models for the modest dress of "the self-restrained man" and later commented on Luke 3:12–13 by observing that God "commands soldiers, through John, to be satisfied with their pay and nothing besides."[25] In his *Exhortation to the Heathen*, Clement may have encouraged military converts to remain in their profession instead of abandoning it, as his pacifist colleagues would have insisted: "Has knowledge [i.e., *gnosis*, or the unique Christian revelation] taken hold of you while engaged in military service? Listen to the commander, who orders what is right."[26] In an entire chapter in his *Miscellanies* (*Stromata* in Greek), he certainly expressed fondness for Moses' skill as a military leader in Old Testament Israel, which, he claimed, the ancient Greeks "had the advantage of receiving from Moses." In that same context, Clement also praised the virtues of military command in general, which Moses exemplified:

> Now, generalship involves three ideas: caution, enterprise, and the union of the two. And each of these consists of three things, acting as they do either by word, or by deeds, or by both together. And all of this can be accomplished either by persuasion, or by compulsion, or by inflicting harm in the way of taking vengeance on those who ought to be punished; and this either by doing what is right, or by telling what is untrue, or by telling what is true, or by adopting any of these means conjointly at the same time.[27]

To be sure, Clement saw the Christian journey as a dynamic process from lower "gnosis" to higher, and hence from lesser virtue to greater and lesser goods to higher. Warfare and the military life might be acceptable to him, but there was always the better way of peace. "For we do not train our women like Amazons to manliness in war," he wrote in the *Miscellanies*, "since we wish the men even to be peaceable."[28] And earlier, in *Christ the Teacher*, Clement compared war unfavorably to peace:

> We are educated not for war but for peace. In war there is need for much equipment, just as self-indulgence craves an abundance. But peace and love, simple and plain blood sisters, do not need arms nor abundant supplies. Their nourishment is the Word, the Word whose leadership enlightens and educates,

from whom we learn poverty and humility and all that goes with love of freedom and of mankind and of the good.[29]

As is well known, the *Pax Constantini* ("Peace of Constantine") brought the Church out of the catacombs and margins of Roman society into the halls of power. Politically and spiritually unshackled, numerous theologians now freely expressed moral support for the military defense of the formerly hostile Empire, most spectacularly Lactantius of North Africa, whose metamorphosis from apocalyptic, sectarian, pacifist critic of the pagan Roman regime to champion of the imperial rule and conquests of Emperor Constantine the Great is virtually breathtaking. Among the many Greek fathers, St. Basil the Great (d. 379) stands out in particular for one brief letter to a soldier written a year before Basil died. Presented below in its entirety, it speaks for itself:

> I have many reasons for thanking God for mercies vouchsafed to me in my journey, but I count no blessing greater than the knowledge of your excellency [*arete*, or "virtue," in the Greek], which has been permitted me by our good Lord's mercy. I have learnt to know one who proves that even in a soldier's life it is possible to preserve the perfection of love to God, and that we must mark a Christian not by the style of his dress, but by the disposition of his soul. It was a great delight to me to meet you; and now, whenever I remember you, I feel very glad. Play the man; be strong; strive to nourish and multiply love to God, that there may be given you by Him yet greater boons of blessing. I need no further proof that you remember me; I have evidence in what you have done.[30]

Other Byzantine-era saints who endorsed war, at least on occasion, include St. Photios the Great, Patriarch of Constantinople, whose letter to the Khan Boris-Michael of Bulgaria in the late ninth century assured him that bravery in battle adorns a good ruler (though not as much as kindness to his subjects). There is also St.

Theophylactos of Ochrid (now in Macedonia), whose prudential advice for princes around 1085 urged that, "while making peace, practice for war, exercising yourself constantly in preparation for every type of warfare."[31]

One more Eastern father warrants some scrutiny here: Aphrahat, author of the Syriac text known in English as *Demonstrations,* which was written in the Mesopotamian fringes of the Byzantine Empire around 336. The fifth section addresses war and provides one of the few sustained arguments on this issue in all of Eastern patristic literature.[32] The text is heavily dependent on the apocalyptic imagery of the Old Testament book of Daniel, which it quotes frequently and from which it derives its framework for reconstructing the rise and fall of empires, including Rome—the last and greatest of all. Aphrahat eagerly anticipated "the kingdom of King Messiah, Who will bring to nought the kingdom of this world, and He will rule for ever and ever." Although Rome, the "fourth kingdom," will be humbled as its predecessors were brought down according to Daniel 2:34, Aphrahat had a high regard for the Romans as the "children of Esau," who had benefited providentially from the failure of the "sons of Jacob" (that is, the Israelites) to prosper in the kingdom that the Lord had originally given to them. He was confident that the Lord, who often intervened in critical moments in the life of ancient Israel, would now protect the "deposit" that He had entrusted to the Romans: "Therefore this Kingdom of the children of Esau shall not be delivered up into the hand of the hosts that are gathered together, that desire to go up against it … [D]oubt not about it, that the Kingdom will not be conquered. For a mighty champion Whose name is Jesus shall come with power, and bearing as His armour all the power of the Kingdom."

That this was not merely a prophecy of the eternal security of the Church in language borrowed from the New Testament book of Revelation is unmistakably clear from the next few sentences. Aphrahat cited Luke 2:1–2 to indicate that, from His birth, Jesus

71

"was enrolled amongst them" (that is, the Gentiles, or Romans). Then the Syrian father declared: "And His standard abounds in that place, and they are clothed in His armour, and shall not be found wanting in war." This obvious pledge of divine acceptance in wartime carried with it an implicit acceptance of warfare on behalf of the Kingdom. But who precisely are the Romans to whom this pledge is given? Are they pagan or Christian or both? Aphrahat avers that before the present Christian rulers—"in the years of the Kings that preceded these"—the empire (or "the beast") was "subdued a little" in wars, "because the chiefs and kings who stood up at that time in the Kingdom of the children of Esau did not wish to lead with them to war the Man [that is, Jesus Christ] who was enrolled with them in the poll-tax." Fortunately, that "beast" was not allowed to be slain, so that God's eschatological plan of salvation for the world might unfold. But it was only the Christian empire, which engages in war in the name of and with the divine aid of Christ, that "shall not be found wanting in war." This was a prophetic principle with far-reaching ramifications for the moral legitimacy of war for Christians.

And yet Aphrahat mitigated the force of his own prophecy of the invincibility of the Christian Roman Empire in war. Citing several biblical passages that teach personal humility and the avoidance of self-glorification, Aphrahat issued a stern reminder that any earthly kingdom, even a Christian one, invariably exalts itself excessively and impiously, particularly through its military conquests: "For even if the forces shall go up and conquer, yet know that it is a chastisement of God; and though they conquer, they shall be condemned in a righteous judgment. But yet be thou assured of this, that the beast shall be slain at its (appointed) time." Thus the Christian Empire was still "the beast" at heart and would be properly overthrown in fulfillment of the divine plan of salvation. There was, for Aphrahat, something inherently unrighteous in military conquest that ultimately merits moral condemnation as a wretched excess, a disproportionate response to a grievance that requires instead a just or righteous response. This cautious, measured approach to justifiable war would become a hallmark of the best Christian reflections on the moral dilemma, both East and West.

Canon Law

Eusebios of Caesarea, a fourth-century Church historian and champion of Emperor Constantine the Great, foreshadowed the dual canonical standard that would later prohibit all clergy from killing any human beings (in war or otherwise), while regulating the conditions under which laymen might serve in the military. Referring in his treatise, *Demonstration of the Gospel*, to two states of perfection that Christians may pursue, Eusebios continued:

> Two ways of life were thus given by the law of Christ to His Church. The one is above nature, and beyond common human living; it admits not marriage, child-bearing, property nor the possession of wealth, but wholly and permanently separate from the common customary life of mankind, it devotes itself to the service of God alone in its wealth of heavenly love! And they who enter on this course, appear to die to the life of mortals, to bear with them nothing earthly but their body, and in mind and spirit to have passed to heaven. Like some celestial beings they gaze upon human life, performing the duty of a priesthood to Almighty God for the whole race ... Such then is the perfect form of the Christian life. And the other more humble, more human, permits men to join in pure nuptials and to produce children, to undertake government, to give orders to soldiers fighting for right; it allows them to have minds for farming, for trade, and the other more secular interests as well as for religion; and it is for them that times of retreat and instruction, and days for hearing sacred things are set apart. And a kind of secondary grade of piety is attributed to them, giving just such help as such lives require, so that all men, whether Greeks or barbarians, have their part in the coming of salvation, and profit by the teaching of the Gospel.[33]

We could not ask for a more explicit statement of the pursuit of justifiable war—albeit by Christian laymen alone—as a "lesser good."

The rich canonical corpus of the Orthodox Church contains three canons and a *novella* (or "new law") of Emperor St. Justinian the Great (d. 565) that allude briefly to Christian laymen in military service, as well as three canons that address the issue more directly.[33] Canon 12 of the First Ecumenical Council addresses a particular historical context—namely, Christian soldiers who had compromised their faith by serving under the militant pagan co-Emperor Licinius in his civil war against Emperor Constantine—that retains little relevance to our modern era, other than its implicit principle that Christian service depends on the moral and religious quality of an army and the government or state it purports to defend by force of arms. The other two canons are, however, profoundly significant in Orthodox moral tradition.[34]

Tucked almost inconspicuously in the body of canon 1 of St. Athanasios the Great (d. 373) is a remarkable argument in defense of the exceptional nature of killing in war. To be sure, the renowned archbishop of Alexandria had sent this letter to the monk Amun in 354 to help him deal with certain problems pertaining to sexual purity. But the small passage in question, intended obviously as an analog to his argument, has endured far beyond its original context and is rendered here in full:

> It is not lawful to murder, but in war [it is] both lawful and worthy of approval to destroy the adversaries. Thus at any rate, those who are bravest in war are also deemed worthy of great honors, and monuments of them are raised proclaiming their successes; so that the same thing, on the one hand, is not lawful according to some circumstances and at some times, but, on the other hand, according to some other circumstances and opportunely it is permitted and possible.[35]

Among the commentaries, only the *Rudder* offers any serious interpretative observations. Its contention that this canon only permits killing in war against "enemies of the faith" may be a valid extrapolation, but it limits the rather indefinite use of the Greek term *tous antipolous* (here translated as "adversaries"). St. Athanasios may intend a more general validity of killing in war irrespective of the identity of the adversaries. The *Rudder* also contends that St. Athanasios proffers this counsel as an example of how the same thing can be sometimes "good" and sometimes "evil."[36] Such a presumption, if correct, bears a striking formal parallel to the classic statement of St. Maximos the Confessor in the seventh century that "nothing among creatures is evil except misuse."[37] An act may in itself be one that is morally neutral—that is, intrinsically neither good nor evil—but requires a personal intention in order for it to acquire moral value.[38] On this interpretation, killing in war could, under certain conditions, be a lawful act with a good intention or goal (*telos* in Greek), such as the defense of innocent and otherwise defenseless persons in the community from aggression or the protection of the honor of the Church from desecration. We might wish to add to St. Maximos's conditions that the war in question have a decisive, salutary, foreseeable effect such as preservation of the commonwealth from foreign conquest, since the concept of intentionality is notoriously susceptible to abuse and ought to apply only to those acts capable of sustaining a noble intention. In light of this parallel, St. Athanasios's canon may be interpreted as sanctioning some wars as moral goods, or at least not evils.

The other canon that we shall consider looms even larger in Orthodox moral tradition. Canon 13 of St. Basil the Great (actually his *Epistle* 188.13 to Amphilokios *ca.* 374) reads as follows: "Our fathers did not reckon as murders the murders in wars, it seems to me, giving a pardon to those who defend themselves on behalf of moderation and piety. But perhaps it is well to advise that they abstain from the [holy] communion for only three years, since their hands are not clean."[39] Among the "fathers" to whom he refers, St. Basil assuredly has in mind St. Athanasios and the canon discussed above, as well as oral tradition or other texts perhaps no longer extant. Several points of contrast with St. Athanasios's canon warrant mention.

First, St. Basil explicitly provides a particular condition for the traditional justification for killing in war: the defense of piety and moderation (or order). Not only does this sharpen the vagueness of St. Athanasios's "adversaries"; it also furnishes an authoritative guide for conduct in war in keeping with St. Maximos's emphasis on intentionality. Thus the Byzantine canonist Balsamon concurs with St. Basil's allowance for the defense of "the faithful about to be taken prisoner" by infidels in a given war.[40] And the *Rudder*, in its commentary on this canon, boldly outlines the result of pacifism in the face of external threats, such as the Byzantines eventually had to endure after the conquest by the Muslim Ottoman Turks: "For, if once the barbarians and infidels should succeed in gaining the upper hand, neither piety will be left, since they disregard it and seek to establish their own wicked faith and bad belief, nor sobriety and maintenance of honor, seeing that their victory would be followed by many instances of violation and ravishment of young women and young men."[41]

Second, the suggested penance entails refraining from receiving the "holy mysteries" (or "sacrament" in Western Christian parlance) of the Body and Blood of Christ, but not expulsion from the Church altogether or reduction to the status of catechumen. Nevertheless, the Byzantine canonists Zonaras and Balsamon regard this penance, respectively, as excessive and irrelevant. Zonaras views even a three-year excommunication from the holy mysteries—in contrast to twenty years for murder and even ten for having or performing an abortion—as unfairly burdensome and an unbearable punishment for Christians who perform so noble a service as defense of faith and empire. For Christian soldiers, particularly the bravest, would never be able to partake of the most precious thing in Orthodox liturgical life throughout their entire military careers, owing to the frequency of wars.[42] In a much less defiant tone, Balsamon coolly (and erroneously, we might add) asserts that this canon is inoperative, or truly moot, because the soldiers are too frequently busy with warfare and the task of destroying enemies to be able to partake of the holy mysteries.[43]

Third, the recommended penance is clearly intended by St. Basil, as the *Rudder* observes, as "an advisory and indecisive suggestion" rather than a definitive canonical requirement.[44] Zonaras feels confident that in opposing the penance he is not violating an injunction.[45] To be sure, the 14th-century Byzantine canonist, Matthew Blastares, provides a dissident counterpoint to his predecessors based primarily on his neo-Augustinian understanding of the complex "closeness of human virtuous actions to evil." Killing in war is rooted in "freely chosen passions of transgression," which require purification through penance "to melt away the filth that clings to their [the soldiers'] way of life." And yet even Blastares acknowledges—together with St. Basil, whose *Epistle* 106, as we have seen above, extols the exemplary virtue of a particular soldier—the good dimension of some warfare when he asks, "[F]or what might be a more worthy reason for praise than to defend on behalf of chastity and piety?" [46]

CHAPTER 4

Orthodox Jus in Bello II:

Saints, Liturgies, Modern Writers

Hagiography

The stylized written accounts of the lives (*vitae* in the scholarly community's preferred Latin) and activities (*acta* in Latin) of the thousands of Eastern Orthodox saints proclaimed officially by the Church constitute a fourth source of the Orthodox moral tradition of war as a "lesser good." A previous study has analyzed the moral significance of those "exceptional saints" who maintained an absolute pacifist witness, but their company is easily surpassed by the number of saints who engaged in or blessed certain military operations as righteous or good acts.[1] On both sides of this moral divide, these generally embellished literary creations share a common theological and social purpose: the proclamation of spiritual and moral ideals for the edification and encouragement of all the Orthodox faithful, whether highly educated or theologically unsophisticated.

Among the dozens of ancient military martyrs who served as Christian soldiers in the pagan Roman army until faced with the dilemma of openly professing paganism or Christ, several are especially revered by the Orthodox faithful.

St. George, a Syrian Christian from birth and a tribune (equivalent to a modern lieutenant colonel) of a famous regiment, was, because of his courage in battle, promoted to the rank of general by Emperor Diocletian toward the end of the third century. Only when he was certain that the emperor's new purge of Christians could not be stopped by other means did he take the dramatic step of resistance that led to his execution. He refused to sacrifice to the

78

pagan gods and was summarily imprisoned, tortured, and killed.[2] Orthodox icons of St. George usually depict him in full Roman military uniform astride a white horse and lancing a dragon, a typical iconographic symbol of Satan. He is, like the other soldier-saints, also popularly regarded by Orthodox Christians as a fervent intercessor before the throne of God and a supernatural protector in time of war. In one miracle story in the Miracles of Saint George, the great martyr was invoked by Leontios, a soldier whose son George was about to fight in the Byzantine army against the Bulgarians after war had begun in 913. The prayer of Leontios before an icon of St. George is probably prototypical of the invocations that were (and still may be) addressed to other soldier-saints as well: "To thee, Great Martyr Saint George, we entrust our only son, whom we called by thy name out of love for thee! Be to him a guide on the way, a guardian in battle, and return him to us safe and sound, so that, having been blessed by thee according to our faith, we may by many good works ever glorify thy solicitude and care for us."[3]

The *acta* of St. Procopios that appears in an 18th-century collection by St. Nikodemos of the Holy Mountain portray him as a devout pagan named Neanian whom Emperor Diocletian appointed "Duke" of Egypt for the purpose of persecuting the Christians in that province. But after he heard the voice of Christ and had a second miraculous confrontation, Neanian felt hopeful enough as a nascent follower of Christ to invoke His aid during a battle in Alexandria with a barbarian tribe. Eventually forced to sacrifice to the gods, Neanian removed his armor and refused to offer sacrifice, knowing the dire consequence of his action.[4] St. Procopios is the only saint, in addition to the Virgin Mary and the imperial Byzantine son and mother, SS. Constantine and Helen, whose name is invoked as an intercessor at the end of the Byzantine Orthodox rite of matrimony.

According to the *acta* of St. Demetrios of Thessalonika, a favorite saint of the Greek Orthodox, the soldier pretended to be an idolater until Emperor Maximillian named him *stratelates* ("general") of the armies of Thessaly at the beginning of the fourth century. Thereafter, General Demetrios openly professed his Christianity and suffered imprisonment for his witness. The immediate cause of his death was, however, most unusual even for *acta* or *vitae* with presumably little historical content. He blessed a certain Nestor (also later canonized as a saint) in his jail cell, who, despite his diminutive size, managed to defeat a pagan giant named Lyaios by killing him in combat in the arena. (The parallel to the boy David slaying the giant Philistine Goliath was not lost on the ancient Orthodox.) The emperor ordered Demetrios put to death when he learned that his general was instrumental in the death of his champion.[5] What commends this popular hagiographic narrative to generations of Orthodox faithful is precisely the captivating drama of the saint's personal moral decision. When compelled, at length, to choose between fidelity to Christ and loyalty to the pagan emperor whom he previously served without question, Demetrios the Roman general cast his lot with the "soldiers" of Christ and consequently forfeited his command and his life. And yet he maintained his vocation as a combatant against injustice—by proxy, to be sure, but in an unmistakably violent setting. Unlike his counterpart, St George, the great soldier-martyr of Thessalonika is often depicted in Orthodox icons astride a horse while lancing an enemy soldier lying prostrate near his horse. That an act of such violence can adorn a sacred image leaves no doubt that the Church regards Demetrios's profession—and his role in particular—as worthy of veneration.[6]

More reliably historical but of equal moral significance are the instances when saints blessed or comforted military commanders or even exhorted them to victory. In the early sixth century *vita* of St. Daniel the Stylite (d. 493), a rumor of a possible attack on Alexandria by the Vandal Genseric moved St. Daniel to assure Emperor Leo I that there was no danger. The emperor, however, was still to decide for himself whether to send an army, in which case "the God, Whom I adore, will both preserve your Piety unhurt and will strengthen those who are sent against the enemies of the Empire."[7] Similarly, in the seventh-century *vita* of St. Theodore of Sykeon (d. 613), the saint gave a prophetic blessing to Domnitziolos (nephew of Emperor Phokas), who had been dispatched with an army to confront the invading Persians. When Domnitziolos learned that the Lazi meanwhile had raided Cappadocia, he beseeched the holy man to pray for him and to advise him concerning the military situation. Exercising this profound privilege of so many Orthodox saints, St. Theodore assured him that the Lazi would pose no problem but that the war against the Persians would proceed differently: "[Y]ou are going to experience great trials and conflicts, but I commend you to God and to his holy martyr George to keep you from harm. When these dangers beset you, you will remember my prayer and God will rescue you from your great peril."[8] In fulfillment of this prophecy, Domnitziolos's army was slaughtered by the Persians, but he himself escaped after calling upon the prayers of St. Theodore to intercede with the Lord. A more hopeful prophecy of victory occurs in a 12th-century Slavic *vita* of St. Methodios (d. 885), which probably derives from a ninth-century *vita* from Bulgaria. At a time when Prince Sventopluk of Moravia was waging an unsuccessful military campaign against "the heathens," St. Methodios sent to him a message with the following proposition: "If you make a vow to spend the feast day of Peter with me, together with your warriors, I believe in God that He will hand them over to you forthwith."[9] The hagiographer hastens to add that this came to pass.

Perhaps the best known example of an unabashed exhortation to military victory by an Orthodox Christian saint appears in the early 15th-century *vita* by Epiphanius the Wise entitled, *The Life, Acts, and Miracles of Our Blessed and Holy Father Sergius of Radonezh* (d. 1392). When the Grand Duke Dmitry discovered that another invasion of Russia by Khan Mamai of the Muslim Tatars was imminent, he consulted the holy Russian ascetic, who, "bestowing on him his blessing, and strengthened by prayer, said to him, 'It behooveth you, lord, to have a care for the lives of the flock committed to you by God. Go forth against the heathens; and upheld by the strong arm of God, conquer; and return to your country sound in health, and glorify God with loud praise.'" Later, shortly before the forces of Dmitry and the Khan clashed, a courier arrived in the camp of the Russian commander with a new message of assurance from St. Sergius: "Be in no doubt, lord; go forward with faith and confront the enemy's ferocity; and fear not, for God will be on your side."[10] The eventual victory by the Russian army certainly helped St. Sergius's reputation as a prophet and national saint; it also served to implant firmly in the memory of the Russian Orthodox Church the decisive encouragement and support for the Grand Duke (recently canonized as a saint himself) and his army that St. Sergius had provided at a crucial moment in the nation's history. This spectacular episode was, however, only the latest in a long series that validated, according to George Fedotov, an emerging Russian commitment to "the idea of a just war." That entailed a specific focus on causation: "Defensive war is always justified, and to defend one's 'heritage' is not only the right of a prince but also his duty towards the inhabitants of his lands."[11]

There are numerous *vitae* of another category of soldier-saint—the warrior prince—among the historic Orthodox nations in the Balkans, particularly Serbia, as well as western lands such as Anglo-Saxon England and Norway before the Great Schism between East and West in 1054. Perhaps the most profound in a prosaic collection of *vitae* of Serbian warrior princes and other saints is that of St. Lazar (d. 1389), last tsar of the medieval Serbian kingdom. His *vita* includes the great national defeat on the plains of Kosovo Polje and the cruel death of the tsar at the hands of the Ottoman Turkish conquerors. With a sense of deep pathos, the hagiographer observes that St. Lazar and his benighted army "fought bravely for Cross and freedom."[12]

Although we ought not speak too confidently about an archetypal *vita* that represents the fullest expression of a type of saint or a specific genre of hagiography, the *vitae* of St. Alexander Nevsky (d. 1263) come closest to the ideal of the regal warrior saint. A 15th-century vita in the *Second Pskovian Chronicle* has the unusual heroic title of *Tale of the Life and Courage of the Pious and Great Prince Alexander*. A recent translator, Professor S. A. Zenkovsky of Vanderbilt University, suggests that the "original version of this *vita* was apparently written as a military tale by one of the warriors of his household who witnessed Alexander's last years of life." This legendary text, known as a *skazanie* in Russian (in contrast to the simpler ecclesiastical *zhitiya*, or *vita*), was then rewritten later in the 13th century by a cleric from the town of Vladimir who displaced some of the references to ancient and Byzantine heroic figures with biblical names and inserted numerous scriptural motifs and passages, the biblical quotes serving variously as panegyrics to St. Alexander or quotations attributed to him.[13]

The result is an idealized portrayal of a prince of the northern region of Novgorod, interspersed with certain clearly historical facts, which remains a living tribute to the leader who saved Russia, in turn, from conquest by the aggressive crusaders from the Roman Catholic West and from total subjugation to the Mongol Golden Horde that had already conquered Kyivan Rus'. His strategy and methods were, in those two missions, extraordinarily different and reveal the depths of St. Alexander's courage and wisdom.

The strong, forceful language describing the campaigns against the Teutonic Knights and Lithuanians is most intriguing. The use of verbs and phrases such as razed, hanged, taken prisoner, campaigned, to show them, captured, liberated, destroyed, cut to pieces, to defeat, killed, captured, jeered, and "attaching them to the tails of their horses" illustrates in no uncertain terms how the indignant targets of foreign aggression defended themselves. For the hagiographer, such vivid expressions engender an abiding respect for the saint's "great glory." But they are juxtaposed to very different descriptions. Whereas St. Alexander accepted the challenge of the Roman Catholic crusaders and met them on the battlefield in 1240 and 1242, his posture toward the Mongol Khan, whose vastly superior occupation forces ruled much of Russia in an appanage state, was one of deference, respect, even humility. St. Alexander became an ambassador of good will on behalf of his beleaguered people. Even after this prince of Novgorod became in 1252 the Great Prince of Vladimir and All Russia, he "went to the Khan and beseeched him not to drive his [Russian] people into misery."[14] Although this image of the great victor over the Western invaders humbling himself before the infidel Khan may have disturbed the hagiographer, whose concept of glory was clearly shaped more by triumph rather than failure, the hagiographer still faithfully recorded this unexpected detail of the saint's life. He cast it in the best possible light, though, by assimilating it to a passage that he (incorrectly, to be sure) attributed to the Old Testament prophecy of Isaiah, which purportedly praises princes who are "quiet, friendly, meek and peaceful ... and hospitable to those who come to him from other lands."[15]

In his *vita*, St. Alexander is the quintessential just prince and righteous warrior. The Teutonic Knights, Swedes, and Mongols may have come to Russia as conquerors, but St. Alexander and his fellow Russians—at least at this juncture in their national history—had no military purpose in mind other than defending their motherland from unwanted invasions. The most eloquent statement of the justice of purely defensive military action on behalf of an entire people occurs before the Battle of Neva, when St. Alexander prayed in tears before the altar of the Church of Hagia Sophia: "Glorious and Just Lord, Great and Powerful God, God Eternal, who created heaven and earth, and who determined the boundaries of the peoples: Thou commandest people to live without oppressing other countries." Then, as he remembered a passage from the Old Testament book of Psalms, he declared: "O Lord, judge those who offended me. Smite those who set themselves against me and come to my aid with arms and shields."[16]

So why, then, was Alexander, Prince of Novgorod, canonized in 1380 by the same Russian Orthodox Church whose precursor in Kyivan Rus' had already formally recognized as saints two 11th-century princes—Boris and Gleb—whose greatest spiritual feat was pacifist nonresistance to their murderous brother Sviatopolk? Russia and Ukraine together boast a proportionately higher number of princes, especially those who defended their Orthodox faith and people, who have been canonized than most other regions of Christendom, save perhaps Serbia. St. Alexander Nevsky was certainly celebrated for his spectacular military victories against the invaders from the West, and for his charismatic leadership and bravery in battle. But the true moral meaning of his life lay not in glorious triumph alone. The actual history of this prince was marked by extreme pathos. When this hero of the earlier victories resorted to personal pleading and submission to the Khan and vigorously opposed any desperate acts of resistance and rebellion by his own people, most Russians apparently accused him of cowardice and heaped calumny and insults upon him and his name. Few realized how his intercessions with the Khan had spared them untold horrors from the ruthless Mongols. Few realized that their wise prince had heeded the timeless counsel of Qoheleth the Preacher in the Old Testament book of Ecclesiastes: "For everything there is a season, and a time for every matter under heaven"—specifically "a time to love and a time to hate; a time for war, and a time for peace" (Ecclesiastes 3:1, 8). St. Alexander died at the age of 42 from too much strain, practically crucified by his own people. But his reputation was resurrected when the people finally realized that a genuine saint had been in their midst, a courageous soldier and brilliant diplomat, a spiritual and moral giant who walked the earth as the closest approximation to the ideal Orthodox prince that the faithful could ever hope to lead them.

There is one more warrior prince whose official status as an Orthodox saint may be somewhat in dispute, but whose exemplary piety and courage in a hopeless battle against Muslim adversaries has special resonance in the post-"Nine-Eleven" world. Blessed Constantine XI Palaiologos, last emperor of Byzantium, perished in defense of Constantinople on May 29, 1453. To appreciate his noble self-sacrifice, it is necessary first to review what happened to the great capital city of the thousand-year empire when the Ottoman Turks finally broke through its walls.

In keeping with Islamic tradition, Sultan Mehmet promised his victorious Turkish troops three days of unrestrained pillage in the Orthodox Christian city, whose inhabitants had resisted his demand to surrender. The prolific British historian of Byzantium, Steven Runciman, described the scene as follows:

> The regiments marched in one by one, with music playing and colours flying. But once they were within the city all joined in the wild hunt for loot. ... They slew everyone that they met in the streets, men, women and children without discrimination. The blood ran in rivers down the steep streets from the heights of Petra towards the Golden Horn. But soon the lust for slaughter was assuaged. The soldiers realized that captives and precious objects would bring them greater profit.[17]

The Turks went on an iconoclastic frenzy, "burning books and icons once the jeweled covers and frames had been wrenched off, and hacking at the mosaics and marbles around the walls."[18] In the monastery of the Holy Savior in Chora, the marauding soldiers destroyed the Hodigitria Mother of God icon, the most sacred of all madonnas, alleged to have been painted by the Evangelist Luke himself. In the great church of Hagia Sophia ("Holy Wisdom") built during the reign of the Emperor St. Justinian the Great in the sixth century, Turkish troops battered down the massive doors soon after the Divine Liturgy had concluded, killed some of the older, weaker worshippers, and bound the rest together by women's veils and scarves. The rapacious soldiers fought over their captives on the floor of the most sacred church in Christendom and again later in their own quarters. As the pillage continued throughout the day (the city's walls having been breached around 8 a.m. after a six-hour assault), "[s]ome of the younger nuns preferred martyrdom to dishonour and flung themselves to death down well-shafts."[19] Byzantines hiding in their homes were taken captive after their homes were ransacked, and those who could not keep up were slaughtered, "together with a number of infants who were held to be of no value."[20]

By late afternoon, however, the sultan called an end to the looting, since there already was plenty of booty and captives to sort out and distribute among the victors. Estimates of the human prizes range as high as 50,000, the vast majority of whom were noncombatants; some 4,000 had perished in one day, including the massacred civilians. Mehmet himself entered the vanquished city, immediately proclaimed that Hagia Sophia would be turned into a Muslim mosque, and soon had various and sundry teenage boys sent to him for his perverse pleasure, even ordering the decapitation of the resistant Byzantine nobleman Lucas Notaras, his 14-year-old son, and son-in-law. Such was the inglorious fate of the once glorious center of the Christian world.

This was what the last emperor of the Byzantines had tried in vain to prevent. Constantine XI (1404-1453) is widely revered in modern Greece as a heroic warrior and Orthodox martyr, despite his tacit support for the ill-fated Union of Ferarra-Florence in 1439 after he assumed the imperial throne in 1448. In a little booklet titled *Constantine the Ethnomartyr: Last Emperor of Byzantium*, Archbishop Chrysostomos of Etna, California, offers a staunch defense of the emperor's fundamental Orthodoxy. St. Constantine XI, the old-calendar Greek hierarch insists, inherited the mess from his older brother, the genuinely Uniate Byzantine emperor John Catacuzenos, who was willing to concede all the theological points disputed by the Byzantine Orthodox and the Roman Catholic pope. The younger brother affirmed the Union only as "a matter of political expediency and not one of theological commitment," and his "unionist actions ... were not willful, deliberate betrayals of his Faith."[21] The best evidence of St. Constantine's own heart was his church attendance during the last Holy Week and Pascha (Easter) before the fall of the capital. Together with the vast majority of the Orthodox faithful, including most of the priests and deacons and all of the monks in the city, the emperor went to the strictly Orthodox liturgies celebrated in the palace church of the Theotokos of Blachernae, instead of the services conducted by Latin clergy and unionist Greeks in Hagia Sophia, the historic patriarchal cathedral. Although the emperor did participate in the Divine Liturgy in Hagia Sophia on the eve of the final assault by the Turks, the entire civilian population had gathered on that at once sorrowful and electric occasion. There, with the fall of the great city imminent, the emperor received the Holy Mysteries of the Body and Blood of Christ from the Greek Orthodox and Latin clergy concelebrating that final Eucharist *in extremis*. St. Constantine tearfully begged forgiveness of the entire congregation and withdrew to his palace, where he did the same with his imperial staff. According to several generally reliable chronicles, he dedicated the rest of his last evening on earth in tearful prayer on his knees, not in fear or for himself but rather for his subjects, his Church, and the last vestige of the once great Orthodox Christian Roman Empire.

Constantine XI forever won the admiration and love of the Byzantines, the future Greek nation, and knowledgeable Orthodox Christians everywhere[22] by his extraordinary behavior as a warrior-emperor on the eve of battle on May 28 and during the military defense of Constantinople on May 29. While the Turks rested beyond the massive stone walls of the city before the day appointed for the final assault, the Byzantine emperor led a procession with icons and relics around the perimeter inside the barricades. Then he addressed the assembled government officials, military officers, and soldiers in a motivational speech whose inspiration and eloquence must rank among the greatest rhetorical achievements in Western civilization—even if the three extant accounts contain certain embellishments.[23] An historian of late Byzantium, Donald M. Nicol, concludes that the shortest version—the one contained in a letter of Leonardo of Chios, Roman Catholic archbishop of Lesbos, to Pope Nicholas V on August 19, 1453—is the most reliable account.[24] It is reproduced below as it appears in Nicol's recent book titled *The Immortal Emperor*:

> Gentlemen, illustrious captains of the army, and our most Christian comrades in arms: we now see the hour of battle approaching. I have therefore elected to assemble you here to make it clear that you must stand together with firmer resolution than ever. You have always fought with glory against the enemies of Christ. Now the defence of your fatherland and the city known the world over, which the infidel and evil Turks have been besieging for two and fifty days, is committed to your lofty spirits. Be not afraid because its walls have been worn down by the enemy's battering. For your strength lies in the protection of God and you must show it with your arms quivering and your swords brandished against the enemy. I know that this undisciplined mob will, as is their custom, rush upon you with loud cries and ceaseless volleys of arrows. These will do you no bodily harm, for I see that you are well covered in armour. They will strike the walls, our breastplates and our shields. So do not imitate the Romans who, when the Carthaginians went into battle against them, allowed their cavalry to be terrified by the fearsome sight and sound of elephants. In this battle you must stand firm and have no fear, no thought of flight, but be inspired to resist with ever more herculean strength. Animals may run away from animals. But you are men, men of stout heart, and

you will hold at bay these dumb brutes, thrusting your spears and swords into them, so that they will know that they are fighting not against their own kind but against the masters of animals.

You are aware that the impious and infidel enemy has disturbed the peace unjustly. He has violated the oath and treaty that he made with us; he has slaughtered our farmers at harvest time; he has erected a fortress on the Propontis as it were to devour the Christians; he has encircled Galata under a pretence of peace. Now he threatens to capture the city of Constantine the Great, your fatherland, the place of ready refuge for all Christians, the guardian of all Greeks, and to profane its holy shrines of God by turning them into stables for horses. Oh my lords, my brothers, my sons, the everlasting honour of Christians is in your hands. You men of Genoa, men of courage and famous for your infinite victories, you who have always protected this city, your mother, in many a conflict with the Turks, show now your prowess and your aggressive spirit toward them with manly vigour. You men of Venice, most valiant heroes, whose swords have many a time made Turkish blood to flow and who in our time have sent so many ships, so many infidel souls to the depths under the command of Loredano, the most excellent captain of our fleet, you who have adorned this city as if it were your own with fine, outstanding men, lift high your spirits now for battle. You, my comrades in arms, obey the commands of your leaders in the knowledge that this is the day of your glory—a day on which, if you shed but a drop of blood, you will win for yourselves crowns of martyrdom and eternal fame.[25]

When the battle was joined and the Turks first managed to scale the outer and inner walls of the city and then breached a gate and began to pour into the city, the warrior-emperor tried to rally his panicking troops. What happened next is by no means historically certain, but some of the more reliable sources indicate that St. Constantine Palaiologos cast off his imperial garb and rushed headlong into the growing mass of Turks at the gate of St. Romanos, fighting to the death with sword in hand as a common soldier. His corpse was probably decapitated along with all of the others, as it was the Turkish custom to mutilate the bodies of their vanquished opponents. (A fresco icon in a Romanian monastery depicts this sorry demise, although Constantine appears bound and very much alive at the time.)[26]

Although his body seems to have disappeared among the many anonymous fallen Byzantine warriors, the legend of St. Contantine XI lives on. His personal piety and courage, his just rule, wise leadership, and loyalty to "faith and fatherland" especially in the face of a vicious, deadly, vastly more numerous foe, have inspired generations of Greeks and other Orthodox for half a millennium. In the current war against Islamic terrorism, the example of this just warrior is perhaps more timely than ever.

Devotional Texts

Eastern Orthodoxy has, from its inception as the New Testament Church, developed an extraordinarily rich liturgical and hymnographic tradition in accordance with the ancient Latin principle of *lex orandi lex credendi est* ("the rule of prayer is the rule of belief"). The worship experience informs and shapes Orthodox theological and moral doctrine at least as much as the converse.[27] That experience yields some weighty evidence for the justifiable war trajectory as a lesser good.

Appeals for "peace" seem to abound in Orthodox worship. The regular daily and weekly liturgical cycles include sets of petitions (usually chanted by a deacon, or, if a deacon is not present, by the higher order of *presbyter* or priest) that begin with invocations such as the following: "In peace let us pray to the Lord" or "Again and again in peace let us pray to the Lord." The priest (or bishop, if he is present) occasionally blesses the congregation while intoning the phrase, "Peace be with you." Toward the end of the Divine Liturgy of St. John Chrysostom, the primary liturgical service of the

Church offered on Sunday mornings and feast days, the priest bids the congregation, "Let us depart in peace."

But that same Divine Liturgy also includes a petition (repeated several times) on behalf of the head of state (emperor, king, or president), the government (or civil or public authorities, depending on the translation), and "our armed forces everywhere." In the Divine Liturgy of St. Basil, an earlier, longer version of the usual Sunday liturgy, which is still celebrated on 10 occasions each year, the prayer of intercession that the priest recites quietly at the altar after the consecration of the bread and wine into the Body and Blood of Christ includes language that seems to entail a hope for righteous public officials and warriors:

> Remember, O Lord, this country and all civil authorities; grant them a secure and lasting peace; speak good things into their hearts concerning Thy Church and all Thy people, that we, in their tranquility, may lead a calm and peaceful life in all godliness and sanctity. Remember, O Lord, every principality and authority; our brothers who serve in the government and the armed forces. Preserve the good in goodness, and make the evil be good by Thy goodness.[28]

Turning to the variable hymns that adorn the various feasts and seasons of the church year, we find a surprising amount of militaristic imagery often juxtaposed with word-images of peace, mercy, humility, suffering, and martyrdom.

The hymnography for the Feast of the Exaltation of the Holy Cross on September 14 (one of 12 "great feasts" eclipsed in import only by Pascha, or Easter, as it is commonly known in the West) is redolent of such military typologies. In its original Greek text, the *troparion* hymn—the key signature hymn of the day—prays for the victory of the Byzantine emperor over the "barbarians." Here's how that hymn would be translated into English: "O Lord, save thy people, and bless thine inheritance. Grant victories to the emperor [*basileios* in Greek] over the barbarians, and preserve thy habitation with thy Cross." To be sure, the post-imperial era has witnessed a spiritualizing of that text, so that now it usually implores the Lord to grant victories to "the Orthodox Christians over their adversary"—that is, Satan. But other hymns from the office of the Holy Cross retain their original bellicosity. Moses and Joshua are depicted as antitypes of Christ on the Cross immediately before their military victories against the Canaanite enemies of Israel. The second *sticheron* hymn at the lamp-lighting psalms for great vespers begins: "Moses prefigured thee, O precious Cross, when he stretched out his hands on high and put Amalek the tyrant to flight."[29] A sessional hymn after the *megalynarion* during matins begins: "In times past Joshua, the son of Nun, stretched out his arms crosswise, O my Saviour, mystically prefiguring the sign of the Cross: and the sun stood still until he had defeated the enemy that resisted Thee, O God."[30] The first canticle for matins credits the Cross with the Emperor Constantine's military triumphs: "Heaven showed the Cross as a sign of victory to Constantine, the holy king and defender of the faith. Through it the proud insolence of his enemies was cast down, deceit was overthrown, and the divine faith was spread to the ends of the earth. Therefore let us sing to Christ our God, for He has been glorified."[31] And the *kontakion* hymn (or second signature hymn) for the feast extends this martial spirit to the present: "Make the Orthodox people [originally "our faithful kings" or "emperor" in Greek] glad in Thy strength, giving them victory over their enemies: may Thy Cross assist them in battle, weapon of peace and unconquerable ensign of victory."[32]

Similarly, the hymnography for the third Sunday in Great Lent—also dedicated to the Holy Cross—contains military images. The second *sticheron* hymn at the lamp-lighting psalms for great vespers poetically lauds the Holy Cross: "Thou art an invincible weapon, an unbroken stronghold; thou are the victory of kings and the glory of priests."[33] The penultimate hymn in the same sequence concludes an appeal to Christ as follows: "Take pity of Thy people in distress, for Thou alone art longsuffering. Rise up and fight against our enemies in Thine almighty power."[34] And the penultimate hymn in the *aposticha* for great vespers clearly calls for military victory:

> O Lord who hast helped gentle David in the combat and enabled him to overcome the Philistine, come to the aid of Thine Orthodox people, and by the weapon of the Cross cast down our enemies. In Thy compassion show us Thy mercy as of old, and make them know in truth that Thou art God, and that we who put our trust in Thee shall conquer. At the constant intercession of Thy most pure Mother, grant us Thy great mercy.[35]

One more hymn warrants analysis as perhaps the most counterintuitive of all. The *kontakion* hymn for the Great Feast of the Annunciation (March 25, which is, either coincidentally or providentially, also celebrated in Greece as the national Independence Day from Ottoman Turkish domination) refers to the Virgin Mary in specifically militaristic language previously applied in the Old Testament to the Archangel Michael: "To thee, O Theotokos [Mother of God], victorious leader of triumphant hosts, we thy people, delivered from calamity, offer hymns of thanksgiving. In thine invincible power, keep us free from every peril, that we may cry to thee: 'Hail, thou Bride unwedded.'"[36] This hymn also serves as a frequent refrain in the special *akathist* matins usually offered in honor of the Virgin Mary on the Fridays in Great Lent. The reference to deliverance in the hymn has an historical antecedent. In A.D. 626, after an unsuccessful siege of Byzantium by the pagan Avars, Patriarch Sergios I of Constantinople led the faithful in a prayer of thanksgiving to the Theotokos that included the hymn for the first time.[37] The victory of the Byzantine army was attributed to her intercession with her divine Son, and the *kontakion* hymn and *akathist* matins to the Theotokos became standard liturgical practice throughout the Church in the Byzantine Empire and its successor kingdoms in the Balkans and the eastern Slavic lands.

In the latter, in particular, devotion to the Theotokos as heavenly patron of the imperial armed forces was perhaps unequaled. There's a telling scene in Lev Tolstoy's epic novel, *War and Peace*, when the protagonist Pierre stumbles upon a procession of Russian troops and Orthodox clergy before the Battle of Borodino in 1812. A huge "wonder-working" icon of the Theotokos is in their midst, borne aloft by soldiers and officers. "This was," Tolstoy narrates, "the ikon which had been brought away from Smolensk, and had ever since followed the army." During the Te Deum service for that particular battalion—the 20th that day, apparently—as the chanters sang to the Theotokos, "Verily we all take refuge in Thee, as in a steadfast bulwark and defence," General Kutuzof himself, future hero of Russia against Napoleon's invasion, approaches and reverences the icon with great piety.[38]

Unfortunately, the historical contexts and original meanings of those liturgical and hymnographic texts are conveniently downplayed or even rejected by those who prefer to restrict the warfare in question to internal, spiritual war against demonic temptation. Even icons of Jesus Christ in the garb of an ancient Roman military officer—such as the stunning mosaic of Christ with a long, sword-like cross over His right shoulder and trampling a lion and an adder, which was installed in the archiepiscopal chapel in Ravenna, Italy, around A.D. 500—may be subject to pacifist deconstruction.[39]

What cannot be so cavalierly spiritualized are the specific prayer services in time of war and the liturgical rites of blessing for military personnel and weapons. In the section on "general calamities" in the *Book of Needs* (actually a multivolume series for the Orthodox clergy that contains special prayers, prayer services, blessings, and sacramental rites), there is a "Molieben to the Lord God Sung in Time of War Against Adversaries Fighting Against

Us." The *troparion* and *kontakion* of the Holy Cross that we examined above figure prominently in that service. A *theotokion* hymn implores the "All-hymned Theotokos" to "make firm the habitation of the Orthodox and save our leaders whom thou hast commanded to govern us. Grant them victory from Heaven, for thou hast given birth unto God..." The hymns in the *canon* of canticles refer repeatedly to Old Testament military victories by Moses, Joshua, David, and Samson over the enemies of Israel as precedents for the Lord now to "grant victory to them that govern us over all adversaries who have risen against us." Even the epistle text, Hebrews 11:32–34, 12:1–2, fits the occasion perfectly: the Old Testament heroes Gideon, Barak, Samson, Jephthah, David, and Samuel "through faith defeated kingdoms ... were mighty in battle, and turned to flight the enemies of the aliens." In one set of petitions, the deacon calls upon the Lord, obviously without mincing words, to let "the nations who have fallen against Thine inheritance and defiled Thy Holy Church ... be assailed by Thy tempests and shake them with Thy wrath; fill their faces with dishonor; let them be put to shame and troubled forever; let them be disgraced; and by the power of Thy judgment let their pride be destroyed." Finally, a long prayer recited by the priest toward the end of the service reprises the hostility toward the enemy: "Rise up to our help and set to naught the evil counsels purposed against us by the evil ones. Judge them that affront us and defeat them that war against us, and turn their impious boldness into fear and flight." Then the prayer immediately accentuates the positive: "But grant unto our godfearing armies that hope in Thee great boldness and courage to drive onward and overtake them, and to defeat them in Thy Name. And unto them that Thou hast judged to lay down their lives for Faith and Country, forgive them their trespasses, and in the day of Thy righteous reckoning grant them incorrupt crowns."[40] The crowns are a standard image for the rewards of faithful and holy martyrs.

96

In the Russian Orthodox tradition, in particular, a special memorial service for Orthodox warriors is appointed for August 29 each year, the feast of the beheading of St. John the Baptizer, one of the most beloved of New Testament saints in the Orthodox world. One petition summons the congregation to pray for "the repose, tranquility and blessed memory of the ever-memorable servants of God, the Orthodox Warriors who have valiantly contended: and for all who have laid down their life in battle for the Faith and the Fatherland." The *canon* of canticles for Orthodox warriors who have fallen in battle echoes this acknowledgement of their valor and noble Christ-like sacrifice. The chanters lead the faithful in praying for "those who have wrought valiant deeds," "those who have served Thee [the Lord] for Thy Holy Church with all their hearts, and have borne Thy yoke upon their shoulders," "those who have perished in battle for the sake of Thy Holy Church," and "Thy servants who have suffered for Thy Holy Church and the Fatherland."[41] Nowhere in either this service or the previous one is there so much as a hint that the work of those soldiers is evil or sinful. On the contrary, these rites clearly extol the virtues of the fighting men who risk their own lives for Church and homeland.

One more text will furnish a fitting conclusion to this section, especially because it has drawn the ire of the Orthodox Peace Fellowship (OPF), a mostly pacifist, international association based in The Netherlands. A recent documentary collection compiled by two OPF activists, Hildo Bos and Jim Forest, includes an English translation of a service for the blessing of weapons that appears in a Serbian edition of the *Book of Needs* published in Kosovo in 1993. After the usual preliminary prayers, the rubrics call for the bishop or priest to read the following prayer "over the weapons":

> Lord our God, God of powers, powerful in strength, strong in battle, You once gave miraculous strength to Your child David granting him victory over his opponent the blasphemer Goliath. Mercifully accept our humble prayer. Send Your heavenly

97

> blessing over these weapons (naming each weapon). Give force
> and strength that they may protect Your holy Church, the poor
> and the widows, and Your holy inheritance on earth, and make it
> horrible and terrible to any enemy army, and grant victory to
> Your people for Your glory, for You are our strength and
> protection and we sing praise to Your glory, Father, Son and
> Holy Spirit, now and ever, and to the ages of ages. Amen.

The bishop or priest then sprinkles the weapons with blessed water, invoking the blessing of the Triune God "upon these weapons and those who carry them, for the protection of the truth of Christ." Finally, the bishop or priest blesses "the soldiers carrying the weapons" and exhorts them: "Be brave and let your heart be stronger and win victory over your enemies, trusting in God, in the name of the Father, Son and Holy Spirit." The concluding rubrics—"This is the way to bless sword and sable"—lead the OPF activists to concede that this text, though not usually included in contemporary editions of the *Book of Needs* published by the various Orthodox Churches in the world, seems to reflect an ancient usage and "an established ecclesiastical custom."[42] What the OPF activists find so disquieting, however, the mainstream Orthodox justifiable-war trajectory deems quite compatible with morality and worthy of a blessing.

Modern Theology and Literature

The final component of Eastern Orthodox moral tradition, though the least authoritative for a religious community that generally prefers the time-tested wisdom of the "ancients" over the opinions of the "moderns," provides additional textual testimony for justifiable war as a moral good instead of an evil.

Particularly bittersweet and quite revealing of a profound inner struggle over conflicting loyalties and patriotisms was the dramatic encyclical of Archbishop Nikolai (Kasatkin) of Tokyo (d. 1912) at the beginning of the Russo-Japanese War (1904-1905).

St. Nikolai was an ethnic Russian whose adopted country, Japan, suddenly found itself at war with his beloved motherland. What an excruciating moral and political dilemma for a bishop! The way St. Nikolai resolved this dilemma for himself and his tiny Japanese Orthodox flock may surprise many Christians today. In an encyclical dated February 11, 1904 (new calendar), St. Nikolai began with an appeal to hope: "It has pleased the Lord to permit a break between Russia and Japan. May it be according to His holy will. We believe that this is permitted for good goals and will lead to a blessed end, because the will of God is always blessed and wise." Then he provided his specific archiepiscopal counsel:

> Thus, brothers and sisters, fulfill all that is demanded from you in these circumstances by the duty of faithful citizens. Pray to God that He will grant victory to your Imperial Army, thank God for all victories He gives, and sacrifice for military necessities; those who must go into battle must fight, not sparing their own lives, not out of hatred for the enemy, but out of love for your fellow citizens, remembering the words of the Savior: "There is no greater love than to lay down one's life for one's friends" (John 15:13). In a word, do all that love for your fatherland demands. The Savior sanctified this feeling by His example of love for His earthly fatherland. "He wept over the wretched fate of Jerusalem" (Luke 1:91). [43]

So far, so good. There was nothing unusual here; rather this counsel was quite reminiscent of the Church fathers on the just conduct of war, particularly St. Augustine.

But his own role would have to be different, according to conscience and his patriotic duty, as he saw it, to the country of his origin. In another public message to his flock, St. Nikolai reaffirmed the counsel in his encyclical:

> Now that war has been declared, your duty is to pray for the victory of Japan and you must thank God for every

> announcement of victory. The Orthodox Church lays this duty
> on all believers in every separate country. Our teacher Jesus
> Christ teaches us patriotism and faithfulness to our homeland.

Precisely because of that universal principle of patriotism, the Orthodox Archbishop of Tokyo would "no longer take part in public services in our church." He had, until now, prayed fervently "for the growth and peace of the Japanese empire." However, in light of the mutual declarations of war in Tokyo and St. Petersburg, he declared: "I, as a Russian, cannot pray for the victory of Japan over my homeland. I also have obligations towards my homeland, and precisely therefore I will be happy when I see you fulfill your duties towards your country."[44]

Having obviously agonized over his decision, St. Nikolai, in effect, blessed both sides in the Russo-Japanese War in 1904, which would conclude the following year with a decisive Japanese military victory. Such an outcome was surely bittersweet for the Russian Orthodox hierarch of the Japanese Orthodox Church, as we might presume the opposite result would have been. St. Nikolai could take consolation only from his more cosmic vision of the "heavenly fatherland" that transcended nationality and earthly fatherlands—that is, "our church," the "one family" in which all Russians and Japanese and people everywhere had the duty to "be confirmed in the faith and flourish in all Christian virtues."[45]

Recently canonized Serbian Orthodox bishop St. Nikolai Velimirovich (d. 1956) reflected his nation's martial spirit in many of his writings. In a Russian Orthodox émigré periodical published in Paris in 1929, he offered the following thoughts:

> War is one of the tools in the hands of God, as well as peace.
> War is a poison, which kills, but which at the same time cures
> and heals.
> It is better to have one great and mighty river than many small
> streams which easily freeze in frost and which are easily covered

with dust and filth. A war which gathers an entire people for a great cause is better than a peace which knows as many tiny causes as it knows people, which divides brothers, neighbours, all human beings, and which hides in itself an evil and hidden war against all.

We have to wish those, whom we love, both a good life and a good death. To die in the struggle for a great common cause is a good death.[46]

Like most Serbs, St. Nikolai admired his saintly predecessor, Tsar Lazar, battlefield commander of the ill-fated Serbian army that lost the decisive Battle of Kosovo Polje to the Ottoman Turks in 1389. In another popular work entitled *The Serbian People as a Servant of God*, St. Nikolai marveled at Tsar Lazar's "holiness and righteousness," primarily because "he laid down his life on the field of Kosovo for the venerable cross and golden freedom. For this the Serbian people have cherished him and praised him in verse, and God has glorified him by making him a saint and crowning him with a double crown, as His servant and as His martyr."[47] Also in the same work, St. Nikolai offers a summary statement concerning "how the leaders of the Serbian people—be they kings or tsars, or despots or commanders or military governors—served Christ their God from their thrones and seats of power; as founders of churches and monasteries, as defenders of the Orthodox faith, as helpers in defense of neighboring peoples, as protectors of the poor, and as cross-bearing warriors against the infidels."[48]

Despite the revisionist views on war as a "necessary evil" advanced by Metropolitan Antony Khrapovitsky of Kiev in 1916, and more recently by the entire leadership of the Patriarchate of Moscow (see Chapter 5 below), many modern Russian Orthodox writers adhere more closely to the mainstream tradition. The enigmatic philosopher and theologian Vladimir Soloviev offered his own views on war and peace through "Mr. Z," one of five fictional Russian characters in his 1899 dialogue titled, *War and Christianity*

from the Russian Point of View: Three Conversations. Mr. Z
responds to a Tolstoyan's pacifism by insisting that "war is not an
unconditional evil, and that peace is not an unconditional good ...
[I]t is possible to have a good war, it is possible to have a bad
peace."[49] St. Tikhon, Patriarch of Moscow (d. 1925) issued a letter
on October 26, 1918 (new calendar), to the Bolshevik government's
Council of People's Commissars, in which he denounced them for
dishonoring the role of the Russian soldier in their haste to conclude
an extremely disadvantageous treaty with Imperial Germany: "You
have taken from our soldiers everything for which they fought
splendidly in the past. You have taught those, who not long ago
were still brave and invincible, to abandon the defence of the
motherland, to run from the battlefields. You have extinguished in
their hearts the conscience that 'greater love has no man than this,
that a man lay down his life for his friends' (John 15:13)."[50] Father
Sergei Tchetverikoff wrote a brief essay in a Russian Orthodox
émigré publication in Paris in 1929 under the bold title, "The
Sanctity of the Military Endeavor." The following passage typifies
his high regard for "the Christ-loving army" of pre-Communist
Russia:

> In the Orthodox Greek [Byzantine] empire, in other Orthodox
> states and in our own Orthodox Russian empire the cross-bearing
> spirit and sense of military service subsequently become so self-
> evident and obvious for the conciliar self-consciousness of the
> Church, that military service as such, as the endeavour of
> defending by the sword the Church and the Christian fatherland
> against paganism and heresies, was itself crowned by an aureoles
> of sanctity. Emperors, princes, generals as well as Christian
> soldiers entered into the host of saints. And the heavenly light of
> their holy glory has forever sanctified all Christ-bearing and
> Christ-loving military endeavours and struggles for the Holy
> Church, Christian statehood and the baptized people, for the
> Kingdom of God on earth.[51]

Arguably the most profound and complex Russian writer since the mid-20th century has been the great Nobel laureate and Orthodox layman, Aleksandr Solzhenitsyn. He himself served in the Soviet Army as a captain, but he was arrested in February 1945 by the Soviet military counterintelligence agency and charged with having written derogatory statements about Stalin in his personal correspondence. As a result of this "offense," Solzhenitsyn endured eight years in *gulags* and three more years in domestic exile. But that unhappy experience with Soviet-style "justice" did not drastically affect his perspective on the Soviet military before he was exiled from the Soviet Union in 1974. Quite to the contrary, he consistently, albeit reluctantly, acknowledged the necessity of the nation's armed forces, even a Soviet Communist military. In his *Letter to the Soviet Leaders* composed in October 1973, amidst a discussion of ecology, the need to colonize the northeastern territories, and the potential threat to the Soviet Union from the Chinese, Solzhenitsyn observed that for the next 50 years "our only genuine military need will be to defend ourselves against China, and it would be better not to go to war with her at all."[52] The use of "our" here reveals an unexpected identity for someone whose opposition to the regime was both spiritual and visceral. Although he proceeded in his *Letter* to decry the excessive quantities of Soviet arms and the vainglorious practice of universal military conscription in the Soviet Union, Solzhenitsyn was not deterred from recognizing the need for defensive forces of his internally subjugated homeland.

Solzhenitsyn reiterated this view in an essay entitled "Repentance and Self-Limitation of Nations," which he published a month later in November 1973. Nations, unlike individuals, he averred, could not make completely self-sacrificing decisions, especially when their neighbors were militarily aggressive: "Defense forces must be retained, but only for genuinely defensive purposes, only on a scale adequate to real and not imaginary threats, not as an end in themselves, not as a self-perpetuating tradition, not to maintain the size and glamour of the high command. They will be retained in the hope that the whole atmosphere of mankind will soon begin to change." Also in that essay Solzhenitsyn amplified his use of "our" with respect to the Soviet military. Operating on the premise that a "nation is mystically welded together in a community of guilt," he asserted that the Soviet Union was no exception: "Even in the most totalitarian states, whose subjects have no rights at all, we all bear responsibility—not only for the quality of our government, but also for the campaigns of our military leaders, for the deeds of our soldiers in the line of duty, for the shots fired by our frontier guards, for the songs of our young people."[53]

A penitential gloom hovers over this kind of support for the military and stands in marked contrast to the passionate, obsequious approval of the Soviet state and military by all of the patriarchs of Moscow after St. Tikhon. It is begrudging at most and does not really cast Solzhenitsyn into the role of cheerleader. Like the Elder Zossima, Fyodor Dostoevsky's exemplary character in his great novel *The Brothers Karamazov*, Solzhenitsyn so identified with his fellow Russians, their Soviet masters notwithstanding, that he felt a mystical bond with everyone in the former Soviet Union—persecutors and persecuted, Communists and Christians alike—that, in turn, entailed a collective responsibility for the sins committed by the leaders in the name of all. By implication, moreover, there were, in his estimation, no substantial differences between the Christian and the non-Christian in the government, the military, or the frontier guards.

This argument from silence is supported by one of Solzhenitsyn's great novels. In *August 1914*, the first in his five-part "wheel" of historical novels pertaining to the end of the tsarist empire and the beginning of the Soviet era, Isaakii (or "Sanya") Lazhenitsyn, a pacifist follower of Tolstoy, resolves to join the army at the outset of the First World War. His reason is as simple as it is profound: "I feel sorry for Russia," he says to his fellow student

Varya.[54] This kind of melancholy compassion is assuredly not the triumphalist or nationalistic kind. Sanya is not moved by an unbridled, militant patriotism. As Fr. Alexander Schmemann perceived, Sanya determines to fight for Russia simply "because Russia *is*, and because she, and not another country, is his motherland, granted him like the sun and the air; because she is his home and body, and no one can be without these."[55] The worst has come to pass—war with Germany and Austria—and so one must fight. Thus, to the proverbial inevitabilities of death and taxation, Solzhenitsyn has added nations and war. Sanya neither extols war nor condemns it, since either of those attitudes ignores the grim reality and necessity of war. But war, when engaged, ought to be conducted efficiently and successfully. For the individual, war is nevertheless a severe challenge. In Schmemann's estimation, the task confronting Solzhenitsyn's Sanya "is a test of the entire man, bringing out the best or the worst in him; it measures his relation to life, and his capacity for sacrifice and selflessness."[56]

In Sanya we are offered Solzhenitsyn himself. For just as Sanya conscientiously responds to the call to serve in the army of autocratic tsarist Russia in 1914 (as did Solzhenitsyn's own father), so the young Solzhenitsyn sought to defend his homeland (and, less happily, its Soviet regime) from the Nazi German invaders in 1941.[57] If there is any planned, universal, Orthodox Christian application of Sanya's decision, it would be similar to the agonized judgment of St. Nikolai (Kasatkin) of Tokyo at the beginning of the Russo-Japanese War: that the Christian ought to serve his country—and no other—in time of war regardless of who happens to be governing the homeland at the time. For the exigencies of birth have located him in that particular place and it is the only country he has. Such service will most likely be a tragic, bittersweet endeavor, a moral necessity and a virtuous activity, but in no way a joy.

CHAPTER 5

Orthodox Justifiable War and Its Critics

The moral proposition that runs through the various biblical, patristic, canonical, hagiographic, liturgical and hymnographic, and modern theological and literary texts presented in the last two chapters is really quite simple. We may call it a **teleology of justice**.

I. A Lesser Good, Not Evil

This particular teleology, like other forms of this moral or ethical perspective, entails a proportionality of morally good (or at least, in some circumstances, morally "neutral") means to morally good ends (that is, purposes, intentions, goals, or *teloi* in Greek). The internal debate within Orthodox ecclesiastical circles (and perhaps also more widely in other religious and scholarly communities) concerns the issue of means. Setting aside the views of the absolute pacifists, for whom any violence against human beings is precluded *a priori*, we may sharpen the question further to whether the resort to war for a good end is itself an evil, or whether it may be a good means to that end. The Apostle John provides a simple but crystal clear moral prescription in 3 John:11 when he writes, "Beloved, do not imitate evil but imitate good." The Apostle Paul offers us important parallels in Romans 12:17: "Repay no one evil for evil, but take thought for what is noble in the sight of all." Also, a few verses later in Romans 12:21 he commands: "Do not be overcome by evil, but overcome evil with good." The defining moment of St. Paul's own teleological approach to morality occurs earlier in the same epistle. In Romans 3:8 the Apostle asks rhetorically, "And why not do evil that good may come?—as some people slanderously charge us with saying. Their condemnation is just." Oxford philosopher John Finnis has dubbed this biblical rejection of evil means to good ends the "Pauline principle."[1]

Further, a sweep of patristic literature would fail to detect even one Church father who gives moral permission to commit an unmistakably evil act, lesser or otherwise. An intrinsic evil may be defined precisely as an unholy, unrighteous, or sinful offense against God, another human being, or oneself, which, irrespective of the particular circumstances, intention, or anticipated consequences, may not be freely and knowingly chosen.

In the medieval Christian West, St. Thomas Aquinas crystallized this fundamental biblical and patristic insight in his forceful argument in the *Summa Theologiae* that the object of one's moral decision (that is, the action that is chosen as the means to one's end) must itself be morally good, or at least not intrinsically evil.[2] How then, may any Christian countenance a course of action—such as war—that he freely and knowingly concedes is "evil," even if he allows that it is a "lesser" enormity than permitting, through inaction, an aggressor to subvert justice and wreak havoc among his or any people? If all war or any particular war is deemed an evil, a Christian nation or people may not elect to go to war, even as a last resort. The logical contrapositive also holds. If a particular war can be justified morally, it must be a good act—or at least a morally neutral act. Perhaps it is a "lesser good" than diplomatic persuasion or nonviolent, nonresistant suffering in full imitation of the "higher" self-sacrificing love of Jesus Christ, but a good nonetheless.

The key to the problem is how to frame the moral decision properly—specifically, how to define accurately and correctly both the means and the end in question. To the familiar refrain among anti-consequentialists that ends do not justify the means, we might offer the flippant rejoinder: If the ends do not justify the means, at least in part, then what else does? The act of cutting human flesh, for example, may be good or evil, depending on the identity of the agent (the person cutting), his intention, and, above all, how he goes about his business. An armed robber assaulting his victim with a switchblade obviously commits an intrinsically evil act, but a skilled

107

cardiac surgeon operating on a patient *in extremis* may be engaged in a good act. To be sure, the immediate slicing of skin and muscle tissue and the cracking of ribs to get at the heart might, in itself, appear to be cruel or violent, but it may also be the only way the surgeon can perform a life-saving operation. In addition, the good surgeon cuts and breaks only the bare minimum of human flesh and bones, thereby safeguarding the life of the patient and treating the entire body with respect and the person with reverence.

In the admittedly much rarer cases when war may be justified in accordance with the *jus ad bellum* and *jus in bello* criteria of the Orthodox justifiable war trajectory elucidated above, the specific acts of harming, wounding, or killing enemy soldiers must similarly be evaluated in the context of a teleology of justice. Orthodox Christian soldiers and other military personnel

- ✓ duly authorized by a legitimate political authority (such as the Byzantine emperor or, currently, internationally recognized governments that do not pose an immediate threat to the Orthodox community, or, to be sure, any other religious community)
- ✓ to defend and protect their Church or homeland from an unjust aggressor such as an invading force (whether a conventional military transgression of internationally recognized borders or lethal violence in the more contemporary form of international terrorism), and
- ✓ who utilize minimal force in direct proportion to the clearly—in their own minds and the expressed will of their constituency—intended restoration of the *status quo ante* (instead of conquest or other kinds of unwarranted aggrandizement),
- ✓ may, in good conscience, engage in warfare as a lesser good, as long as that military activity targets the unjust aggressor

instead of civilian noncombatants and is exercised with a minimum of necessary lethality and destruction.[3]

Such limited or proportionate warfare in pursuit of just ends becomes a function of justice. Since justice is one of the four "cardinal" virtues introduced by Plato, acknowledged in the *Septuagint* (Wisdom 8:7), and amplified through the entire patristic tradition, justice in war—both as an end and the means to that end—may also be virtuous and, hence, morally good.[4] This is the ineluctable conclusion that we must draw from the scores of texts adduced above. Whenever the Holy Scriptures, Church fathers, canons, lives of the saints, liturgical and hymnographic texts, and modern theologians and literary authors speak of military activity in terms of right or righteousness, nobility, valor, or heroism, their individual and collective impact alike is the same: a justification of such activity as a moral good and of the soldiers who carry it out as virtuous warriors.

This highly constrained use of armed might—which is even more limited in scope than the secularized just war theory as it is currently enunciated by Western Christians—offers a stark, sobering contrast to the ideology of international Islamic terrorism. The latter promotes the conscious, deliberate targeting of innocent civilians and a maximum of destruction and disorder as a matter of *preference*, no less—to inspire fear and terror among the masses that might weaken their resolve and pave the way for an eventual Islamic takeover. Those extremists exult in evil means to supposedly "good" ends. The stakes for Western civilization could not be higher. The Orthodox justifiable war tradition is obviously needed now more than ever.

II. Lesser Morality

Oddly enough, the Orthodox justifiable war tradition seems to be facing a frontal assault, or is, at least, under siege, by a growing cadre of Eastern Orthodox bishops and theologians. As we have seen in the last two chapters, this moral trajectory—like its parallel trajectory, absolute pacifism—enjoys an unbroken continuity from its origins in Old Testament Israel through two millennia of Orthodox moral reflection and praxis as an "aretaic" (or virtue) tradition. And yet justifiable war has been recast as a mere concession to human weakness and sin, a "lesser evil" than the alternative failure to resort to such unsavory military means in pursuit of justice. This has, in turn, created the spectacle of highly respected religious leaders of one of the venerable Christian communities advocating what may be charitably dismissed as a "lesser morality."

The Orthodox proponents of the "lesser evil" approach to war do, indeed, constitute a formidable phalanx of notables. To be sure, some appear to be more enamored of pacifist principles than the justifiable war tradition. Father George Dragas, dean of Holy Cross Greek Orthodox School of Theology near Boston, repeats a familiar refrain: "There is no just war, no just violence, no just revenge or recompense, no just accumulation of wealth."[5] Similarly, Dr. Vassilios Giultsis, professor of Christian ethics at the University of Thessalonika in Greece, expresses horror at the destructive magnitude of modern warfare, which, he asserts, "forces Orthodoxy to condemn in the strongest terms all the causes of war and means of destroying God's gift of human life." Giultsis also disdains the view that "accept(s) war and injustice as 'natural' states of human society, and consequently a necessary evil."[6]

But it is precisely the latter view that has become *de rigueur* among his colleagues. In May 1989, the 40 Orthodox theologians who gathered in Minsk (then in the Soviet Union) under the auspices of the politically left-wing World Council of Churches declared: "The Orthodox Church unreservedly condemns war as evil. Yet it also recognizes that in the defence of the innocent and the protection of one's people from unjust attack, criminal activity and the

110

overthrowing of oppression, it is sometimes necessary, with reluctance, to resort to arms."[7] On March 7, 1991, when the decisive victory of the U.S.-led alliance in the Persian Gulf War was only a week behind them, the otherwise cautious, generally conservative Holy Synod of Bishops of the Orthodox Church in America (OCA) issued a surprising statement on that military operation. The OCA bishops insisted that what they called the "just war theory" (instead of the more accurate "justifiable war tradition" as used in the present work in deference to the insight of the late Princeton theologian, Paul Ramsey) "does not reflect our theological tradition," because war may never be "theologically justified." And yet they hastened to add, "[A] lesser evil must sometimes be chosen to resist a greater evil."[8]

The OCA still appears quite squeamish about military operations. On September 13, 2001, only two days after the terrorist attack on the World Trade Center and the Pentagon, Metropolitan Theodosius and the Holy Synod of Bishops of the OCA asked their clergy to include among the petitions in the litany that follows the Gospel reading in the Orthodox Divine Liturgy a specific appeal "that the Lord our God may bring us speedily to victory." In a special prayer to be recited on bended knees toward the end of the liturgy, each parish priest was to ask the Lord to "rise up to help us, and grant our Armed Forces in Your name to be victorious." That prayer was to conclude with a doxology that began, "For You are the Protection, the Victory and the Salvation of those who hope on You. ..." The benediction at the end of the liturgy was to include an unusual invocation of martyred soldier-saints including George, Demetrios, Theodore Stratelates ("the General"), and Theodore the Recruit. The use of the imperfect tense here is intentional, for those texts were radically revised in the next couple of weeks, owing to what a member of the staff at the OCA chancery in Syosset, New York, reported had been a "flurry of complaints from disgruntled priests." In the September 20 version of the special prayers, all

111

references to victory and the warrior-saints mysteriously disappeared. The only hint of support for the armed forces of the United States was the following petition: "Again we pray for the President of our country ... for all civil authorities and the armed forces: that the Lord our God will bless them to protect and defend our land, and grant them wisdom and strength, sustaining and guiding them in the days to come." A week later, to this stripped-down version of the petitions, the OCA chancery added a reference to "our enemies, known and unknown: that the Lord our God would soften their hearts, stay their hands from base deeds, and free them from hatred and every violent passion."[9]

Nor is the "mother" church of the OCA immune from such moral confusion. In a comprehensive statement on "The Basis of the Church's Social Concept" issued in August 2000, the Moscow Patriarchate swings back and forth between militant Russian nationalism and patriotism, on the one hand, and excessive caution about the military on the other. Early in the statement, the Russian Orthodox bishops quote St. Philaret, Patriarch of Moscow, who, during Napoleon's invasion of Russia in 1813, exhorted the faithful: "If you avoid dying for the honour and freedom of the Fatherland, you will die a criminal or a slave; die for the faith and the Fatherland and you will be granted life and a crown in heaven." A few chapters later, however, the Russian Orthodox bishops offer a mixed message. First, they concede the following: "While recognizing war as evil, the Church does not prohibit her children from participating in hostilities if at stake is the security of their neighbors and the restoration of trampled justice. Then war is considered to be a necessary though undesirable means." But then they make moral room for the measured pursuit of justice in war:

> The Christian moral law deplores not the struggle with sin, not the use of force towards its bearer and not even taking another's life in the last resort, but rather malice in the human heart and the desire to humiliate or destroy whosoever it may be. In this

regard, the Church has a special concern for the military, trying
to educate them for the faithfulness to lofty moral ideals.[10]

However, one must ask how soldiers can be educated in this way if
their vocation is fundamentally evil?

Even the most esteemed Orthodox moral theologian in the
last half century has, by his own admission, experienced a profound
metamorphosis in his moral reflections on the problems of war and
peace. In a widely read article published as a book chapter in 1981,
Fr. Stanley S. Harakas, dean emeritus of Holy Cross Greek Orthodox
School of Theology, declared, "The just war theory holds that war is
an evil and seeks to make it less so."[11] Five years later, he elaborated
on this theme of war as "a necessary evil" in an essay entitled, "The
Teaching of Peace in the Fathers." The Church fathers in the
Christian East, he contended, "rarely praised war, and to my
knowledge, almost never called it 'just' or a moral good." Following
their example, then, the Eastern Orthodox Churches "cannot speak of
a 'good war,' or even a 'just war.'" What Fr. Harakas termed the
"peace ideal," though not absolute pacifism, "continued to remain
normative and no theoretical efforts were made to make conduct of
war into a positive norm."[12]

In his most recent contribution on this issue in the aftermath
of the terrorist attacks in 2001, Fr. Harakas expresses an extreme
hostility toward military operations as thoroughly immoral and
detestable, though sometimes necessary. He confidently proclaims
that "Jesus's teaching regarding the Kingdom of God excludes the
idea and practice of war among nations," owing, in particular, to "the
awful killing, maiming, destruction, horror and evil which is war."
The task of the Church is "to constantly and persistently remind civil
leaders that war—and terrorist war in particular—is an unacceptable
alternative in international relations." And yet, he balances this
quixotic advice by allowing realistically for the "necessary evil" of
war "sometimes." When a nation such as the United States of

113

America cannot influence an aggressive enemy through peaceful means "to deal with us righteously," the "most which we can do ... is to defend ourselves without seeking to harm the other beyond what is necessary to stop the attack." To fail "to defend the innocent," Fr. Harakas concedes, is "paradoxically consenting and contributing to their extermination." But he mitigates the value of that insight by adding that "war can never be our goal, [sic] it can only be a falling away from our goal for which repentance is the only appropriate response."[13] Again, one must ask how a nation can conduct defensive military operations without having war—especially military victory—as a "goal"? War may never, of course, be the ultimate goal, or an end in itself, in any decision to resort to armed force. We've already established that in the two previous chapters. But Fr. Harakas's conclusion makes no sense teleologically.

Finally, it might prove illuminating to bring this unhappy story up to date with the public moral witness of Orthodox bishops and theologians on the controversial war in Iraq that began on March 19, 2003. The OCA bishops continue to eschew military action as *ipso facto* unworthy of Orthodox Christians. In his archpastoral message on March 21, Metropolitan Herman, the primatial bishop of the OCA, laments that the "world today" is "unwilling to pursue His [the Lord Jesus Christ's] divine peace in its conflicts and disputes." And so the bishop prays that "that which is evil might be transformed into that which is not only good, but godly"—an obvious rejection of the U.S.-British intervention as "evil."[14] A subsequent statement by the entire Synod of Bishops of the OCA issued on April 3, 2003, removes any doubt: "As bishops we are aware that acts of violence are not the proper responses of mankind to the unique gift of life." The OCA bishops also beseech "our Good God to have mercy on us all and to soften the hard and stubborn hearts to end this war so that terror and killing cease and peace can have its place."[15] Within a week, Baghdad fell to Coalition forces and the regime of Saddam Hussein was toppled.

The OCA bishops' critique was nothing compared to the denunciations from Orthodox hierarchies abroad. Before the commencement of hostilities, Patriarch Petros VII of Alexandria, Patriarch Alexis II of Moscow, Patriarch Ignatius IV of Antioch, the Serbian Orthodox Church, and the Orthodox bishops of Germany, among others, issued warnings of the dire consequences that would ensue if the U.S. carried out its planned military operation in Iraq. These included, supposedly, humanitarian catastrophes, an escalation of terror in the world, incalculable ecological damage from burning oil wells, exacerbation of the Arab-Israeli conflict, and the lasting enmity of Muslims in the Middle East and perhaps the entire world. As we now know after the fact, virtually none of those predictions proved accurate. On the very day of the initial air strikes, Patriarch Bartholomeos of Constantinople, first-among-equals of all Orthodox bishops in the world, declared with seeming finality that the "one God and Father ... is not a God of war and battle but of reconciliation and peace."[16]

By far the most ambitious—and extreme—Orthodox statement on the impending war in Iraq came from the North America chapter of the Orthodox Peace Fellowship (OPF), an organization that we encountered in Chapter 4 above. A 10-person council headed by John Brady and Jim Forest drafted "A Plea for Peace" in October 2002, which 146 persons had signed by March 19, 2003, the first day of the U.S.-led intervention in Iraq.[17] The list of signatories is admittedly quite impressive and includes seven Orthodox bishops (three from the United States), the majority of the faculty of St. Vladimir's Theological Seminary in New York, and a potpourri of faculty from the other major Orthodox seminaries in the United States, as well as many prominent Orthodox clergy and laity on both sides of the Atlantic. What is most striking about the statement, especially in light of its distinguished proponents, is its shrill tone, simplistic analysis, and fundamental moral error.

115

We need only cite a few passages from this grievously flawed document. In the opening paragraph, the "Plea" concedes that Saddam Hussein "is an enemy of the United States and of the people of Iraq;" but, it hastens to add, "there are better ways to respond to terrorism than to respond in kind." That blanket characterization of the then anticipated U.S. military action is, to use the familiar term from international relations, an example of "moral equivalence" of the worst kind. It is startling to realize that so many Orthodox leaders would equate U.S. military intervention with "terrorism." The "Plea" also asserts that the "United States is ready to overthrow him by any means"—an egregious falsehood. The official military policy of the U.S. government, at least since the adoption of the "counterforce" nuclear strategy in the mid-1970's, is firmly grounded in the Western just war tradition, particularly the *jus in bello* criteria (shared, as we have seen above, with the Orthodox justifiable war tradition) of the proportional use of force and immunity of civilian noncombatants from direct attack. There are other profound shortcomings in the document, such as an incorrect use of the concept of "pre-emption" in war, dire predictions about the consequences for the Middle East, and a naïve understanding of "friendship" in international relations.

But the most extreme assertion comes in the fourth of its 14 short paragraphs. The "Plea" declares: "the Orthodox Church has never regarded any war as just or good, and fighting an elusive enemy by means which cause the death of innocent people can be regarded only as murder." The first contention in that passage is what the present volume is all about. Once again, a group of Orthodox leaders has mischaracterized the Orthodox moral tradition concerning war and peace. There is, unfortunately, nothing new there. But the charge of intended "murder" places this document into a class by itself. Perhaps the OPF and its signatories resort to this legal (and ethical) term out of sheer frustration with their presumed adversaries in the administration of President George W. Bush or the

U.S. military itself. Perhaps the signatories are somehow unaware of the ramifications of impugning the motives and divining the intentions of U.S. public officials with such certitude. Perhaps not everyone who signed the "Plea" agrees with its entire content.[18] Whatever the circumstances that gave rise to this accusation, a charge of "murder" is a rhetorical weapon of mass destruction that demands a moral rebuttal. As it happens, the prolific Orthodox author and publisher, Frank Schaeffer, managed to land an opinion-editorial essay in the *Washington Post* on April 6, 2003, that provides such a response, albeit one rooted in very personal circumstances. His son, John, an enlisted man in the U.S. Marine Corps, had recently been deployed to the Middle East, when Schaeffer wrote from his heart:

> I don't see my son as a murderer. I don't see my country as evil. I see my country and my son's cause as just. But maybe I'm wrong. If I'm wrong I don't want to drag God down with me. I don't claim that Jesus is on my side. I'm hoping that God is on the side of my pacifist friends too. And I assume God is hearing the prayers of Iraqi parents worried about their sons who are serving their country.
>
> How can a church comfort all its children when it plays political favorites? I believe that the Greek Orthodox whose sons and daughters are marching in peace rallies should find as much comfort in our beloved church as I do. I don't want them excluded or condemned in the name of God. Yet as the father of a Marine I feel excluded from my church at the very moment when I most desperately need to be included. Why have so many priests and bishops traded their call to pastoral care for a few fleeting moments of political "relevance"?
>
> My son is gone to war. I am sad and frightened. I am also proud of my Marine for his selfless service. But I am being stripped of the comfort of my church in the name of "peace" by people who seem determined to make God as small as we are.[19]

III. What Went Wrong?

The brief review of encyclicals and statements above highlights the lack of moral clarity and consistency that besets contemporary Orthodox bishops, theologians, and activists in their reflections on the morality of war—or, to be sure, the *immorality* of war, according to an emerging consensus. We hope the abundant textual and iconic evidence adduced in the present volume will restore among them the longstanding traditional moral position that war may be engaged and conducted as a virtuous or righteous act, or at least as a "lesser good" instead of a lesser or necessary evil.

But whence the lesser morality that seems to have displaced this Orthodox justifiable war tradition? What has caused so many Orthodox hierarchs and theologians to veer off the mainstream trajectory? To be sure, there are occasional glimpses in the historical sources of a "lesser evil" or "necessary evil" approach to the question. One such instance, popular with proponents of that approach, is an anonymous treatise on Byzantine military strategy dating from the reign of Emperor St. Justinian the Great in the sixth century, which concedes that "war is a great evil and the worst of all evils."[20] But that comment is remarkable for its extreme rarity among the texts. The likely influences of the modern revisionism in Orthodox thinking on war are external to Orthodox tradition and have, beginning in the first quarter of the 20th century, infiltrated Orthodoxy as a result of a flurry of ecumenical contacts with Western Christians and an accelerated emigration of Orthodox Christians to Western Europe and North America.

First, there is the enduring legacy of one of the fundamental anthropological claims of the Protestant Reformation in the 16th century—namely, the inherent sinfulness and depravity of all of mankind after the original Fall from grace. To summarize the views of Martin Luther and many Anabaptists, for example, the human will was so corrupted by Adam's sinful rebellion that every moral choice—unaided by divine grace—is fraught with danger.[21] In fact, a person can only elect evil of one kind or another, lest, through his self-justification through ostensibly good works, he fool himself into thinking that he has grounds to boast before God and render the atoning sacrifice of Christ irrelevant or superfluous. The most for which one might hope in this vale of tears is to minimize, but not overcome or transcend, his sinful tendencies: to choose an evil assuredly lesser than its more grievous alternatives. Such a dim view of human nature in its present fallen state has little in common with the essential patristic heritage of Orthodoxy Christianity.

The second suspect is contemporary Roman Catholic "proportionalism." Pope John Paul II himself took square aim at this movement in his monumental encyclical *Veritatis Splendor* ("The Splendor of Truth") in 1993. In Europe and North America, in particular, the proportionalists, or "mixed teleologists" as they are also known, greatly outnumber the more traditional Thomist or neo-Thomist moral theologians in the Roman Catholic Church. The proportionalists withhold moral judgment of particular acts until they can calculate the likely proportion of good and evil effects of the alternative choices; for them, *contra* St. Thomas Aquinas and the Church fathers, personal intent and particular circumstances have weight at least equal to that of the specific means. Indeed, the proportionalists generally maintain that it is impossible to establish moral absolutes that prohibit certain behaviors at all times and everywhere. Through a remarkable ethical sleight-of-hand, they manage to absolve persons who, it would appear *prima facie*, violate universal negative norms (such as those prohibiting lying, premarital sex, or military violence against civilian noncombatants) by elevating their "good" intentions and the presumably "good" consequences of their decisions, while downplaying the "evil" quality of the act itself considered objectively. Such a seeming evil is not really intrinsic, but rather only "physical," or "ontic," or "premoral," or even "nonmoral." Sometimes the evil is of a "lesser" magnitude than the presumed alternatives and hence acceptable.

Finally, in his doctoral dissertation at the University of Virginia, Professor Darrell Cole identified the kind of "Christian realism" popularized by Reinhold Niebuhr and his many academic and ecumenical disciples in the middle of the last century as the primary cause of the preoccupation with war as a "lesser evil" among Protestants and Roman Catholics.[22] On that view, Niebuhr, prescinding from his interpretation of the gospel ethic as a "pure ethic of love"—an ideal toward which men and women must strive if they hope to act morally, especially as individuals—conceded that the perfect morality modeled by Jesus Christ is not practical in human society and must be moderated by a pragmatic or realistic ethic of responsibility that requires a choice of lesser evils on behalf of justice for the community. The fatal flaw of this approach is the self-evident moral incongruity of Niebuhr's logic: "Jesus's ethic of love impels us to do vicious things." Specifically in terms of war, Niebuhrian realism creates a slippery slope that could facilitate a slide into total or unlimited warfare: "Once we begin to believe that we are acting viciously by the very nature of the case, then the temptation becomes to be a little more vicious and guarantee victory."[23]

Niebuhrian and other early 20th-century varieties of Christian or secular ethical realism may be unsurpassed in their impact on the revisionist Orthodox proponents of the lesser morality approach. Paul Robinson of the University of Hull has demonstrated convincingly that Ivan Il'in, for example, was such a relentless realist. Author of a controversial 1925 treatise, *On Resistance to Evil by Force*, Il'in categorically rejected any association of justice or good with war and endorsed some wars as *"unsinful* [!] perpetration[s] of injustice" that may, nevertheless, entail means that are "necessary in all their injustice" as a "spiritual compromise."[24]

120

Il'in and his ilk, as it were, furnish, unwittingly to be sure, a *reductio ad absurdam* of the embrace of the "lesser evil" or "necessary evil" approach to the moral problem of war. It is an unnecessary "compromise," a counterfeit of the genuine, mainstream Orthodox justifiable war trajectory. This kind of consequentialism has not been nicknamed the "dirty hands" approach in vain. Ironically, the "lesser evil" approach, whether Western or Eastern in provenance, opens a Pandora's box of rationalizations for all manner of evils in war and even other apparent or real ethical dilemmas. If a decision to resort to war is an acceptable evil, then why not embrace other morally unsavory options as acceptable evils? What moral restraints may be imposed on the use of military means if the whole business is a carnival of evils in which we may, nonetheless, have to participate? This is not merely a matter of semantics. Countless lives and the moral health of Western civilization hang in the balance. When we justify any evil in war, we take a dubious path that could lead to the obliteration bombing of civilian populations, to the mistreatment and torture of enemy prisoners-of-war, even, perhaps, to various forms of terrorism. We become vicious, not virtuous, and practically indistinguishable from the barbarous enemy we are sworn to resist and eventually defeat in battle. The "lesser evil" approach to war makes us "lesser" human beings.

Orthodox Christians and those who desire to know and understand the authentic Eastern Orthodox moral tradition on war and peace should accept no substitutes.

CHAPTER 6

The Roman Catholic Tradition

When St. Ambrose, St. Augustine, and St. Thomas Aquinas flourished, the church was able, at least to some degree, to exercise discipline over the empire's rulers. The church no longer exercises such discipline as a matter of course over the rulers of liberal, pluralistic, democratic regimes. But the church still plays (or ought to play) a role in determining for its flock when and how force is to be used for the cause of justice, and it uses that determination as a witness to the state. This is what the Western just war tradition is all about and it owes much to the three figures discussed in this chapter. To St. Ambrose, St. Augustine, St. Thomas, and their theological heirs we owe our understanding of the charity that compels Christians to seek justice, even if it means using force, as well as the fact that the church witnesses to a tradition that determines how force is to be used by its members and exercises discipline over those who do not do it well.

I. St. Ambrose of Milan

It is commonly thought that, before St. Augustine, the early Christians were pacifists, or if not entirely pacifists, at least not thinking about war enough to formulate a distinctly Christian response to it.[1] This understanding is far from accurate. The falsity concerning the hegemonic pacifism of the early church has been told elsewhere and does not need repeating here.[2] The falsity of there being no distinct Christian approach to warfare before St. Augustine is what we address first in this chapter. St. Ambrose of Milan is the real beginning of a distinct Western Christian approach to the moral problems of war and a direct influence on St. Augustine (and thus the entire history of Western Christianity). In St. Ambrose we find the two ingredients that make Western Christian just war doctrine

122

Christian: the role of charity, which compels justice, and the role of ecclesiastical discipline in keeping just war just. St. Ambrose's influence in this area is inestimable: St. Augustine, Aquinas, Luther, Calvin, and Grotius—to name but five (four of whom are the most important figures in Western Christianity, while the fifth is the recognized father of international law)—are all deeply indebted to St. Ambrose on matters of how Christians should respond to the moral problems of war.

The Church and Empire

Military matters, in St. Ambrose's time, were matters of empire. We begin, therefore, with St. Ambrose's understanding of the empire before turning to the Christian's involvement in political duties; for how he views the empire makes Christian participation in it possible. In short, St. Ambrose's understanding of the state (or, as the modern ethicist would say, his "theological politics") gives us the proper context within which we can describe accurately his understanding of soldiering and warfare. St. Ambrose, who held a high government office before becoming a Bishop, knows that political order is a necessity for communal life. Government is a divine institution created to insure that life. "Man was made for the sake of man," claims St. Ambrose, and hence, "in accordance with the will of God and the union of nature we ought to be of mutual help to one another, and to vie with each other in doing duties" (*On Duties of the Clergy* 1.134,135).[3] St. Ambrose took this to mean that the emperor and his army have a duty from God to preserve political order, which includes the church.

In an epistle to the emperor Valentinian, St. Ambrose tells him, "you yourself are also in the service [*militatis*] of almighty God and of our holy faith" (*Epistle* 17.1).[4] Here we find an important assumption: the emperor is not responsible directly to God for his use of the sword, but to the church. The emperor's duty to the state is a duty to "almighty God," and hence under the church. This is key, because if the responsibility of the use of the sword is under the church, then we should find something distinctly Christian about how that use is carried out in actual practice.

The distinctiveness of Christian rulership and soldiery is repeated time and again in St. Ambrose's epistles to various emperors. First, in St. Ambrose's epistle to the emperor Theodosius concerning the massacre of innocent civilians at Thessalonica (*Epistle* 51), St. Ambrose uses the biblical figure of David as a measuring rod against the behavior of Theodosius. The striking thing about this exchange is that Theodosius's actions, though severe by today's standards, were by no means unheard of in antiquity. In any event, the incident was an act of state, and as such, a coercive act entrusted by God to civil authority. We would ordinarily understand this to mean that the emperor is responsible directly to God. But, as we can see, St. Ambrose will have none of it. He subjects the emperor's civil action to ecclesiastical control. Theodosius's humbling of himself before St. Ambrose as penance has become famous in the annals of history. Whatever we might say about the political motives of Theodosius, McLynn is surely right in observing that his penance before St. Ambrose "gave full expression to the deep religiosity and abiding sense of human frailty that (we need not doubt) he shared with his Christian contemporaries."[5] In doing penance for a civil act, Theodosius acknowledges his responsibility within the church for the proper use of his sword. The use of the sword by the state, therefore, is not an action that falls entirely outside the church's sphere of authority when members of the Church are the ones holding the sword.

St. Ambrose's epistle to Theodosius concerning the burning of a Jewish synagogue in Callinicum (the emperor had ordered the Christian bishop there to bear the cost of rebuilding it) suggests further the proper relationship between church and state. St. Ambrose asks the question, "Which is of more importance: a demonstration of discipline or the cause of religion?" (*Epistle*

40.11). There is no doubting St. Ambrose's opinion on the matter: maintenance of civil law should be secondary to religion. Moreover, St. Ambrose reminds the emperor that his victories come from Christ, and, as he did in the epistle concerning the affair at Thessalonica, he holds up David as the model for Theodosius to follow, reminding the emperor (as Nathan reminded David) that God "has brought your captive enemy into your power" and has "brought you to victory within the very ramparts of the Alps" (40.22). Theodosius is victorious only because God makes it possible. So, to spurn matters of religion (that is, the church) is to spurn the very foundation and security for order in public matters. The good of the church, then, can never be at odds with truly good public order.[6]

Finally, we have St. Ambrose's first two books of *On Christian Faith*, which praise the emperor Gratian as a Christian eager for instruction and encourages him to go forth to war "protected by the shield of faith and girt with the sword of victory" (2.136). The new twist here is that military victory is now dependent upon fidelity to the Christian faith. To abandon God or the Church is to abandon all hope of defeating the enemy.

Let us sum up so far: the responsibility of the use of the sword is, at least in part, under the church's guidance. The state does not have a completely free reign in how it preserves civil order but is under ecclesiastical discipline to some degree. Furthermore, the state is successful in preserving civil order only in so far as God makes it possible. The state, therefore, cannot ignore ecclesiastical guidance and advice on the proper maintenance of civil order without ignoring the very power behind its success and victories. Finally, because the church determines in part how the sword is used by the state, we should be able to see a distinctive Christian characteristic of this use. That is what we turn to now.

Christian Soldiering and the Virtues

For St. Ambrose, Old Testament figures are models of right action for Christians. Christians can find guidance in shaping their lives by looking at the virtuous behavior of God's children. The key text here is St. Ambrose's Christian reworking of Cicero's account of the virtues in *On Duties*:

> Meanwhile they [the three books of *On Duties*] offer you a large number of examples, for almost all the examples drawn from our forefathers, and also many words of theirs, are included within these three books; so that ... a succession of old-time examples set down in such small compass may offer much instruction. (3.138)

The lives of the Old Testament fathers are to be "a mirror of virtue, not a mere collection of shrewd and clever acts. Let us show reverence in following them, not mere cleverness in discussing them" (*On Duties* 1.116). Not the least of these "mirrors" of virtue are the valiant warriors in God's service. The military virtues are praised time and again by St. Ambrose as virtues that Christians should emulate. The battle prowess of Joshua (1.205) and Judas Maccabeus (1.209) in particular are urged for Christian emperors and soldiers. But King David is the epitome of the just warrior. David is "brave in war, patient in time of adversity, peaceful at Jerusalem, in the hour of victory merciful" (1.114). David exhibits all the virtues incumbent upon the Christian ruler: he never enters war without seeking the counsel of God, he wages war only when necessary, and when war is necessary (and thus the will of God), he always enters it with a prudence combined with fortitude (1.177).

Quietism, Justice, and Charity

The Old Testament figures represent the paradigm of the just warrior; they can serve admirably as models for Christian rulers and soldiers. How the Old Testament figures can serve as models for

126

Christian rulers and soldiers—men who take their name from the figure who provides a <u>New</u> Testament—is made clear by turning first to a problem within the tradition: Christian quietism. By exploring how St. Ambrose deals with the problem we can bring into focus exactly how the Christian's character is so constituted that he acts virtuously in the face of violence, and we will be able to see why the brave Old Testament warriors in *On Duties* are the models for Christian soldiers and commanders.

The pre-Constantinian tradition was generally quiet in nature; that is to say, early Christians did not participate in the political life of the empire, especially soldiering. The consensus among historians is that the early (pre-Constantinian) opponents of warfare and military service objected to it on a variety of grounds (the role of pagan religious practices in the military being the main objection), but that at least from the end of the second century there is evidence of a divergence in Christian opinion, and that practice and Christian support for military service grew.[7] Thus, by the time St. Ambrose begins his duties as a bishop, Christians are in ever-increasing numbers giving up their quiet ways and participating in the political life of the empire. How was the church to deal with this phenomenon?

St. Ambrose deals with the phenomenon by placing it within the context of the relationship between the virtues of justice and charity. When St. Ambrose discusses justice in *On Duties* he says:

> ... in accordance with the will of God and the union of nature, we ought to be of mutual help one to the other, and to vie with each other in doing duties, to lay all our advantages as it were before all, and (to use the words of Scripture) to bring help one to the other from a feeling of devotion or of duty. (1.135)

He follows this by saying that the glory of justice lies in its authority to "bring help to others and supply money; nor does she refuse her services, but even undergoes dangers for others" (1.136). Here we

127

see that the very essence of justice is charity, or, as Paredi accurately describes it, justice is "integrated with charity."[8]

Furthermore, all virtue and usefulness are one. In one of his many discussions of the story of Susanna (*On Duties* 3.90), St. Ambrose emphasizes her desire to face a "virtuous death rather than to endure and live a shameful life in the desire to save herself." From this St. Ambrose extracts the moral axiom that "whatsoever is shameful cannot be useful, nor, again, can that which is virtuous be useless. For usefulness is ever the double of virtue and virtue of usefulness." So there is never a conflict between virtue and expediency, and hence the virtuous should always aim for right moral action and never do evil for a good cause. But how does the virtue of courage operate with charity—the perfect virtue? "Charity is perfect," says St. Ambrose, "it is the fulfilling of the law" (*Epistle* 29). If charity is not quite the form of all virtue (as it will be for St. Augustine), it is certainly the form of all justice. Why is this so? Because charity eliminates motives of self-interest, and this allows justice, the virtue that "assigns to each man his own, does not claim what is another's, and disregards its own advantage in order to safeguard the rights of all" (*On Duties* 1.115), to work more perfectly. Self-interest is that vice that vitiates just acts. Charity is the virtue that especially combats self-interest, for charity keeps our eyes away from self and on God and neighbor.

What this means for soldiers who must display courage on a regular basis in order to act well in their duties can be seen in St. Ambrose's discussion of John the Baptist's conversation with the soldiers who came to him to be baptized and to seek advice. St. Ambrose concentrates on the part mercy plays in John's advice and argues that, for Christian soldiers, mercy is the virtue for which they must strive above all else. Christian soldiers are to be marked by the virtue of mercy, for they should be soldiers only because they desire to protect their neighbors from harm (*Commentary on Luke* 1.77). Thus the virtue that is most befitting a Christian soldier is not

128

courage, or even justice per se, but mercy. Soldiers who possess the virtue of mercy can have the courage and self-control to be just. We see here in St. Ambrose the birth of what will become the dominate Christian just war view in the West: the soldier is an office of mercy and love.

We should emphasize that St. Ambrose is not twisting the logic of charity in order to make allowances for the use of force. The early fathers rarely talk about the role of the Christian in the military in a direct way, but they do talk about how Christians possess virtue in such a way that will guide them in leading a holy life. The revolution in St. Ambrose occurs in how he uses charity in the Christian moral life. St. Ambrose conceived of charity as the motivating force behind the Christian's use of force in a just cause. Charity (and its ever-present cohort, mercy)—gifts of virtue bestowed only through the Holy Spirit—shape people in such a way that the virtuous cannot stand by while preventable evil is perpetrated.

Moses is the perfect example of this process in action. According to St. Ambrose, Moses:

> ... feared not to undertake terrible wars for his people's sake, nor was he afraid of the arms of the mightiest kings, nor yet was he frightened at the savagery of barbarian nations. He put to one side the thought of his own safety so as to give freedom to the people. (*On Duties* 1.135).

Moses, a virtuous leader, was shaped by God in such a way that he was afraid not to use force for justice. Now we see how the courageous Old Testament figures of *On Duties* can be models for the Christian soldier. Moses, Joshua, Judas Maccabaeus, and David are to be emulated by charity-driven soldiers who know how to use force when it is fitting. The days of quietism are over—mercy and charity demand it.

129

Duties for Soldiers and Duties for Civilians and Clerics

St. Ambrose's just soldiers are virtuous soldiers, and he never claims that soldiers ought to give up soldiering if they wish to be Christians. On the contrary, just soldiering is entirely consonant with following God's will for political order. This does not mean that just soldiers can do anything in the line of duty. Because they are virtuous soldiers, there are certain rules in combat behavior that should be observed. In *On Duties*, St. Ambrose lists three such rules: (1) no unfair advantage of the enemy should be taken (1.29.139), (2) agreements with the enemy should be kept (2.7.33), and (3) mercy should be accorded a foe in defeat (3.14.87). This is what just combat looks like. If one wants to be known as a virtuous Christian soldier, these are the sort of acts one strives for so that others will say of him: "he always does these things."

Never does St. Ambrose claim a soldier must lay down his arms, yet he forbids civilians to take up arms. St. Ambrose even frowns upon Christian civilians using force in self-defense. St. Ambrose argues that "I do not think that a Christian, a just and a wise man, ought to save his own life by the death of another; just as when he meets with an armed robber he cannot return his blows, lest in defending his life he should stain his love (*pietatem contaminet*) toward his neighbor" (*On Duties* 3.27). This clear prohibition of using force in self defense would be repeated by St. Augustine and Luther for the same reason: the self-defender may not act in a loving way in the process of self-defense.[9] The difference between the civilian and the virtuous soldier is that the latter does not act for revenge and does not act out of any motive of self-interest. In fact, the soldier, whose duty it is to protect others, is just that person who fulfills the duty to defend the neighbor at risk. "The law of courage," claims St. Ambrose, is exercised "in driving away all harm" (*On Duties* 1.179). Here the very duty of civil courage is to protect the weak from harm. When protection of others is concerned, it is a stain on Christian piety not to use force in defense.

Clergy, too, are forbidden to take up arms. After St. Ambrose distinguishes two kinds of courage in *On Duties* (courage in war and courage in domestic affairs), he expressly denies the clergy a role in warfare, since the "thought of warlike matters seems to be foreign to the duty of our office, for we have our thought fixed more on the duty of the soul than on that of the body; nor is it our business to look to arms, but rather to the affairs of peace" (1.175). Elsewhere, St. Ambrose expressly states that the church does not fight with "temporal arms but with the arms of the spirit" (*On Widows* 8.49). So, when it comes to deciding who can use force, it is a matter of office (our very word for "offices" is taken from the Latin word for "duties"—"*officiis*"). There are various duties to be performed by various people. The duty of the soldier is to protect the innocent with force. The duty of the clergy is to pray· for the success of that force. No one, except clergy, are forbidden to soldier. No one, except soldiers, should take another's life.[10] The soldier and political leader has Moses as an example to follow in using force to protect the neighbor. When Moses came to the aid of his neighbor who was "receiving hard treatment at the hands of an Egyptian, he defended him" and "gave this as a first proof of his fortitude in war" (*On Duties* 1.179).[11] The clergy have the apostle Paul as an example to follow, both in praying for the victory of just use of force, and in the willingness to abstain from violence when attacked.

II. St. Augustine of Hippo

St. Augustine's ideas on war and the use of force are based entirely upon his assumptions concerning human nature and the role of the governing authorities in the human state. The basic assumption is original sin. In St. Augustine's thought, Adam's fall tainted the entire human race. Humanity is a "mass of sin" (*To Simplicianus on Diverse Questions* 1.2.16) inherently at odds with God, and under just condemnation (*City of God* 21.12). Humanity's essential goal is to bring itself into right relation with God, or, in other words, to seek its

131

proper place in the divine order. This is, in fact, the sum total of Christian behavior. Because human beings are so tainted by original sin, and the lust for domination that results from it, St. Augustine does not allow for a basic change in the human condition. Human beings are not going to improve appreciably from a moral perspective. If St. Augustine was right about nothing else, surely history has proved him right on this point.

The earthly city is a human construct dealing with the "mass of sin." The earthly city is formed to hold evil actions in check (*Epistle* 153.6.16). The state's task is to minimize disorder and hence to provide a place for its citizens to reach their ultimate good: God (*City of God* 19). Because the state is formed to prevent disorder and chaos, it has an absolute need to protect its liberty and safety (*City of God* 3.10 & 22.6). Consequently, Christians should value the peace of Babylon (*City of God* 19.26), for the Christian as well as the pagan benefits from the protection of order.

In granting the state an absolute need to protect its liberty and safety, St. Augustine did not intend to give the state carte blanche on how it performs this task. He provided earthly rulers with a standard for just ruling (*City of God* 5.24). This "mirror for princes" requires the ruler to put his power in the service of God. The advice to earthly rulers can be summarized into three basic duties: to provide a place for the worship of God, to carry out the judicial task, and to take vengeance on wrong because of the necessity to "direct and protect the state." Essential to the success of each duty is the establishment of peace and order.

St. Augustine's estimation of human nature led him to concentrate his political philosophy on the fundamental needs, and the need most fundamental for human beings is peace. Nevertheless, war among fallen humanity is inevitable. No one is secure from war, but everything works to the good under God's providence, including war. However, because peace is the ultimate goal of war, the peacemaker who uses the word is better than the peacemaker who uses the sword

(*Epistle* 229.2). Nevertheless, when the word and prayer fails, the Christian takes violent action. The intention, then, is always peace; preferably by the word, but if not, then it must be by the sword. Thus, St. Augustine's model of war follows St. Ambrose: choosing to go to war is not a choice between two evils. For St. Augustine, we can never do evil that good may come,[12] so war can never be the choice of a lesser evil. Justified violence for St. Augustine is something that is demanded partly for the sake of justice and peace, and ultimately for charity. So justified violence is a good to be practiced by the Christian.

The end goal in war is always peace, just as doing good is always the goal in human actions, and it is not war that forestalls doing good, but malice of the heart: a lack of charity (*Sermons* 302.15). The emphasis St. Augustine places on this inward disposition, and its subsequent influence on Aquinas, cannot be overstated. Proper Christian behavior seeks to get the person in harmony with the divine order, so a good action is one taken in relation to the wider order where everything is in proper relation to God (*On Christian Doctrine* 1.22.21). Therefore, a correct inward disposition places a person in the right relation to God, and the love of God must inform any correct inward disposition. It is this charity-informed disposition that guides our right actions, and this charity-informed disposition sometimes demands acts of violence.

Here is where we find St. Augustine's legacy to the West. All "just" violence, therefore, is the product of a charity-informed disposition that seeks the good—in this case, peace. War is not to be viewed in terms of the dangers to material interests or even human survival (cf. *Against Faustus the Manichaen* 22.78 and *City of God* 1.11). Instead, the evils of war lie in the moral evil of disordered desire and twisted inward dispositions. Consequently, then, it is only the virtuous citizen—the true Christian—who can know when to use force, for only the Christian is sufficiently detached from the earthly goods and lust that lead to disordered desire. All Christians should seek the preservation of the moral order: rightly ordered dispositions and desires, which can only be achieved by the grace of God (charity).

III. St. Thomas Aquinas[13]

St. Thomas follows his predecessors by concentrating upon virtue and the common good. We should point out that the *Summa Theologica*, where the bulk of Aquinas's thought on war occurs, was intended as a handbook for clerics—people who are expressly forbidden to fight in wars. Why, one may rightly inquire, do clerics need to know about war when participation in war is forbidden to them? Because the people who read the *Summa* are a body of people representing the risen Lord and Savior; they embody practices that witness to the governing authorities. The governing authorities must respond, and when they do, an account of the just use of force must be articulated. The governing authorities cannot fulfill their true function, to be a sign on earth of God's just rule, without the witness of God's people on earth. The just war tradition enables St. Thomas's clerical audience to give such witness concerning warfare.

Charity, like it was for St. Ambrose and St. Augustine, is the driving force behind St. Thomas's moral approach to war. St. Thomas's logic is impeccable: charity is the virtue necessary for acquiring all other virtue and, hence, for acquiring excellence in any worthy practice. Love and war are not incompatible, and to be morally acceptable, war-making must be a work of love. This means that a soldier cannot be an excellent soldier *qua* Christian soldier without charity. The account of excellence in soldiering leads to a potentially troubling aspect of Aquinas's approach: the relative absence of rules for fighting in war (what we commonly refer to as the *jus in bello*). The scarcity of rules in St. Thomas's approach is one of its most noticeable features. Although St. Thomas offers a few criteria that define the just war, he has little to say about how a war should be fought. This is not to say that Aquinas is unconcerned with how soldiers fight, but that he locates the questions about proper behavior in right intention and virtue—especially the virtue of charity.

St. Thomas on the Morality of Human Acts

Roughly speaking, for St. Thomas, any human act is an act that can be called praiseworthy or blameworthy. "Moral acts and human acts are the same" [*Summa Theologica (ST)* I-II 1.3]; consequently, all human acts contribute to the virtuous or vicious character-in-formation of the human being. These acts proceed from a "deliberate will" (*ST* I-II 1.1), and because the "object of the will is the end and the good," the starting point of human acts is the end (*ST* I-II 1.3). That is to say, the principle of human acts is the end, and "in like manner it is their terminus: for the human act terminates at that which the will intends as the end" (*ST* I-II 1.3). Intention is that which makes a plurality of acts one moral act (*ST* I-II 12.1), so now we can say with more precision that intentional human acts are those acts we call praiseworthy or blameworthy.

What makes an intentional act good or bad is, first of all, its object (*ST* I-II 18.1), but St. Thomas expands this when he discusses the fourfold goodness of the human act: its genus, species, circumstances, and end (*ST* I-II 18.4). The genus of an act is good in an ontological sense; that is, it is good insofar as it has being, for all being has goodness. Moral appraisal of acts begins with an act's species, "which is read from the fitting object," hence, insofar as reason judges some object fitting, it is a good act. Circumstances are those accidents surrounding any act that can add to the goodness or badness of it. The end is that to which an action can be referred; it is what is most closely bound to intention. So to sum up: a good act must be a good kind of act, done at the right time and at the right place (the appropriate circumstances), and for the purpose of achieving some good end (right intention). Moral virtue is a reliable disposition toward acting well, time and again.

135

Properly formed habits allow the person to act well consistently. Acquiring such habits depends upon properly governed passions—passions that operate in accordance with reason. When St. Thomas talks about having passions in the right way, he means our passions need to be ordered not only by reason but also by our passion for God, since supreme happiness (union with God) is the final goal, which all rational appetite apprehends and by which it is drawn.

We will not be able to react to things correctly, however, if charity does not inform all our loves. For St. Thomas, objects that cause passion (that cause us to want to draw near) must be fitting for a rational animal. When we love a fitting object, the object perfects and improves us; so we are most perfected and most improved through the love of God (*ST* I-II 28.5). Therefore, the most fitting and most rational thing to do is love God; and by loving God, all our passions can be ordered. This means that charity enables us to give the most meaning to God. When we possess the ability to react to things correctly, we can also act correctly. We then acquire those habits constitutive of the moral life we wish to lead.

The Cardinal Virtues and Charity

With this in mind, we turn now to St. Thomas's discussion of the four cardinal virtues. As we begin this discussion of the cardinal virtues, we must keep in mind that charity—not justice—is the crucial virtue in Christian soldiering in the West. Justice is, of course, the key cardinal virtue insofar as we want to know what a just war looks like, but the virtue of charity is what will give the impetus for Christian participation. St. Thomas classifies each virtue in terms of its formal principle (what each one is moved by) and in terms of the subject matter with which it deals (*ST* I-II 61.2). Prudence is the exercise of reason, and its subject matter is the way reason should operate in practice—that is, it enables us "to apply right reason to action" (*ST* II-II 47.4). Prudence is essential in the decision to go to war and in formulating battle plans. Justice is the employment of reason in human conduct, and its subject matter is how the will is directed toward good acts. Justice, then, is that virtue that grants the person "the perpetual and constant will to render each one his due" (ST II-II 58.1). Justice is the measuring stick to which we apply prudence in figuring out the justice of a proposed war or battle plan. Courage is the proper steering of the passions that drive us to act irrationally in the face of danger or hardship (ST II-II 123.1), and its subject matter is the irascible appetite, which can urge us to act unreasonably (ST I-II 61.2). Courage enables leaders to make the appropriate decisions for or against war depending on what prudence dictates. Courage enables soldiers to stand firm when tempted to run away from battle. Temperance is the restraint of the passions when they are contrary to reason; it is the virtue "that inclines a man to something in accord with reason" (ST II-II 141.1), and its subject matter is the concupiscible appetite, which provides the passions with their force. Temperance enables leaders to recognize in themselves motivations for certain actions based upon hate and revenge. The role it plays in combat behavior is enormous and obvious.

It is important to note that neither justice nor the other cardinal virtues can exist as complete natural virtues for fallen humanity unless they are informed by the infused (i.e., granted by grace—the Holy Spirit) supernatural virtue of charity (caritas). According to St. Thomas, charity is the form of all virtue; it is the friendship of a human being for God, and no true virtue is possible without it (ST II-II 23.7). Charity, a gift of grace from God (ST II-II 23-44, especially 23.7), is what guides the virtues in the right direction; it is always ordered to the good.

For St. Thomas, there is an order of charity, a hierarchy of loved objects depending on circumstances and fittingness (ST II-II 26; cf. On Charity Q.9). It is in this idea of an order of charity that St. Thomas argues explicitly for the fittingness of some acts of force as charitable acts.[14] Of course, there is one order of love that does not change with the circumstances: love of God. There can be nothing more fitting than loving God above anything or anyone else. Regardless of circumstances, regardless of the people involved, we should love God supremely, for it is by loving God most of all that all other loved objects will be loved fittingly with respect to circumstances. Prudence, guided by love of God, informs us who is to be preferred in acts of charity: in matters of politics (which is the locus of warfare) we should prefer our fellow citizens over family members. So, in warfare, charity demands that we seek the good of the community over the good of individual families. Charity and acts of force are compatible. One does not have to forget about God when one goes to war. On the contrary, it is only by loving God that the Christian is able to order his loves rightly so that he is able to choose the good of the community over individual goods.

The Presumption Is Against Injustice—Not Violence

St. Thomas approaches the moral problems of war through the virtues and the common good. War and peace can be either good or bad for the common good. The virtue of love compels the Christian to exercise prudence in judging when war is called for, and to exercise courage and self-control in making decisions to go to war and in fighting. War is not a vice. War is not necessarily opposed to charity (*ST* II-II 34–43). Peace is not a virtue, and those who make an idol out of peace often find themselves supporting a political order that is not worth preserving (*ST* II-II 40). St. Thomas follows St. Augustine in conceiving peace as the tranquility of order that all things desire. War is one means to this peace. This bears repeating. Because true peace can only concern the good, peace is not a virtue in itself. Peace can be both pleasing to God (a just peace) or displeasing to God (an unjust peace). Just citizens should keep the peace and fight just wars (when necessary) because these are meritorious acts of charity (*ST* II-II 29.4 and 40.2).

That St. Thomas considers fighting just wars to be acting meritoriously suggests a divergence from the modern presumption against violence (all acts of force) found in many recent just war accounts both Protestant and Catholic. Stanley Hauerwas, for example, has argued that Christian just war advocates and pacifists share a presumption against violence and that this presumption generates just war criteria. Indeed, Hauerwas goes so far as to say that "Christians created just war reflection because of their nonviolent convictions."[15] St. Thomas knows of no such presumption against violence in this modern sense of the term. The abundance of texts that testify to St. Thomas's rejection of the idea of a presumption against war are too many to list. A few examples will suffice. First, St. Thomas, similar to St. Ambrose, argues that the just vindication taken by the Old Testament heroes of faith is a virtue that is "sought out of love of justice ... and this remains still in the New Law" (*ST* I-II 107.2, cf. 108.3). Second, in his commentary on Paul's letter to the Romans, he argues that it is not only allowable (*licet*) but positively "meritorious for Princes to exercise vindication of justice with zeal against bad people (*in malos*)" (*Commentary on Romans* 13, lect. i). Third, he argues that it is both "praiseworthy and advantageous" for someone with the proper authority to kill someone dangerous and infectious to the community (*ST* II-II 64.2). Thus we find St. Thomas arguing for a moral approach to unjust violence that demands Christians to do what they can to put an end to it, even if it means using force to do so.

One might reply that, given what we have said about the use of force as a positive obligation, what, then, is the point of the just war doctrine? If the use of force is a moral imperative in some cases, then why, for example, do we need *jus ad bellum* criteria to justify a war? Put another way, if there is no presumption against war, then why does war need to be justified? War needs to be justified because going to war will lead inevitably, but not intentionally if the war is just, to collateral damage, which causes all kinds of unintended suffering. Also, because fallen human beings can never be certain of their intentions, especially in desperate situations, we can never be sure that we will not commit unjust acts in war. Indeed, just warriors know that they will do unjust things in war because they can only approximate what the *jus in bello* demands in proportion to their always incomplete virtuous characters. Thus, those who decide upon war must have their own intentions sifted as much as possible for evil desires that may lie behind the decision for war. Warfare is not something to be entered into lightly, and must, as time permits, be considered carefully. But it is exactly this time factor that increases the need for the virtues to be in place before a crisis appears.

Another possible objection here is that, if there is no presumption against violence, then why do we not immediately jump to violence when we see an injustice being done? First, on the international level, the question is, in part, answered in the preceding paragraph. War often entails a lot of suffering, but we do not say that we have a presumption against war because of the suffering; rather we say that we must make sure of the justice of our cause before we proceed. We do this in order to prevent the intended evil that would occur should we enter a war for unjust reasons. Second, on a personal (and sometimes even international) level, the virtuous may, in fact, immediately jump to violence when they see a great injustice being done to others. Only those with the virtue of prudence will be able to do so, and such actions would, in fact, demand a high level of prudence.

Of course, the just warrior might agree that there is a presumption against war, but what the just warrior means by this presumption differs from what most people, especially pacifists, think the presumption means. Should just warriors use the language of presumption against war, they would mean that a presumption exists not because the proposed activity (use of force) is somehow evil in itself or disconsonant with holy Christian living and therefore in need of justification, but because unintended suffering (which is a misfortune but not a moral evil) may come from the proposed activity.

140

Rules and Right Conduct in War

St. Thomas has three rules that define a just war: proper authority, just cause, and right intention (*ST* II-II 40.1). These three rules comprise the *jus ad bellum*, the criteria that allow us to decide if a particular war is worthy of Christian participation. Right conduct in war is dependent to some degree upon the virtues of the soldiers and especially the commanders waging the war. Following Aristotle, St. Thomas views the military as a place where virtue can and should be cultivated.[16] Excellence in soldiering depends especially upon courage (*ST* II-II 123.5 and *Commentary on the Ethics* III, lect. xiv), while excellence in leading soldiers depends especially upon prudence (*Summa Contra Gentiles* 3.128). How do soldiers acquire military virtues? St. Thomas has nothing directly to say about this, but there seems to be no reason to doubt that virtue is acquired by those in the military as it is acquired by anyone seeking excellence in some practice: we learn excellence in a pupil-master relationship. Military commanders, then, must be virtuous soldiers who are able to teach the soldiers under them. The rules hammered into recruits-in-training are all commanded for the purpose of making the recruit a soldier of excellence.

Rules, therefore, are not entirely discarded but are given a certain secondary place. Or perhaps it would be better to say that there are two kinds of rules in this account of moral action: the primary ones that guard the boundaries of acceptable practice and the secondary ones that are crucial to moral formation. The former are always kept because they actually define the parameters of the activity within which excellence is sought. To act contrary to these would be to abandon the practice. But the latter are only rough and ready rules—they are not absolutely binding.

An analogy (though imperfect, as we will later explain) would be helpful in clarifying this point. Let us take the game of baseball as an example of what is going on here. There are two kinds of rules in baseball. Most important are those rules that help define what baseball

141

is: a player gets three strikes before he is called out, a team gets three outs before they must quit batting, a player must tag each base as he rounds the base path, and so forth. These are all rules that define the game of baseball. To break these rules would mean that you do not want (or you do not know how) to play baseball, for you will not be playing baseball if you do not play by these rules.

The second set of rules is what we can call rules of training. Rules of training are imposed upon would-be players who are learning how to play the game well. These rules are "rules of thumb" learned through experience by coaches and passed on to those learning how to play. A good example of such a rule is the standard proper "classic" swing of the bat (back straight, shoulders square, back elbow high) taught to every person who ever tried to learn how to play the game. Yet a glance at a professional baseball game, where those who have achieved excellence in this practice display their abilities, reveals that very few of those who have attained excellence in the practice of baseball actually use the "classic" swing of the bat. That is because they learned over time and through experience that deviation from the rule-of-thumb enables them to be better players. In short, they develop virtues. In summation, we can say that training rules are a means of developing excellence in a practice, but excellence in a practice cannot be reduced to any set of rules; thus, as excellence grows, so does the freedom to depart from the formative rules by which the skill was nurtured.

One of the lessons learned from this account of rules in the moral life is that there is no need to get entangled in the language of absolutes. It adds nothing to the discussion to say the rules defining some practice represent absolute rules. Because such rules define an area of proper moral practice, it goes without saying (or should go without saying) that these criteria cannot be ignored. In the same way, it is pointless to say that it is, for example, an absolute rule in baseball that a batter gets only three strikes. The "absolute" here is redundant. Three strikes for a batter is part of what makes baseball what it is; so

142

we do not have to say the rule is absolute—instead, we say that it is baseball. Similarly, rules defining the just war *are* just war.[17]

How virtuous behavior plays out in St. Thomas's virtuous soldier suggests part of the reason why he does not enumerate *jus in bello* criteria. As James Johnson has shown, rules for right conduct in war in St. Thomas's time come from a two-fold secular tradition: the chivalric code and the *jus gentium* (itself influenced by canon law).[18] This suggests that right conduct in battle is largely culture-dependent; what counts as praiseworthy or blameworthy action in combat will vary from place to place. We see something like this at work in St. Thomas. One objection to St. Thomas's proposition that all acts of virtue are prescribed by law is that "acts of virtue are not common to all: since a thing is virtuous in one and vicious in another" (*ST* I-II 94.3 obj. 3). St. Thomas's answer is that "it is owing to the conditions of men, that certain acts are virtuous for some, as being proportionate and becoming to them, while they are vicious for others, as being out of proportion to them." So the specific rules used to approximate virtue vary from place to place. Custom, in other words, can help specify what a virtuous act may look like.

Something more, however, must be said from St. Thomas's point of view: rules governing just acts in combat must be, to some degree, rules-of-thumb for soldiers. That some moral rules are not absolutely binding is made clear from the following passage:

> Thus it is right and true for all to act according to reason: and from this principle it follows as a proper conclusion, that goods entrusted to another should be restored to their owner. Now this is true for the majority of the cases; but it may happen in a particular case that it would be injurious, and therefore unreasonable, to restore goods held in trust; for instance if they are claimed for the purpose of fighting against one's country. And this principle will be found to fail the more, according as we descend further into detail ... because the greater the number of conditions added, the greater the number of ways in which the

> principle may fail, so that it be not right to restore or not to restore. (*ST* I-II 94.4)

Clearly St. Thomas recognizes certain precepts that do, for the most part, ensure correct acting, but these precepts are not always binding since circumstances may require other acts. It is the prudent person who knows how to act appropriately in given circumstances; the prudent person knows when to disregard the rule-of-thumb. I suggest that the absence of a specified *jus in bello* is due in part to the uncertain circumstances that constitute the context of right acting in combat. Rules that govern how one should fight in a war are very difficult to formulate in any way that is permanently binding. The rules that define a just war, however, can never be disregarded; for to disregard any boundary marker means that you are no longer "playing the game," or waging a just war. The main point is this: the virtuous soldier is not constrained by the rules-of-thumb in just warfare, but he is constrained by rules constituting what a just war is.

St. Thomas quotes St. Ambrose in maintaining certain rights of war and covenants that ought to be observed among combatants (*ST* II-II 40.3), but he does not tell the reader what they are. He no doubt has in mind the sort of rules we found in St. Ambrose's *On Duties*. If our argument is correct, we can say that St. Thomas does not discuss these rules for two reasons: they are largely under the province of local custom, but more importantly, such rules are of only secondary importance in a virtue-governed account of just war. To put the matter more bluntly, for St. Thomas the just soldier may be in circumstances where, for instance, to refuse mercy in defeat or to break an agreement may be the right course of action.[19] It takes only a moment of thought to formulate circumstances when this could be true (the wars of Israel under Joshua's leadership readily come to mind).

None of the above denies the usefulness of the *jus in bello* in controlling warfare. The rules of fighting are rules-of-thumb, but not merely rules-of-thumb, and this is exactly where the analogy with baseball breaks down. The end of the *jus in bello* is to approximate virtuous behavior in battle, but the specified approximations can never be set in stone. Put more clearly, what the *jus in bello* strive for— proportion and non-combatant immunity—are always binding upon the soldier and commander, but what is not (cannot) be binding is what may count as meeting the criterion of proportion or non-combatant immunity. If we attempt to stretch the analogy with baseball, we might say that it is always binding upon the batter to hit the ball where it cannot be fielded by an opponent, but how the batter goes about doing this will vary from era to era, from game to game, and from player to player. In the same way, it is always binding upon soldiers to do their best not to kill innocent people and to attack and defend in such a way that the expected good of those acts will outweigh the expected evil, but how soldiers go about doing this will vary, depending upon time, place, and individual soldier.

However, no such latitude applies to the rules constitutive of just war as a practice.[20] This point is emphasized in St. Thomas's discussion of murder (*ST* II-II 64) and injuries to the person (*ST* II-II 65), a discussion in which he insists that only one in authority can kill or maim for the welfare of the community (64.3, 65.3). It is just for one in authority to kill, but it would be a species of injustice for a private person to kill or maim for the good of the community. Moreover, attacking those who do not deserve it or attacking with any intention other than a rightful one is always an unjust act. To break one of these rules is to opt out of waging a just war.

Virtue, Double-Effect, and Proportion

One could argue, of course, that two of St. Thomas's defining or constitutive rules of a just war—just cause and rightful intention— assume both the modern *ad bellum* rules (and in this instance there is complete identity) and the modern *in bello* rule of discrimination (noncombatant immunity). In other words, one could argue that just cause and rightful intention in St. Thomas encompass both the right

145

reasons for going to war and the intention not to harm those who do not deserve it, therefore entailing the prohibition against killing innocent people in war. Regrettably, innocent people may be killed in just wars, but in just wars they should be killed only unintentionally. In other words, it does no necessary harm to the justice of a war when innocent people are killed. We must first ask if those deaths were intentional or not. If they were unintentional, then those deaths do not harm the justice of the war. For St. Thomas, the rule of double-effect applies in such cases. St. Thomas argues that "nothing hinders one act from having two effects, only one of which is intended, while the other is beside the intention" (*ST* II-II 64.7). We can apply this principle to combat behavior.[21] No just soldier will intend to kill innocent people. Nevertheless, he may be required to take action against the enemy that he knows will cause injury to innocent people, but in such cases, he does not intend those injuries; he only intends to injure the enemy.

When St. Thomas talks about double-effect, he does not mean that anyone can direct his or her intention a certain way in order to make any act just. The danger this poses to proper just war thinking is obvious. The temptation is for any soldier to justify acts simply by directing his intention in a certain way and denying all the evil consequences. Let's take an example. Imagine the Nazis operating a heavy water plant during World War II. The plant is located in a residential district. To bomb the plant from the air would mean the deaths of thousands of innocent civilians. The leaders and pilots of such a mission could simply say that "what we mean by bombing this plant is the destruction of the enemy's nuclear weapons program." St. Thomas would determine the intention of the military personnel not by asking them about their "directed intention" but by first observing the completed acts, for intention is a communal concept. Roughly speaking, for St. Thomas, what you intend is what you do. Intention, in other words, is how we make our or another's action intelligible to us. This makes intention a communal concept; that is to say, no person can possess intentionality as one possesses personal property. For the intelligibility of our acts is something that others may know more about than ourselves. Of course, the community can make mistakes as well, but it may be a more reliable judge of our intentions than we are, at least when the community possesses virtuous people. For the community does not suffer from the same level of temptation to justify vicious acts of force, which is not to say that it suffers no such temptation. What matters here are the observable circumstances. Do the acts in question contain elements of callousness, intemperance, impatience, or cruelty? Was this particular act the only way to achieve the good in this instance?

We may describe the act as one of bombing a heavy water plant in order to sabotage its nuclear program or we may describe the act as one of bombing the plant in order to demoralize the civilian population as well as sabotage the nuclear program. This is why St. Thomas insists that the most important circumstances of human acts are the "why" (*ST* I-II 7.4). Because intention is an "act of will bearing on the end" (*ST* I-II 12.1), when you answer the question of why you do something, you have a good idea what your intention is. In other words, when the will chooses to act in a certain way, it chooses to do so for some end. That end sought best answers the question why someone does something. Thus, if the end of the above example is only to knock out the heavy water plant, then that action is best described as such (the intention is to attack an enemy objective). On the other hand, if the end is to demoralize the civilian population as well as to knock out the plant, then the act is best described as one of attacking civilians as well as military objectives (the intention is to attack civilians and a military objective). We can look for traces of vice in the way the bombing mission was formed and how it was carried out—examining issues like patience in planning, the attempt of alternative actions, such as the use of underground fighters for sabotage, the carefulness of the bombing runs, and so forth. All of these would help us answer the question of what exactly was the intention of the action.

An agent, of course, may not intend every consequence of an act. St. Thomas says that "since the end is willed in itself, whereas the means, as such, are only willed for the end, it is evident that the will can be moved to the end without being moved to the means" (*ST* I-II 8.3). So, although the soldier and those who plan his mission know his act will kill innocent people as well as destroy the depot, they do not intend their deaths (that is, he bombs the plant for the sole purpose of crippling the enemy's nuclear program). The soldier and war planners, if just, will not wish to kill the innocent people, and they wish that there were no innocent civilians living in the area they must attack. Another way of looking at this is to say that their only purpose is to destroy the plant and they would have done it even if no innocent people were living nearby. That is to say, the presence of innocent people serves no part in their motivation to bomb the target, nor can the presence of innocent people play any part in telling us why they bombed the target. The presence of regret might be key.[22] But we do not determine this merely by asking them to report their intentions, but also through observation of the soldiers' acts, and the acts of those who planned the mission, which tell us why the act was performed. The act is good in its species in so far as it has a fitting object, which, in this case, is bombing an enemy heavy water plant. Also, the end is good in so far as the bombing is carried out for the sole purpose of defeating a proper enemy. Lastly, it should be pointed out that soldiers must take sufficient care if they are to incur no guilt. When St. Thomas argues that what is not actually and directly voluntary and intended is voluntary and intended accidentally, and hence imparts no guilt on the agent, he argues that guilt still accrues to the agent if he "be occupied with something unlawful, or even with something lawful, but without due care" (*ST* II-II 64.8). To sum up: if the act of bombing itself is a species of injustice or if sufficient care is not taken in the act, the soldier is guilty of murder.

One further thing would have to be settled before we could judge acts of bombing as just or unjust: we would have to examine them under the criterion of proportion. This concerns the circumstances of the act, and in this case we have to ask whether the anticipated good (elimination of the plant) outweighs the consequence of the innocents killed. Prudence is the virtue that helps us arrive at an answer, and the fact that there is no hard and fast rule for such cases is no argument against the pursuit of virtue. There is no chart we can read that will tell us, for instance, that a heavy water plant of such and such a size can be destroyed as long as the projected loss of innocent life does not exceed some number. The only hope for acting rightly in such circumstances is to exercise prudence concerning the likely success of the mission (destroying the heavy water plant), the positive effect of the mission (debilitating enemy nuclear power), the negative effect (killing innocents), and to determine when the positive outweighs the negative.

The knowledge of when to carry out such acts falls within the province of the prudence of the soldier and especially the commander. The soldier cannot attain this prudence without the grace of God and the skill learned through training and practice under a master of soldiering. The virtuous commander knows when and with how much force to attack. Like most knowledge in skillful practice, it becomes habitual. This is not to deny deliberation on the commander's part. Perhaps the commander will have sufficient time to deliberate concerning the course of just action. The point is that the commander *qua* virtuous commander is the product of experienced deliberation and practice in warfare. His "snap decisions" are always made, if rational, with the final temporal goal in mind: a just fight that leads to a just peace.

Conclusion

St. Thomas's just war approach is an account of a practice embedded in the way of life of the virtuous in the face of a fallen world that has been at war almost from the very beginning.

St. Thomas follows St. Ambrose and St. Augustine in making the virtue of charity primary for just Christian participation in war. No true virtue is possible without charity, for the love of God is necessary to make practices truly excellent, that is, constitutive of our final end: the beatific vision of God. The virtuous Christian soldier obeys the just war *ad bellum* criteria in going to war and fights virtuously in war (with the *jus in bello* as a guide) because to fail to do so would destroy his character and prevent him from achieving the ultimate end of this practice: a just peace. Moreover, failure to fight virtuously would hinder his progress toward God. The virtuous Christian soldier is the kind of person who knows how to act on the field of battle because he is who he is. The Christian soldier is that soldier who fights because he loves God and his neighbor, and justice and temperance always govern his fighting.

We can now make some concluding observations about how the Christian's character, within the context of the role of church discipline in society, is so conceived that it produces a Christian view on soldiering, and about how the Christian's response to violent situations says something important about Christian character. Christians can use violence when they have a duty to do so; in other words, when they are soldiers (or policemen). Such Christians respond to violence from enemies that threaten peace and order—not passively, but with force. Christians, however, who are not responsible for safe political order do not respond to violence made upon their lives as individuals, for this may taint the very virtue that guides Christians soldiers in their use of force: charity (love of God and neighbor). Lastly, Christians—both the soldiers who fight and the clergy who pray for victory—do this for the sake of others. Christians fight in the army and pray for victory because they are formed by the perfect virtue of charity. Charity is the ruling virtue in the moral life. To end with a paraphrase of Flannery O'Connor's dictum: how Christians react to violent situations says a lot about them— they greatly value the virtue of charity.

CHAPTER 7

Protestant Reformers on the Just War

Traditional Protestants have a rich heritage to draw from when it comes to handling the moral problems of war. That heritage is founded on the moral approaches to war found in the Church fathers and St. Thomas Aquinas. So, on this point at least, the great Reformers saw themselves as continuing on the same unbroken path of thought begun by St. Ambrose. Martin Luther and John Calvin are without doubt the two most influential Reformers. The two main streams of the magisterial Reformation—Lutheranism and Reformed—trace their roots to these figures. Although their theological differences were sometimes great, there is a strong similarity in how each approached the just war tradition. Because Luther and Calvin looked to their predecessors for guidance in the questions of war, traditional Protestantism and Catholicism have a unified voice in witnessing to the Christian just war tradition.

I. Luther

In Luther's essay, "Secular Authority: To What Extent It Should Be Obeyed," he argues that the civil law and the sword are in the world by God's will and ordinance. It is God's will that the law and sword be used for the punishment of the wicked and the protection of the upright. Christ's words are not counsels of perfection but exist in the heart, in faith and love. For such people, there is no need for temporal law and sword. This is because the righteous do all the law demands and more out of their own free will. But the unrighteous need the law and sword to coerce them to do right. So, the law is for the lawless, which is to say, law is for the majority of humankind. Because there are few true Christians, God provides humankind with a different kind of government than the government of the kingdom of God.

151

Christians should get involved with the earthly government because true Christians live and labor on earth not for themselves but for their neighbors—including their non-Christian neighbors. These non-Christians neighbors need the law and the sword in order to preserve the peace, which is beneficial to all, so Christians get involved with the government for the sake of their neighbors. In such cases, Christians do not seek their own advantage but the advantage of their neighbors. In fact, Christians ought to make the best holders of sword and authority, because these duties are a particular service to God (it is one of the few jobs God has actually ordained Himself).

Luther made two replies to the objection that Christ did not use a sword. First, he argues that Christ's words are for true Christians—they guide the conduct of Christians toward other Christians, and not toward non-Christians. Second, he points out that neither did Christ take a wife, become a tailor or many other things, but we don't say that therefore no one else ought not to do so. Christ pursued his own office, which was that of redeemer of humankind, and as such could offer no resistance.

Luther's attitude toward soldiering in the essay, "Whether Soldiers, Too, May Be Saved," is very revealing. Whoever fights with a good and well-instructed conscience can also fight well, but a timid and insecure conscience makes a bad fighter. Luther writes the essay in order that his Prince's men will fight with a good and well-instructed conscience. Luther plans to show soldiers how they can go to war and not lose God's favor and eternal life. He makes much of the distinction between the occupation and the person: an occupation may be good in itself, but evil if done by the wrong person or done wrongly. If one uses public office in order to gain riches and popularity, it is done wrongly. Of course, to do rightly in office does not merit you salvation; only faith in Jesus Christ can do that. The goal is external righteousness. The problem is this: is the Christian faith compatible with being a soldier, going to war, stabbing and killing, robbing and burning, as military law requires us to do to our enemies in wartime?

Luther follows his Roman Catholic predecessors by arguing that soldiering is a work of love. The very fact that the sword has been instituted by God is proof enough that war and killing has been instituted by God. War is the punishment of wrong and evil. Slaying and robbing do not seem to be a work of love, but they are. Luther offers the famous analogy with doctors performing surgery: in both cases we should not concentrate on the brutality but at what the consequences would be if the brutality did not occur. God instituted the sword in order to preserve peace. Some say that God ordained war for the Old Testament period only, where God explicitly commanded His children to fight. Luther counters that God never "un-ordains" war in the New Testament. More to the point for Luther, John the Baptist, Paul and Peter sufficiently refute the idea that war was ordained only for the period before Christ.

Luther also addressed the question of how we know when the military profession is being used properly. First, it is impossible to establish hard and fast rules and laws for this matter, but in general we ought to make the law yield and justice take its place. So, we must say that equal may fight against equal, and overlord against subject, but never subject against overlord. Subjects ought to suffer wrong before rebelling, for the mob knows no moderation of violence. Besides, God says that "vengeance is mine". Lastly, it does no good in the long run to rebel; there is simply too much destruction involved. The same goes for noblemen who wish to rebel. Second, whoever starts a war is in the wrong. God has instituted the sword to maintain peace and not to start wars. Wait until war is necessary, a necessity that we would rather avoid. In fact, we ought to wait until the thought of war is distasteful to us, then we will know that we do not have any bad motives. Third, self-defense is a proper reason for war. Such a war is a war of necessity.

Fourth, even if you fight a proper war, you need to be careful that you fight it properly. The cause does not justify the means, nor does the cause guarantee success. We should commit ourselves and our cause to God before going to battle. Fifth, any war is a proper war that God commands. When a war is just, there is no need to feel guilty about fighting. We should go forward with joy into battle if the cause is just because we do no evil by fighting just wars justly.

II. Calvin

Calvin's approach to the moral problems of war is inextricably tied to his interpretation of the life and work of Christ. Calvin argues for a unity between the God of the Old Testament and the God of the New such that we cannot conceive of Jesus Christ in the New Testament as commanding anything different from what Yahweh commanded in the Old Testament. For Calvin, it is precisely within that unity that we can understand the positive role that Christ plays in the Christian's relationship to political order and war.

The norm for interpreting Christ, as most theologians would admit, is not actually the New Testament itself but the New Testament as interpreted within a later theological scheme. For Calvin, it is Paul's letter to the Romans that provides us the key text through which we understand the person and work of Christ and so all other Scripture. Calvin argues that we learn from Paul that God, because of human disobedience, sees to it that many are killed justly, including through war. We learn that it is part of God's character to use force against evil and that it is part of his character to use human beings—including Christians—to restrain the evil actions of other human beings.

Calvin's theological formulations of the problem are especially useful since he is always mindful of his radical opponents who insisted on complete pacifism. The one position that underlies all of Calvin's arguments against his radical opponents is that we
154

may never reject the Old Testament and spurn the law (Com. Jeremiah 26:4). Calvin wished to counter the claim that spiritual perfection could be found only for New Testament believers and not for those living before Jesus (*Institutes* II.10.7). Calvin argued against those who claimed that the two testament periods are totally different, especially with regard to God's relationship with his chosen people. He was especially keen to counter the position that the Old Testament law was for the Jews alone and had no authority for Christians. For Calvin it is a scandal to argue that the new covenant obliges Christians to live according to the moral precepts of the New Testament, which supersede the Old Testament moral precepts.

Calvin argues that there is no conflict between law and Gospel (Com. Matthew 5:17).[1] Christ did not bring a new law but his Spirit to renew our hearts so that we would want to obey and please God, which means following the moral law (Com. Matthew 5:20). Calvin insists that the love command is wholly consonant with the Decalogue (Com. Matthew 5:45). So the Sermon on the Mount is not a code of perfection for the few but for all that live in this world. Two of the main lessons to be learned from the Sermon are that all must break with seeking personal vengeance if they wish to obey and please God, and that charity and justice are synonymous (Com. Matthew 7:12).

The passage in Romans that Calvin felt to be normative for Christian politics occurs in the first seven verses of the 13th chapter. Here is how the passage reads:

> Let every person be subject to the governing authorities. For there is no authority except from God, and God has instituted those that exist. Therefore he who resists the authorities resists what God has appointed, and those who resist will incur judgment. For rulers are not a terror to good conduct, but to bad. Would you have no fear of him who is in authority? Then do what is good, and you will receive his approval, for he is God's

servant for your good. But if you do what is wrong, be afraid, for he does not bear the sword in vain; he is the servant of God to execute his wrath on the wrongdoer. Therefore one must be subject, not only to avoid God's wrath but also for the sake of conscience. For the same reason you also pay taxes, for the authorities are ministers of God, attending to this very thing. Pay all of them their dues, taxes to whom taxes are due, revenue to whom revenue is due, respect to whom respect is due, honor to whom honor is due. (Romans 13:1–7)

The key verses fall into what is known traditionally as the parenetic section of Paul's letter to the Romans (12:1–15:13). As Calvin notes, we should not assume that the passage has no theological connection with what has gone before and could therefore be ignored without loss to the general sense of the letter. Paul, as Calvin argues, has spent the previous part of the letter showing us "those things necessary for the erection of the kingdom of God" (Com. Romans preface to 12). In particular Paul argues that the righteousness of God is to be sought from God alone, that salvation comes from God's mercy, and that "all blessings come from Christ only" (Com. Romans, preface to 12). These things are the foundation of Christian morality, and all the "duties of holiness" that we find in chapters 12 through 16 are duties that "flow" from what Paul teaches in the first 11 chapters.

Before going directly to the passage in question, Calvin directs our attention to the beginning of the parenetic section (12:1–2), since Paul's remarks on the governing authorities find their roots just at this spot. Paul begins by saying, "I appeal to you therefore, brethren, by the mercies of God, to present your bodies as a living sacrifice, holy and acceptable to God, which is your spiritual worship." The "therefore" is crucial since it alerts the reader that what has gone before is to be carried over into the moral teaching. Paul then says, "Do not be conformed to this world but be transformed by a renewal of your mind, that you may prove what is the will of God, what is good and acceptable and perfect." Paul's

156

appeal to the "mercies of God" indicates that Christians serve God "not by servile fear, but by the voluntary and cheerful love of righteousness" (Com. Romans 12:1). The opening parenetic verses are an exhortation stressing the Christian's commitment to and dependence on God. This commitment and dependence is the foundation for morally correct behavior; hence it governs everything that follows. Now we turn to the passage in question.

The situation Paul addresses—Christians living in the imperial capital—lends urgency to his advice, so he simply goes straight to the point: Christians must be subject to the governing authorities. The everyday political realities facing the Christians in Rome force this urgency. Calvin points out that the governing authorities "not only hated [Jewish-based] impiety, but persecuted religion with the most hostile feelings" (Com. Romans 12:1). What kind of relationship are these Christians then supposed to have with such a rulership as this? What is the justification for this particular relationship? These are the questions Paul answers in 13:1–7.

First and most important to Calvin, Paul declares that God is the ultimate author of all earthly political order. That the powers have been established by God means that those earthly powers are subject to the limits God has placed upon their authority, namely "to provide for the tranquility of the good and restrain the waywardness of the wicked" (Com. Romans 13:5). Consequently those in power who either abuse their authority or seek to go beyond the ordained limits will have to answer to God. Thus, according to Calvin, Paul provides us with a picture of God's wrath and judgment working through human agency and, in particular, the agency of human political order.

For Calvin, Paul's declaration of the state as "God's servant" means that civil magistrates do not rule for their own interests, "but for the public good" (Com. Romans 13:4). In short, he wishes to emphasize that the innocent are protected only through the divine goodness instantiated in the governing authorities. Paul reminds the

157

reader that "God's servant" does not "bear the sword in vain." This phrase can take on a wide range of meaning, but, as Calvin insists, most obvious and *sine qua non* is the power of life and death in waging war and capital punishment. Paul immediately follows this reminder by repeating the "God's servant" motif with the added force of an "avenger" for God's wrath.

Paul's use of "must" (*anagke* in Greek) in warning that Christians "must be subject" is of particular note because of its philosophical sense of divine necessity. We should also note how Paul's use of "conscience" (*sunedesin* in Greek) indicates his unwillingness to make proper Christian civil conduct a matter of fear alone. Calvin therefore argues that Christians obey the state not simply because of fear (though that is part of the formula), but also because it is a service acceptable to God.

According to Calvin, Paul tells us in effect that the soldier is an agent of God's wrath, but it is important not to lose sight of the fact that God' s wrath is encompassed by God's love. As Calvin argues: "Paul meant to refer the precept of respecting power of magistrates to the law of love" (Com. Romans 13:8). So the soldier who does his duty well is modeling his behavior on God's actions as revealed in Scripture: he is as much an agent of love and wrath together, for the two characteristics are harmonious in God.

We are now in a better position to see how what Paul says about the governing authorities meshes with his advice to forgo vengeance. Just before his comments about the governing authorities, Paul exhorts his readers to "repay no evil with evil, but take thought for what is noble in the sight of all. If possible, so far as it depends on you, live peaceably with all. Beloved, never avenge yourselves, but leave it to the wrath of God" (12:17–19). The keys here are "If possible" and "so far as it depends on you." Calvin rightly argues that Paul realizes that peace does not always lie with us, and this leads Calvin to caution that:

158

... courteousness should not degenerate into compliance, so as to lead us to flatter the vices of men for the sake of preserving peace. Since then it cannot always be, that we can have peace with all men, he has annexed two particulars by way of exception, *if it be possible,* and, *as far as you can.* But we are to conclude from what piety and love require, that we are not to violate peace, except when constrained by either of these two things. (Com. Romans 12:18)

Although Christians ought to bear much for the sake of peace, they ought to do so, "in such a way, that we may be prepared, whenever necessity requires, to fight courageously: for it is impossible that soldiers of Christ should have perpetual peace with the world, whose prince is Satan" (Com. Romans 12:18). When a soldier uses force justly, he is not repaying evil for evil, for a just act is not an evil act. By using force justly, he does what Paul advises him to do: something "noble in the sight of all." Here Calvin is close to Aquinas on vindication (*vindicta*) as a virtue. Aquinas argues that vindication is a special virtue when the vindication sought is intended to prevent further evil (*ST* II.II.108). So virtuous vindication is a vengeance sought for the good of the commonwealth and not purely personal reasons. The soldier who fights justly is an agent of God's vengeance—not of his own vengeance. Just soldiers fight in order to execute God's wrath, which is in harmony with his love, and that is exactly what they do when they fight justly in a just war.

The Moral Law

Calvin taught that God's character is reflected in his moral law, and that Christians follow the moral law because it pleases God. God is pleased when we follow the moral law, for by doing so we are made more fitting for union with him; that is, we are made more like him. Calvin followed Aquinas, who argued that the moral precepts of the old law are an obliging force to Christians, but not a

159

compelling force, for Christians are compelled by the Holy Spirit to act well. Charity, therefore, inclines the Christian to do what the moral law requires (Com. Galatians, ch. 5, lect. 5). Charity inclines believers to do that which brings them closer to God. One of the things charity inclines us to do is to follow the moral law. The Holy Spirit makes us fitting for union with God by turning us into creatures more like God. In short, the Holy Spirit begins the job of instilling in human beings divine characteristics here on earth in preparation for our ultimate end as human beings. One way in which the Holy Spirit does this is to impel us to follow the moral law. The role of the moral law in all this is to provide a guide for virtuous behavior. To borrow from Vigen Gurorian on Orthodox ethics: the commandments "indicated those modes of behavior which are in accord with the Word of Life and appropriate to the sanctifying work of the Spirit both in persons and in the church."[2]

Calvin holds that the moral law, which finds its purest form in the Decalogue, commands virtue as well as forbids vice. So, the commandment, "Thou shall not kill" has a positive thrust to it, namely, that we ought to do all that is in our power to help our neighbors preserve their lives. Here is the key passage:

> We are accordingly commanded, if we find anything of use to us in saving our neighbors' lives, faithfully employ it; if there is anything that makes for their peace, to see to it; if anything harmful, *to ward it off*; if they are in danger, to lend a helping hand. (*Institutes* II.8.39, emphasis added)

Calvin argues that the God is so concerned with the welfare of human beings because to violate a human being is to violate the image of God:

> Scripture notes that this commandment rests upon a twofold basis: man is both the image of God, and our flesh. Now, if we do not wish to violate the image of God, we ought to hold our neighbor

> sacred. And if we do not wish to renounce all humanity, we ought to cherish his as our own flesh ... The Lord has willed that we consider those two things which are naturally in man, and might lead us to seek his preservation: to reverence his image imprinted in man, and to embrace our own flesh in him. (*Institutes* III.8.40)

Calvin warns us that by failing to use force to protect others—by failing "to ward off" those who attack the innocent—we do harm to the image of God. We also fail to take an additional step on the road to our being made more fit for beatitude with him. In short we fail to act like God when we refuse to use force in a just cause. This is why Calvin argues that "he who has merely refrained from shedding blood has not therefore avoided the crime of murder" and "unless you endeavor to look out for his safety according to your ability and opportunity, you are violating the law with a like heinousness" (*Institutes* III.8.40). In other words, there is no moral difference between murder and failing to save an innocent person from being murdered that you could have saved.

Earthly Political Order

Calvin also taught that earthly political order reflects the character of God. Just as the Trinity exists peacefully and harmoniously as one, so should human beings, and political order is what allows human beings to live together as such. This means that the state is not the result of sin. We cannot identify Calvin (nor any of the major Christian thinkers we have referred to) as a proto-member of the moral-political realist camp, which insists that all political order is the result of sin and the disorder it brings. There would have been a political order had there never been a Fall. Thus we must agree with pacifists such as John Howard Yoder and Stanley Hauerwas that politics, considered abstractly, does not necessarily presuppose violence. Nevertheless, on this side of the fall, we cannot conceive of a political order without violence. Because all human beings have fallen short of the glory of God and

161

love themselves more than they love God or even each other, the use of force will be a necessity in achieving a peaceful and just human society. But the Christian tradition insists that the use of force be used for moral purposes—for just purposes. All peaceful order demands protection from enemies both internal and external. A police force provides one, while the armed forces provide the other.

For Calvin, civil government is the external means whereby human beings are given the opportunity to be made fully human— flourishing human beings (the Holy Spirit is the internal means). Because civil government uses force to protect order and promote good, it makes being a human being possible. This is an extremely important point. The pacifist communities exist only at the good graces of the larger communities around them that are willing to use force even to protect those who will not protect themselves. Thus, for example, the many Mennonite and Amish communities in the Unites States can exist only because the United States government threatens to use force against those who would do harm to those pacifist communities.

Calvin reminds us that those who reject the use of force reject God himself. The virtuous use of force is action modeled on God's action, which allows Calvin to make strong claims such as this one:

> A Christian man, [under the] order of the country, be called to serve
> his prince, doth not offend God in going to the wars, but is in a holy
> vocation, which cannot be reproved without blaspheming of God.
> (*Short Instruction*, 78)

Seen in this light, we can see why Calvin argues that, if we refuse to use force in a just cause, we "become guilty of the greatest impiety" (*Institutes* IV.20.10).

Calvin argues that the best form of government is probably an aristocracy, or a system of aristocracy mixed with democracy, for a virtuous king is a very rare thing and we are safer from human failing when rulership is divided. Yet, whatever the kind of government, it must be concerned with both tables of the law: it must be concerned with piety as well as civil virtue. The public welfare will suffer if true piety is not established. Religion has to be the first concern of the government if the commonwealth is to run smoothly. As it was for St. Ambrose, David is the pattern for all good rulership: despise the vicious and seek out the upright. Good government must provide justice and judgment: it must keep safe and prosperous the virtuous and judge the impious and punish their evil doing.

When the government takes up arms to execute public vengeance this is a lawful war. For God has given earthly government the power to maintain public order and peace with the sword. Calvin holds that "kings and people must sometimes take up arm to execute such public vengeance. On this basis we may judge wars lawful which are so undertaken" (*Institutes* IV.20.11). When states use force to pursue those who would do harm to its citizens, it is doing something just and good. Nevertheless wars should not be waged with disordered passion. When our disordered passions prompt us to use force, we do not use force virtuously. God does not make us more fitting for beatitude with him when we use force unjustly. This is why Calvin argues that Princes should not go to war but through necessity and regard for the public good (Com. Isaiah 3:4). Because soldiering is conceived as an office of love, Calvin rejects outright mercenary soldiering. Soldiers who fight merely for money do not fight out of love for their neighbors (Com. Matthew 3:11ff.).[3]

Following Christ from a Distance

Luther and Calvin considered just soldiering as a holy vocation. God loves his children so much that he provides earthly political order to restrain the chaos and evil that would make life so miserable where the ordered use of force is absent. So, the just soldiers' acts are imitative of God's acts—they are loving acts of force—but this does not mean that just soldiers perfectly imitate God when they use force justly in a just cause. For one thing, soldiers cannot redeem humankind with their acts. They may be able to save the mortal lives of their neighbors but they cannot save their immortal souls. As Paul Ramsey once pointed out, the Reformation fathers used to talk a lot about following Christ at a distance. Here is an instance where that imagery seems apt.

We believe that we can make the point clearer by taking a very short excursion through Hans Frei, who has discussed the various patterns of Jesus's identity and how they relate to the believer. One pattern is the pattern of exchange. The pattern of exchange is particularly important for Frei, because it unites the individuality of Jesus as Savior and the cosmic scope of his identity—two patterns that the believer cannot hope to duplicate. Frei uses a literary example to illustrate a case of this "mysterious exchange." The example is the priest in Graham Greene's *The Power and the Glory*. According to Frei, the priest "follows Christ without trying to become Christ, at a distance rather than from too nearby; or with that intimacy of total contrast which is paradoxically one with total identity."[4] The priest's humility allows him to love his neighbor, which means that he can follow Christ at a distance, but the sort of love he has shows that he cannot overcome the distance.[5] We are saying much the same thing about the just warrior. The just warrior follows Christ without trying to become Christ. The just warrior possesses a desire to protect his neighbor because he loves his neighbor, and this desire allows him to follow Christ at a distance. But the just warrior also loves the neighbor who is acting unjustly and the acts of force he uses against this neighbor do not have a redemptive quality. Thus, this sort of love cannot save the unjust aggressor—it cannot overcome the distance between Christian and Christ.

III. Grotius

The Christian desire to protect the neighbor found its way into international law via Hugo Grotius. Grotius, a Dutch Calvinist, built his account of warfare in *On the Laws of War and Peace* on two solid foundations: the Roman law found in Justinian's *Corpus Iuris Civilis* and the word of God found in the Christian Bible. Moreover, Grotius gathered the bulk of his moral authority from the traditions of these foundations: the Western heritage of the Greek and Latin authors informing Justinian's laws and the interpretation of Christian scripture by the Greek and Latin Church fathers. Following the tradition of St. Ambrose, Grotius believed war to be a human enterprise subject to the limitations of human decision. Again, following St. Ambrose, Grotius locates the Christian limitation on force in the theological virtue of charity. Grotius grounds war in a wide-reaching concept of natural law self-defense that allows for offensive measures. Charity, however, limits the amount of force that can be used in self-defense:

> It was ... very well said of Aquinas, if it be rightly understood, that in a true defensive war, we do not intentionally kill others; not but that it may sometimes be lawful, if all other means of safety fail to do that purposely whereby the Aggressor may die. But that this death was not our choice, nor intended primarily (as in capital punishments) but our last and only refuge, there being no other visible means then left to preserve our own lives, but by killing him that seeks to kill us; nay, and even then, he that is violently assaulted ought to wish rather that some other thing would happen, whereby the Aggressor might be either affrighted, or some ways disabled, than he should be killed. (*On the Laws of War and Peace*, Book II, Ch. I, 2)

The Christian soldier, therefore, uses only what force is necessary to repel the enemy. Grotius's entire treatment of the *jus in bello* in the third book is based on this principle: only use force that is truly necessary.

The idea of using a limited amount of force in a just cause sheds light on how Grotius is able to treat civil police action as an analogue of just war. In fact, the idea of just war as analogous to just police action is as old as the idea of just war itself, but Grotius is the first to make it the very foundation of what a just war is supposed to look like. Pacifist theologian John Howard Yoder takes exception to the analogy.[6] For Yoder, the police function has built in limitations not found in warfare. The limitations are: (1) the force used by policemen is applied only to offenders of the law, (2) the force used by the police is subject to review by a higher authority, (3) the police and the potential offender agree that the police has the authority to use force on him, (4) safeguards are set to keep the innocent from being hurt when the police have to use force, and (5) the power of the police is so much greater than potential offenders that resistance is pointless.

Fortunately, these so-called limitations, which amount to objections against the police/just war analogy, can be met on every point. First, the force used in a just war is aimed at the offending party only. Innocents are certainly more likely to be killed in a just war than in a just police action, but the intention is the same for both. Second, the force used in a just war is subject to review by two higher authorities: the Church and international courts of law. The former may not carry much weight with nonbelievers in modern society, but it ought to carry a lot of weight with Christians. Christians ought not participate or support any unjust war. If the Church could teach its members to be just warriors, a great impact may be made on how the governing authorities, who rely on a good number of purportedly Christian members in their armed forces, approach proposed conflicts. Third, agreements about the use of force are achieved more often in police action than in war, but it should be pointed out that such agreements are by no means found in all police actions (e.g., the very civil laws are sometimes in question) nor are such agreements absent from every war (e.g., international law). Fourth, just war too has safeguards for the innocent. We call this noncombatant immunity. Fifth, the relative capabilities for destruction between two or more warring parties varies a great deal. Sometimes resistance is pointless (e.g., the Gulf War), sometimes not (e.g., the early days of World War II). Also, the pointlessness of resistance does not guarantee that no resistance is forthcoming from the criminal.

The analogy is, of course, imperfect, as are all analogies. Strictly speaking, Yoder is perfectly right, if we are talking about war abstractly. That is to say, the phenomenon of one group of people exerting its will on another group of people by means of force does not have inherent limitations exactly like those found in the police function. But just war comes very close. In fact, we call a just war "just" partly because certain limitations are built into it. And just as we refuse to call police acts legitimate when they depart from their built-in limitations, so do we refuse to call a just war "just" when its built in limitations are abused. We should also note that Yoder, in arguing against the police analogy, attempts to cut the link between the police function and war-making by arguing that Roman "warfare" was more like what we think of as "police action" since Rome did not have large enough enemies to engage in "war" as we conceive it. The goal here is to undercut the very term "just war," since what we traditionally consider a just war is really, in modern terms, simply a just police action. This is an interesting argument by Yoder, for he seems to be admitting that the use of force (if limited in scale and scope) is indeed consonant with holy Christian living. Such an admission would place him squarely in the traditional just warrior camp in so far as just warriors have to fight limited wars if they are to be just, but it also seems to be a blow to his very point that the Christian life is nonviolent to the core.

Grotius realized that, unfortunately, charity does not always inform the soldier on the battlefield, for not all soldiers are Christians. Justice, then, derived from a concept of international law, takes the place of charity in governing battle conduct. For law will govern all soldiers. It is important to emphasize that this move is for the restraint of the soldier who does not possess the virtue of charity. As we have seen, a soldier who possesses charity already possesses justice (the similarities with Luther here are obvious), but Grotius believes that a

167

soldier who lacks charity (of whom there must be many) can be constrained by justice interpreted by law. Grotius, consequently, treats war as a police action: it is only for the enforcement of justice and must be kept within the bounds of justice and good faith. So war is waged against those who cannot be constrained by courts of law and must be conducted as scrupulously as judicial proceedings (*Laws*, Preface, 23).

Charity, as illuminated by St. Ambrose, St. Augustine, and Aquinas, is the virtue without which no just war can be fought. This is the theological sphere of the western account of warfare. Not all soldiers, however, possess the virtue of charity; yet wars must be fought when the cause is just, hence the secular responds to the theological by striving for charity but finding a kind of justice instead: a justice governed by law. In effect, the secular says that it cannot always be charitable, but the Christian witness forces it to be at least just, and this justice takes the form of a juridical action. Notice, however, how charity is not entirely absent from this scheme. Justice, conceived as a police action here, seeks a limitation demanded not by natural law justice (Grotius is very clear about this) but by charity. Charity, then, forces the secular to respond, and that response is justice *qua* international law. Christendom, consequently, bequeathed to the West an account of the just war that limited the use of force with charity and law.

CHAPTER 8

Opponents of Traditional Just War Thinking

There are two main tenets in our look at the classical Christian just war tradition that need to be emphasized. First, warfare need not be a lesser evil. Once the *jus ad bellum* criteria have been met, once Christians have decided that they ought to make a proposed war their war, warfare is a positive good to be pursued. The Christian just war tradition—East and West—teaches that we do not engage in anything evil when we use force justly. As a matter of fact, we become more like creatures fitting for beatitude with God when we use force against evil. Second, as a positive good to be pursued by the virtuous, just warfare must be enjoined if we are going to be a virtuous people. This means that a failure to engage in a just war is a failure of virtue both natural and supernatural. An odd corollary of this conclusion is that it is worse–that is, a greater evil– when Christians fail to engage in a just war than when unbelievers also fail to do so. When an unbeliever fails to go to war, the causes may be a lack of courage, prudence, or justice. The unbeliever may be a coward or just indifferent to the evil that might be prevented. This is a failure of natural moral virtue. When Christians fail to engage in just war, it may involve all these natural failures as well, but it will certainly involve a failure of charity.

The Christian who fails to use force in the neighbor's aid when prudence dictates that force is the best way to aid the neighbor, the Christian who fails to protect the innocent from evil in this sort of circumstance, is an uncharitable (i.e., not agapeic) Christian. So, from the Western Christian point of view, those who willingly and knowingly refuse to engage in a just war do a vicious thing: they fail in natural and supernatural virtue (or, from the Orthodox perspective, a failure in virtue pure and simple, since traditional Orthodox thought rejects the dichotomy between nature and grace). There are

169

two kinds of thinking that tend to facilitate failure in proper just war thinking: a form of ethical consequentialism known as "Christian Realism" and the mixture of pacifism with just war doctrine.

These opponents of proper just war thinking contribute to the decay of the virtues a citizenry needs in order to deal with warfare justly. Reinhold Niebuhr's Christian Realism and the U.S. Catholic Bishops' pacifism tend to corrupt the ability to discern when certain actions are intrinsically bad. The unrestrained political realism of Christian Realism and the confusion of pacifist assumptions in just war doctrine tend to recognize certain acts as intrinsically bad, but accepts them as part of a "dirty hands" scheme of political philosophy that approves of (indeed, finds necessary) our choosing the lesser of many evils.

Pacifist theology is fundamentally incompatible with the just war tradition, for the admission of pacifist principles in war leads the Christian to be psychologically and spiritually distanced from the good that comes from using force justly in a just cause. In other words, if we reject a God who hates injustice so much that He uses His creatures to stem it and punish evil-doers, or if we reject the just use of force as one way of following Christ, or if we view acts of force as inherently evil acts that need to be justified before we can sully our hands with them, then we have no way of grounding the Christian's acts of force in the Christian's way of life such that the Holy Spirit uses those acts of force to make the Christian more fit for beatitude with God.

The just war tradition—East and West—offers of a way of seeing how these opponents of just war thinking are a moral hindrance to a virtuous citizenry able to handle the moral problems of war. We can combat these opponents by insisting (1) on the intrinsic evil of some acts, especially with regard to evil intention; (2) that proper Christian just war thinking demands that we act justly regardless of the consequences; and (3) that soldiers who fight just wars justly are charity-governed soldiers who do no evil when they fight just wars justly.

I. Reinhold Niebuhr's Christian Realism

Robin Lovin has argued that Reinhold Niebuhr was the most important voice of the movement called "Christian Realism." Christian Realism is itself a version of political realism, which is simply to say that it takes into account "the multiplicity of forces that drive decisions that people actually make in situations of political choice."[1] Niebuhr wished to counter Rauschenbusch's moral vision of the New Testament as a "simple possibility."[2] Niebuhr complained that Rauschenbusch's social gospel did not understand justice, for it failed to take into account sufficiently individual and (especially) collective self-concern. For Niebuhr, not only can we not always seek to do the right thing, but in some cases, we should not even seek to do so, for the very efforts to do the right thing may make a situation worse. Also, selfish interests and the pursuit of power may lie behind the most benevolent-looking pursuits of justice. Realism therefore takes self-interest and the pursuit of power into account. Niebuhr wanted a "realistic liberalism" that sought gains in justice, yet with the realization that the goals must be limited if we are going to do more good than harm.

One of the main tenets of Niebuhr's realism is that Jesus's life and work do not offer us a social ethic. In "The Ethic of Jesus and the Social Problem," Niebuhr argues that the ethic of Jesus was a "personal ethic" or "individual ethic" inasmuch as Jesus's goal was to change the quality of the individual's life.[3] Jesus offers us a pure ethic of love, an ethic "too pure" to be realized by anyone in this life, but an ideal toward which we must strive if we hope to act well. This charge is echoed in a later essay in which Niebuhr argues that the personal ethic derived from the Sermon on the Mount is an absolutist, individual ethic in need of a social ethic, for human beings love not each other but themselves.[4]

Christian pragmatism is the solution according to Niebuhr, for it incorporates definite principles of justice, freedom, and

171

equality. The biblical sources of a Christian social ethic are a sense of divine providence, an emphasis on the tension between humanity's social and political freedom and the fact that all human beings are sinners, and a passion for justice as an expression of the love command. Jesus's love ethic as exhibited in the Sermon on the Mount is not a simple possibility, but human beings must respond to it. How can they do so? For Niebuhr, people respond to Jesus's moral teaching by adopting a "critical attitude" to all political arrangements. This critical attitude both spurs the Christian to seek better arrangements and to realize how woefully short all human politics is of the ideal we see in Jesus's teaching. On its own, Jesus's moral teaching would be disastrous for human beings. So Jesus's ethic must be balanced with a "responsible" attitude that forces the person to choose a lesser evil for the sake of the community.

In "Christian Faith and Natural Law," Niebuhr argues against the Roman Catholic concept of natural law, which allows human beings the capacity of knowing justice when they see it, and argues instead that all statements of justice are corrupted by interest. Justice requires an equilibrium of power to offset competing interests.[5] Nevertheless, human beings are not completely corrupted by self-interest, for they retain the law of love (what Niebuhr sometimes refers to as "the law of our being"), which is boundless self-giving. Between these two forces we formulate "ad hoc restraints," and this we can call natural law. The end of law is justice, but justice is related to love in that the law, in seeking a tolerable social harmony, is both "an approximation of the law of love" and "an instrument of love."[6] Put a different way, Jesus's love ethic "supports, maintains and contradicts mutual love" which is the highest kind of love we can hope for in this life.[7] In short—love "rises above justice to exceed its demands."[8]

We should not take Niebuhr to mean that the Christian love ethic plays no role in the Christian moral life. When we ask the question, "why does the Christian seek justice?" Niebuhr replies that love is the reason we seek earthly justice. For Niebuhr, the ideal impels us to do the mundane, and even try to transcend the mundane, though we realize that our attempts will always fall short of the ideal of *agape*. As Niebuhr puts it: "For the Christian the love commandment must be made relevant to the relativities of the social struggle, even to the hazardous and dubious relativities."[9] Thus, while the Christian must admit that Jesus's ethic of love is an impossible ideal, that ideal is nevertheless essential if we want to achieve worthwhile mundane goals such as earthly justice.

We can understand what is going on here if we interpret Niebuhr in Aristotelian terms. Aristotle argues that some virtues can be likened to target areas between two means of extremes (*Nicomachean Ethics* II.6-9). A virtuous act is one where we are able to hit the target squarely between the two vicious acts on the extremes. A courageous act is, for example, the targeted area between the two extremes of cowardice and foolhardiness. Aristotle argues that when we are predisposed toward one extreme, we often have to "aim beyond" the target area in order to hit it. In short, we must overcompensate for an existing defect. So, for instance, cowards must aim at foolhardiness if they wish to be courageous; for if cowards aimed at courage itself, they would fall short of it because of their natural cowardly dispositions. For Niebuhr, all human beings are predisposed toward sin, and sin (especially the sin of pride and self-interest) predisposes us to miss the target of justice if we simply aim at justice. Thus human beings, if they wish to achieve justice, have to aim beyond it. Niebuhr's "beyond" is Jesus's ethic of love. In short, sinful human beings will always fall short of worldly justice if they do not aim at otherworldly agape. What this means for warfare we turn to now.

Christian Realism and Warfare

Niebuhr's arguments against the Roman Catholic concept of natural law suggest a certain emphasis on the consequences of actions as opposed to the actions themselves, which, in turn, both erodes confidence in justice itself and relativizes the goodness and badness of acts. The first, of course, is something Niebuhr and the Niebuhrians do not wish to deny. Indeed, it is the very confidence human beings think they have in establishing real justice that indicates the lasting presence of original sin. The second point, however, that the morality of acts becomes relative in deference to the consequences, is something Niebuhr and the Niebuhrians would probably want to deny.

In *The Nature and Destiny of Man* (vol. 1) Niebuhr argues that the limitations of Catholic natural-law theories are evident when those theories are applied to the field of international relations. The limitations of the Roman Catholic theory of a just war are offered for evidence. While admitting that the Catholic just war theory "is infinitely superior to Lutheran relativism," Niebuhr nevertheless finds fault with just war theory, because "it assumes that obvious distinction between 'justice' and 'injustice,' between 'defense' and 'aggression' are possible."[10] Against these assumptions of just war theory, Niebuhr argues that not "all wars are equally just and not all contestants are equally right." Therefore, no war can be waged "with completely good conscience." Niebuhr, of course, is not leading the reader toward pacifism; on the contrary, he argues against those who would have us "refrain from all war."[11] We may not possess a clear case of justice, but a war "may yet concern itself with the very life and death of civilizations and cultures."[12] So, to summarize: we cannot make "obvious" distinctions between justice and injustice, nor can we make them between defense and aggression—all wars are just and unjust to some degree. Nevertheless, we should engage in wars (when, for example, our civilization and culture are threatened) even though we know that we will be unjust to some degree in so doing.

The trouble with Niebuhr's position is that it does not safeguard against evil acts employed in the name of things like "saving civilization." In short, good consequences may trump evil actions if the cause justifies it. Put differently, Niebuhr is going to be at pains to show why a civilization or culture should not perform vicious actions in order to save itself. He has admitted that all warfare is unjust to some degree; we already, to use present popular terminology, possess "dirty hands" when we engage in any war. Even "just-for-the-most-part"-wars are won with dirty hands. So how "dirty" can the hands get in a good cause? Can any amount of dirt on the hands render a war "unjust-for-the-most-part"? Niebuhr seems to have no way of telling us. But the very credibility of a moral position on war, if it is to be a critical (criticizing) position, rests with the ability to say "no" to some wars and to some acts in war. Yoder summarizes the just warrior's stand on this quite nicely when he argues that "if the tradition which claims that war may be justified does not also admit that it could be unjustified, the affirmation is not morally serious."[13] In sharp contrast to Niebuhr's Christian Realism, Roman Catholic just war theory, because it claims the ability to judge the difference between at least some just and unjust acts, provides a way for us to say, for instance, that the bombing of centers of cities during World War II was unjust, because thousands of innocent civilians were intentionally killed. It is telling that Niebuhr was unable to condemn those same bombings. In his essay "The Bombing of Germany," Niebuhr defends the Allied bombing strategy by arguing that:

> It is not possible to defeat a foe without causing innocent people to suffer with the guilty. It is not possible to engage in any act of collective opposition to collective evil without involving the innocent with the guilty. It is not possible to move in history without becoming tainted with guilt.[14]

The just warrior does not hide his head in the sand. The just warrior knows that some innocent people will suffer with combatants and those closely connected with war-fighting capabilities. The just warrior knows that collective force against evil will inevitably involve innocent people in suffering. That is why no war should be entered into lightly. That is why there are *jus ad bellum* criteria that must be

175

met before any war can be joined justly. It is the third sentence that brings dissent from the just warrior, and rightly so. Those responsible for the decision to fight in a just war and those who fight virtuously in war do not become necessarily tainted with guilt (i.e., there is nothing inherently evil about deciding to fight in a war or about fighting in war). Such virtuous people know that innocent people will suffer, but they do not intend this suffering, and the success of their war-fighting plans are not in any way dependent upon the suffering of innocent people. The vicious persons responsible for the war are the ones necessarily tainted with guilt, as are those who, though fighting on the just side, fight unjustly. The Allies of World War II, for example, were not guilty of any suffering caused to the innocent people of Europe as long as they did not behave viciously in battle—that is to say, so long as they approximated the *jus in bello* as best they could. The Nazis were responsible for the suffering of the innocent people caught in a battlefield *created by the Nazis*, except of course the suffering caused by the Allies when they engaged in vicious practices like saturation bombing.

The trouble is that, as soon as we start wringing our hands with self-imposed guilt, our own evil actions may follow—as they seemed to do in both World Wars. Once we begin to believe that we are acting viciously by the very nature of the case, then the temptation becomes to be a little more vicious and guarantee victory. Dirty hands thinking tells us that we have already crossed a moral threshold in fighting a war to begin with, and once having crossed that threshold, we may be tempted to make sure that it was worth it and guarantee victory. And once we have victory guaranteed, we may be tempted further to go ahead and be even more vicious in order to put an end to the whole sordid affair. In short, once the first moral threshold is crossed, psychologically speaking, it becomes easier to move further away from that threshold. It is just this kind of reasoning that may be traced in the Allied war planners in World War II. Certainly, it is just this kind of thinking that drives Fussell to defend the Allied use of atomic bombs on Japan.[15]

We must remember that, for Niebuhr, love is the very reason we are trying to be just in the first place and it is the only way we can actually be just. So, Niebuhr's logic seems to lead us to claim that vicious acts in war are sometimes needed to get the job done, but when we do such things, we do them out of love. In other words, Jesus's ethic of love impels us to do vicious things. There is something wrong about this. Timothy Jackson has rightly characterized this way of thinking as one in which love, "claiming to transcend justice, actually falls below it in embracing too violent means to political ends."[16] Some acts cannot be described as loving acts. Deliberately and willfully killing innocent people is a vicious act to which we cannot ascribe anything like Jesus's ethic of love. When our Christian ethic allows us to do things like deliberately kill innocent people, we should be worried that we have separated Jesus from our moral behavior. Oddly enough, Niebuhr and the Christian Realists were not alone in this particular moral failure. In their efforts to make human beings more than human, the liberal-humanists too approved of moral viciousness in the cause of human progress.

Niebuhr's Jesus and the Jesus of Messianic Pacifism

Stanley Hauerwas has claimed that Niebuhr's ethic of "responsibility" severs Jesus from the church, and we have found reasons for agreeing with this claim. Yet, as Lovin rightly observes, Niebuhr and the pacifists are in essential agreement on Christian moral demands. Lovin finds the dividing line between the two in the role of criticism. For pacifists such as Hauerwas and Yoder, the Christian critic, the Christian who stands against the nations (though is oddly for the nations in the sense of being a witness to a more truthful way of living),[17] cannot be a "responsible" citizen such as Niebuhr envisions. To the pacifist's eyes, the "responsible" citizen has to make too many "deals with the devil" in order to be a good witness to the ethic of Jesus

177

Christ. Niebuhr argues that the Christian must choose a lesser evil for the good of the community, while the pacifist realizes that to choose any evil deliberately is to stray too far from Christ. So, for the pacifist, criticism and responsibility, as Niebuhr defines it, are mutually exclusive. However, for Niebuhr, criticism and responsibility are not two opposed forces, but two attitudes held by one person.

What is not at issue between the two camps, however, is how to interpret the person and work of Jesus Christ. Niebuhr may have argued that the Sermon on the Mount could not be a "simple possibility" for human beings, but he certainly interpreted the Sermon simplistically. Both Niebuhr and the pacifists look at the person and work of Jesus Christ simplistically. This is not to say that their interpretations of the Christ event are "simple." Far from it. It is merely to say that each camp believes that it can understand what the person and work of Christ means for the Christian by interpreting the person and work of Christ primarily (when not completely) through the Gospel writers. Thus, both Niebuhr and the pacifists fail, in some sense, to "see" Christ through Paul and the larger concerns of the Old Testament.

Jesus's love commandments are not to be understood simply by looking at the Gospel narratives, but by looking at the Gospel narratives in conjunction with Paul, the other New Testament writers, and the Old Testament. Jesus's love commandments are not "otherworldly." They are, to refer back to the Aristotelian scheme, "targetable," and if they are targetable, then human justice certainly is. For politics, the love commands mean that we do not, for instance, use political force to seek personal vengeance. In fact, we forgo all personal vengeance. Christians do not have to do anything to make the love commands "relevant." They are relevant as they stand, so long as we do not think that we have grasped them apart from Paul and the Old Testament's broader concerns.

The pacifist rightly attacks Niebuhr for making Jesus's ethic an "otherworldly" ethic. Jesus's ethic is very much a "this-worldly" ethic.

But the sort of theology we see at work in the early fathers, St. Thomas, and Calvin insists that Jesus's ethic be read harmoniously with God's "this-worldly" ethic as revealed in the Old Testament. Those adhering to classical just war doctrine, we suggest, would make one with Hauerwas and Yoder that Niebuhr's position is mistaken, but they part company on how to remedy the mistake. If by the term "responsible citizens" we mean what Niebuhr means (i.e., citizens who must leave the personal ethic of Jesus behind and get their hands "dirty" if they wish to be "responsible"), then the just warrior is solidly in the pacifist camp. The just warrior agrees with the pacifist that no deals should be made with the devil. The just warrior along with the pacifist refuses to get his or her hands "dirty." Just warriors nevertheless insist that they are responsible citizens in so far as they are willing to use force when the cause is just. They merely deny that using force means that we have to get our hands "dirty," and when we have to get our hands "dirty" in order to be effective politically, just warriors will remain "ineffective." That much again they have in common with pacifists. To sum up this last point: the just warrior is able to agree with the pacifist about "dirty hands" while disagreeing with the pacifist about what this means for being a responsible citizen.

II. Contemporary Roman Catholic Failures

The U.S. Roman Catholic bishops' 1983 pastoral, *The Challenge of Peace: God's Promise and Our Response* (henceforth cited as *CP*)[18] exhibits the faults mentioned at the beginning of this chapter. These faults are still evident in the bishops' 10-year-anniversary reflection of the pastoral, *The Harvest of Justice is Sown in Peace*. A mixture of pacifism and an evolutionary theory of religion that denies the God of the Old Testament any place in the New Testament exacerbate the problem. The bishops effectively strip themselves of any theological grounding that could make acts of force constitutive of a way of life that makes the human being more fit for beatitude with God. Worse, the mixture of pacifism and Christian just

179

war doctrine actually leads to internal incoherence, for pacifist principles make uneasy bedfellows with just war principles.

The bishops' attempt at just war thinking is sorely lacking on two fronts: theology and morality. The pastoral is on shaky theological grounds because it relies upon an evolutionary theory of religion, which, in turn, allows the bishops to co-opt pacifism into their just war model. The introduction of pacifism also places the pastoral on shaky moral grounds. The confusion it causes leads to the presumption against war, the willingness to engage in "dirty hands" morality, and an unwillingness to stick with honest just war thinking. Perhaps worst of all, the bishops employ the criterion of comparative justice, a criterion that guarantees to debilitate virtuous warfare. The pastoral seems to do its best on nearly every count to give God very little to work with when it comes to His elevating us through our virtuous acts in war.

The Challenge of "The Challenge of Peace"

The bishops declare two purposes for the pastoral, *The Challenge of Peace*: one is to help Catholics form their consciences with respect to questions of war, peace, and deterrence. The other is to contribute to the public policy debate on these issues (*CP* 16). The goal, of course, is peace, but the bishops realize that peace is achieved fully only in the kingdom of God. In forming the conscience of the flock and contributing to the public policy debate, the bishops want to lead their flock and the public toward policies more consonant with realizing the kingdom of God on earth.

The bishops admit to the great influence of Vatican II, particularly the Pastoral Constitution, in shaping their thought. Specifically, the influences are three: (1) John Paul II's declaration that the world wants peace and needs peace; (2) the declaration that the arms race is a curse upon the human race, especially the poor; and (3) the nuclear arms race requires the fresh application of traditional moral principles. The traditional moral principles that comprise Roman Catholic teaching on war and peace stretch back, according to the

180

Bishops, to the Sermon on the Mount. The prominent place given to the Sermon on the Mount as one of the foundations of Roman Catholic thought on war and peace indicates the influence of recent pacifist thinking on this letter. Pacifism, of course, is not recent, but the extent to which it has permeated official Roman Catholic thought, at least in the U.S., is new.[19] This permeation, as we will see, may cause problems for the coherency of the bishops' letter.

The bishops begin with theology; that is to say, they formulate their religious perspectives and principles before applying those principles to the actual political situation. The bishops find their principles in the Biblical conception of peace and the kingdom of God. God may have been conceived as a God who approved of bloodshed in Old Testament times, but this conception gradually changed, according to the bishops, and is completely gone by the time of Jesus. Love and forgiveness characterize God much more accurately in the New Testament. Justice, however, is not forgotten, since peace must be built on the basis of justice. Because we live in the "already but not yet" period, the peace and justice of this world will always be compromised (*CP* 58). Nevertheless, peace must be sought, for it is the indispensable condition for improving humanity.

How do we achieve peace and justice? According to the bishops, the church's teaching on war and peace establishes a strong presumption against war (*CP* 70). Peace and justice are nevertheless sometimes achieved by means of a just war. The presumption against war indicates the supposed complementary relationship between just war theory and pacifism: each presume that violence is wrong but differ on how the common good is to be defended most effectively. Just war is meant to restrain evil and protect the innocent, but in order to override the presumption against war, certain criteria must be met; this is popularly known as the just war criteria. The bishops, however, do not wish to give the impression that the just war is the only effective way to restrain evil and protect the innocent: pacifism is an option (for individuals but not for nations). Indeed, even those who take the just

181

war road are encouraged to incorporate pacifist thinking in their just war formulations (*CP* 118).

The Bishops, Jesus, and Just War

There is much in *The Challenge of Peace* that should give the just warrior pause. The root of much that is troubling—though not all—is a pacifism that does not mix well with traditional Roman Catholic just war teaching, which ignores pacifism (and thus retains its coherence). The mix of pacifism and just war theory also tells us why neither traditional just warriors nor vocational pacifists may be satisfied with the pastoral. In the words of James Finn, pacifism and just war thinking "corrupt each other."[20] For the just warrior, the problem for the bishops begins at their beginning: the underpinning theology. The bishops fail to show us how the Old Testament God who uses force and approves of bloodshed can be reconciled to the New Testament God of forgiveness and love when forgiveness and love are conceived by the bishops in ways that presume as evil the use of force. The bishops, in short, cut the umbilical cord between the use of force and Christian moral and spiritual formation.

The first theological problem, at least from the just warrior's perspective, is to focus on the Sermon on the Mount, without any reference to Paul or the Old Testament, for moral principles relating directly to the just war. The bishops make the problem worse by relying upon an evolutionary theory of religion. Or, perhaps it would be fairer to say that, given the pacifist influence at the conference that produced the pastoral, the evolutionary theory of religion is the one way they could justify the pacifist influence on the letter. None of this is to deny the Sermon on the Mount a place in Christian morality as it relates to warfare. Insofar as wars are sometimes started over slights of personal honor, which lead to acts of personal vengeance, the Sermon suggests that such wars as illegitimate. This is no small point. Donald Kagan, for example, has argued that Thucydides got it right in declaring that, generally speaking, people go to war for three reasons:

honor, fear, and interest.[21] Just warriors accept the necessity of warfare out of fear, and, to a certain degree, interest (so long as those interests do not force us to act unjustly). But slights of personal honor are not acceptable reasons for the just warrior. Christ effectively ended all divine-like participation in warfare (or any other activity) for the sake of personal revenge.

Just warriors may also be troubled by the bishops' evolutionary theory of religion. The Old Testament conception of God as a divine being who uses force and approves of bloodshed did not, *pace* the bishops, fizzle out gradually, or, more to the bishops liking, evolve into a more morally and spiritually worthy conception of the New Testament God of love and forgiveness. Just warriors (and many other Christians besides) claim that love and forgiveness are just as much a part of God's character in the Old Testament as in the New. None of this is meant to deny progressive revelation; it is simply to deny that what is progressively revealed can contradict what has already been revealed.[22]

Pacifism and the So Called "Presumption Against War"

One area in which the bishops diverge from traditional Roman Catholic just war teaching is their claim that there is a presumption against war in just war theory. Just warriors make one with traditional Catholic just war teaching in denying this claim. There is no presumption against war, at least in the common sense of the term, in proper just war theory. The presumption against war, a characteristic the bishops tell us just war theory shares with pacifism, is actually the result of pacifist thinking in just war. The Catholic just war tradition has never, at least before this century, carried any presumption against war; instead, the presumption has traditionally been against injustice. The presumption, for example, is nowhere to be found in the Catholic "founding fathers" of just war theory: St. Ambrose, St. Augustine, and St. Thomas.

Charles Curran has argued that the bishops are simply trying to point out that the church's desire for peace on earth means that there is always a strong presumption in favor of peace, but that limited self-defense cannot be denied to nations, and this is where the just war doctrine becomes useful.[23] But what does the presumption of peace purchase ethically? Perhaps it gives the message to everyone that the church desires peace. Fair enough, but that should not be a part of just war doctrine, which presumes that the peace in question is unjust, does not deserve a presumption in its favor, and the only question left is whether we can and should do something about it.

The main trouble is that it is hard to find a complementary relationship between just war and pacifism apart from the insistence by both that we never do evil that good might come. In other words, just warriors and pacifists are one in denying that we should ever get our hands "dirty" in a just cause. But the complementary relationship ends here. There is little else to be agreed upon by just warriors and pacifists. For just warriors hold that we can use force justly and well in a good cause and that such acts bear no stain of evil. Pacifists, on the other hand, hold (as do the bishops) that there is something inherently wrong about using force. For pacifists, this is enough to preclude any act of force, but for the bishops (and all pacifist-influenced just war accounts) this only means that such evil acts (sometimes called "prima facie" evils)[24] have to pass a test (the just war criteria) that will tell them if they ought to get their hands dirty.

Just warriors as we have conceived them deny that the just war criteria allow us to do evil—even prima facie evil—that good might come. They hold in fact that the just war criteria rule out evil altogether. For just warriors, the just war criteria help us see when our proposed acts of force mean getting our hands "dirty," and thus when we must say "no" to certain proposed acts of force. For anyone who holds that acts of force are somehow inherently evil acts that need justification, that same person as a matter of logic is committed to hold that we restrain a greater evil with a lesser one. Just warriors refuse to

184

play the lesser evil game. They refuse to restrain evil with evil. If we cannot prevent an evil without doing evil ourselves, then we throw ourselves on God's mercy and trust in His will for us, even if it means dying; for such dying is a noble death, and noble dying always beats ignoble living. The just warrior views vicious living and not death as the worst evil. Those who play the lesser-evil game play a vicious game, and just warriors refuse to call that game a Christian "just war." They refuse to embrace the "lesser morality," as we have seen also in Chapter 5 above.

Curran nevertheless insists that "pacifism and just war are distinct but interdependent methods of evaluating warfare, with each contributing to the full moral vision we need in pursuit of human peace."[25] Again, from the Western just war perspective, this is just plain wrong. Pacifism considers all bloodshed as evil, while just warriors consider just bloodshed as good and unjust bloodshed as evil. The two are at fundamental moral odds. This does not mean that a pacifist cannot think about just war, nor that a just warrior cannot think about pacifism. It only means that each must suspend his or her moral vision of the world in order to think like the other. Thus, when a pacifist gives advice about just war-making, it is, for the pacifist, similar to giving advice to prostitutes about how to prostitute in a less evil manner.

Comparative Justice and Virtuous Warfare

One further thing must be said about the bishops' use of just war theory: the incorporation of the criterion of comparative justice into the *jus ad bellum* (*CP* 93). Comparative justice, as Davis argues, is a "thesis about moral epistemology"[26]—a way of knowing what sort of moral knowledge can be had by human beings—and a skeptical one at that. Comparative justice says that we cannot be sure who is really just or whose side God is really on. We cannot know these things because no one is absolutely just. We have already seen in Niebuhr's thought the problems such thinking can cause in morality in warfare. It is as if the admittance of epistemic fallibilism gave us free reign to do all sorts of evil things (e.g., threatening to kill millions of people unjustly) in the name of preserving a good (e.g., our nation). Yet, as Davis rightly reminds us, "admitting epistemic fallibilism does not mean embracing the view that there is no truth, in science or ethics."[27] Britain and the U.S. did not, for example, have to be absolutely just to recognize that the Nazis were unjust and needed to be stopped.

Why do the bishops incorporate comparative justice? Perhaps it is because the bishops have no account of the virtues in war. Since the virtues play no role for the bishops in shaping warfare, they must invoke another rule in an attempt to get the same job done; namely, the suppression of hubris that may lead to vicious war-making. The cultivation of prudence aids just warriors in deciding when and how to combat injustice. Just warriors realize that they too "have fallen short of the glory of God," but they are able to recognize when others fall so short that they need restraining (that is one reason we call them "just warriors"). For the bishops the just war criteria seem to be merely a set of rules that comprise a test that enables us to see if we can employ a lesser evil (force in a comparatively just cause) to avoid a greater evil (defeat at the hands of a comparatively evil regime). So conceived, the just war is not something the virtuous can engage in with a clear conscience; hence there should be few if any virtuous people involved in this sort of "just war." If history tells us anything, the people who will be involved will be prone to hubris, more than likely created and fed by a government that must get its citizens on the bandwagon for war by inciting a crusading spirit. As a result, the enemy has to be dehumanized in some way in order to maneuver citizens into the necessary mood to want to kill the inhuman enemy. In order to curb this unfortunate but necessary tendency, concerned groups such as the bishops introduce the notion of comparative justice.

Thus the criterion of comparative justice may be valued because it somehow short-circuits the hubris of those who think themselves thoroughly just to the point of holiness and think the enemy

186

thoroughly unjust to the point of beastliness. In short, the bishops hope that comparative justice will prevent us from dehumanizing the enemy. It is right to worry about the dehumanization of the enemy; for if the enemy is not human, there is no need to treat them like humans. But comparative justice is not the best way to go about it, for comparative justice makes justice nearly impossible to achieve.

The *jus ad bellum* are those criteria that define just war as a distinctive practice, and we have already compared them to the rules of baseball in Chapter 6 above. We noted that such practices have a developmental capacity; new rules can be added in the attempt to make the practice a better practice. The criterion of last resort in just war and the allowance of the designated hitter in baseball were given as comparative examples, and we argued that whether either addition actually improved the practice or not was a hot topic. The criterion of comparative justice should not be a hot topic; it should be a dead topic. Comparative justice harms the practice of the just war. Comparative justice divorces justice from the other virtues and turns justice into a mere principle, and a shaky one to boot. Comparative justice says that we cannot know were true justice lies; so it divorces justice from prudence.[28] Comparative justice says that, because we cannot know where true justice lies, we should be hesitant about restraining evil, seeing that we are evil ourselves; so it divorces justice from courage. Comparative justice leads us to say that, because we know that we are not fully just (and thus a bit unjust) and the enemy is not fully unjust (and thus a bit just), let us go ahead and do anything to end the mess or let us do a lesser evil in order to prevent a greater one; so it divorces justice from temperance. For the fathers and St. Thomas, charity guides justice and all the other moral virtues toward their proper end. Justice, prudence, courage, and temperance work in harmony to bring the believer in beatitude with God. Fighting just wars is one way this is done. Comparative justice denies that this could ever be done, denies that the soldier can ever use force in such a way that those acts of force bring the soldier closer to God. The just warrior's prudence is at one

187

with his conscience, but comparative justice separates justice from prudence, which leads the bishops to abandon justice for desired consequences, that is, an unjust peace. In summation, comparative justice takes the "justice" out of just war.

The Challenge of "The Harvest of Justice"

The goal of *The Harvest of Justice* (*HJ*) is "to build on the foundations of our 1983 pastoral"(*HJ,* Intro.).[29] The challenges of peace involve: "renewing and reshaping national commitment to the world community, building effective institutions of peace and alleviating the injustice of oppression which contribute to conflict" (*HJ,* Intro.). The goal certainly sounds worthwhile. World community, peace, and alleviating oppression are all worthy goals that any Christian should find praiseworthy. Christians can also applaud the renewed attacks on abortion as a consequence of the growing influence of the "culture of death" so well described by John Paul II. The bishops wish to see "engaged and creative U.S. leadership" that avoids the pitfalls of isolationism and unwise intervention. Again, the goal seems entirely praiseworthy. We don't wish to see the U.S. hide its head in the sand in the face of every injustice, but neither do we wish to see the U.S. go to war every time an injustice is committed. Unfortunately, all the mistakes made in *Challenge* repeat themselves in *Harvest*, which, again, proves an axiom true: bad theology makes for bad ethics, which, in turn, makes for bad advice to the faithful.

The bishops have become so tainted by a liberal-humanist pacifism (cloaked in Christian symbols) that they verge on turning peace into an absolute good—and idol—that is to be sought at all costs. The bishops, for example, are fond of referring to God as "the God of peace" (and so He is), but He is also "the Lord of Hosts" (The God of Armies). The bishops claim that peace is "a gift and grace from God" (*HJ,* Sect. I). All peace? Was the peace established by Nazis in France and Poland in the early 1940's a gift and grace from God? Was the peace established by Saddam Hussein in Iraq with the brutalization,

188

torture, and murder of thousands a gift and grace from God? There are places where the bishops seem to recognize the apparent absurdity of such conclusions: "Peace does not consist merely in the absence of war, but rather in sharing the goodness of life together" (*HJ*, Sect. I), but none of their platitudes about peace or actual advice evidences the good sense of this conclusion. The favoring of sanctions as a "nonmilitary alternative to the terrible options of war or indifference" (*HJ*, II.5) is a perfect example. For the innocent, sanctions can be and usually are more terrible than military options. The innocent are the first (and often the only ones) to be effected in any great way by sanctions. The advice by the bishops to target sanctions at those directly responsible for injustice is politically naive and practically impossible. Anytime goods are made scarce, those directly responsible for injustice—the ruling regime and those that preserve its power—feel the crunch last.

Ill-conceived pacifism leads to additional troubling practical turns in the bishops' advice, such as their call for "peacemaking institutions." Here is a typical paragraph in full:

> The World must find the will and the ways to pursue justice, contain conflict and replace violence and war with peaceful and effective means to address injustices and resolve disputes. Through the United Nations and regional organizations, our nation must be positively engaged in devising new tools for preserving the peace, finding ways to prevent and police conflicts, to protect basic right, to promote integral human development and to preserve the environment. (*HJ*, Intro.)

Paragraphs like this lead one to think that the bishops are simply confused. They want the U.S. to pursue justice and contain conflict while at the same time replace violence and war with peaceful means. To call such an idea "utopian" would be kind. How is this to be done? The United Nations? How will this organization "prevent and police conflicts" and "protect basic rights" without using force? The bishops remind us that Jesus called us to be peacemakers, but they forget to add that Jesus did not give directions on how to achieve peace. The bishops and the Pope place a great deal of weight on the U.N. as a peacemaking organization, but their hopes for this all-too-human institution seem ill-founded. The U.N. will never, in the words of the bishops, "fulfill the promise of its charter to save succeeding generations from the scourge of war," because war will always be a part of sinful humanity. The bishops and, more sadly, recent Popes seem to act as if the U.N. were not populated by people tainted with self-interests like everyone else in the world. We must remember that the U.N. is not a holy institution, but an organization of human beings, sinful human beings, who do sinful things for sinful motives like all other human beings in a fallen world.

The bishops also place too much weight on the development of peoples as a way of eradicating war. They quote with approval the Pope:

> [It] must not be forgotten that at the root of war there are usually real and serious grievances: injustices suffered, legitimate aspirations frustrated, poverty and the exploitation of multitudes of desperate people who see no real responsibility of improving their lot by peaceful means. [quoted from *On the Hundredth Anniversary of Rerum Novarum*, no.23]

Of course, the development of all peoples is a praiseworthy goal and, indeed, would eliminate some wars, but not all. In the case of the first Persian Gulf War, at root was a rapacious Saddam Hussein. Hussein had no real or serious grievance. He had suffered no injustice, though he certainly perpetrated injustice. He was not suffering poverty, though he certainly impoverished many and tortured and exploited thousands. Could it be that the bishops are losing the ability to admit that, when evil doers have enough power (and demonstrate a willingness to use it) they must be stopped?

190

The bishops often overestimate the effectiveness of nonviolent means to eradicate injustice. For example, they claim that "dramatic political transactions" in Eastern Europe "demonstrate the power of nonviolent action, even against dictatorial and totalitarian regimes" (*HJ,* Sect. 1). Without denying the role played by the "solidarity movement" in Poland during the Cold War, we have to point out the obvious: there was a Cold War and the tactics used in that war by the West played a large role in bringing about the "dramatic political transactions" in Eastern Europe.

Lastly, in the third and last section entitled "Concluding Commitments: Blessed are the Peacemakers," the bishops give a great deal of advice to the faithful about seeking peace, but not one call to join the organization most likely to be the one that makes any peace secure: the military. Why is there no call for Christians to join the military and thus leaven the institution responsible for securing peace? Do the bishops not think that more Christians—people shaped by the church's teachings on justice and peace—in the military may mean a more moral military, and thus a military more likely to do things consonant with what the church believes to be just?

Conclusion

We have argued that the Christian just war tradition is most usefully approached with classical notions of justice and Christian notions of God and charity ,and that this approach receives its brightest theological formulations in the West in the Church fathers (especially St. Ambrose) and in St. Thomas. In this chapter we have suggested that our approach to the just war offers useful critiques of the moral approaches exemplified by Reinhold Niebuhr and Christian Realism and the mixture of pacifism and just war tradition as attempted by the Roman Catholic hierarchy particularly in the U.S. The Christian conception of justice gives rise to a just war approach that avoids the pitfalls of a consequentialism that may allow any vicious act whatsoever, as long as it is for some ultimate good cause. It also

191

avoids the utopian ideal of ending all war, which actually issues in defending wars where any sort of evil can be perpetrated so long as war is ended. The Christian just war approach also helps us locate the problems of "realist" and "dirty hands" thinking.

The main lesson we have learned from the U.S. Catholic Bishops is that it is hard to mix pacifism with just war theory. Attempts to mix the two merely lead to incoherent just war thinking. Through the eyes of the just warrior, the faults of the bishops are obvious: a mistaken presumption against war in just war doctrine, the acceptance of consequentialism and "dirty hands" morality, and the employment of the criterion of comparative justice. According to just warriors shaped by the Church fathers and St. Thomas, the presumption in just war doctrine is against injustice; we never allow the consequences of an act to render an evil act "acceptable;" we do not consider acts of force as intrinsically evil and thus allow ourselves to do a lesser evil in order to prevent a greater one; and we find the criterion of comparative justice particularly troublesome, for it tends to debilitate justice in war. This last item cannot be stressed enough. To accept the criterion of comparative justice is to give up hope for virtuous warfare.

Just warriors believe that God elevates them through their virtuous acts in war. The bishops' model of the just war undercuts this notion entirely, for the virtuous cannot participate in "just war" so conceived. The virtuous cannot engage in evil acts for any reason, so the virtuous cannot participate in a "relatively" just war that is also "relatively" unjust. The just warrior declares that the *jus ad bellum* can tell us when we ought to go to war, and when it does, it has declared us just—not relatively just—in doing so. This is not a guarantee that all our acts in war will be just acts, for the *jus in bello* are restrictions we can only approximate according to our virtue. But it is to say that, when Christians decide that under legitimate leadership their nation has a just cause to go to war and the right intent in prosecuting the war, then they are just in so far as this decision to go to war is concerned.

192

They do not engage in anything evil when they decide to fight a just war. They know that they will be made fitter for beatitude with God by soldiering virtuously in war. This being the sole reason they are going to fight, they would render null and void their whole reason for fighting should they do evil that good may come. They will not be perfectly virtuous warriors, but they will be warriors who enter a battle with a clear conscience, and have every intention of exiting battle the same way.

CHAPTER 9

Penance, Just War, and Recent Conflicts[1]

The Christian just war (or justifiable war) tradition is a body of thought centered on two goals: to enable Christians to distinguish just from unjust wars and to enable Christians to distinguish justice from injustice in war. When we look at how the tradition is applied to specific wars and actual combat practices, we notice that the practice of penance looms large. In fact, it is impossible to talk about applying just war criteria to concrete wars without also talking about applying penance. Hence, any discussion of how the Christian just war tradition works in actual practice leads inevitably to a discussion of penance. We have written much about the just war tradition and a little about Canon Law. Now, as we seek to apply the just war criteria to recent conflicts, we must say more about penance, which is an ecclesial practice regarded with necessity in both the Christian East and West.

Aristotle reported that some peoples rewarded their warriors returning from battle in proportion to how many they killed and punished those who had not killed enough (*Politics* VII.1324b10–22). Christians have not followed the example of such peoples. In the place of rewards Christians have often demanded penance for those returning from battle. Exactly why penance was thought necessary in some cases is not perfectly clear, but it is clear that penance was demanded at least from those who fought unjustly, and sometimes even from those who fought justly. So, from the very beginning of Christian involvement in warfare, ecclesiastical authorities demanded that at least some, if not always all, Christian soldiers should do penance.

The Christian just war doctrine has always played a large role in shaping Christian moral approaches to war. When the Church did not demand penance from all soldiers, the just war doctrine is what allowed it to judge exactly who needed penance. For the just war doctrine is the tool that allows the Church to distinguish justice from injustice in war, and thus to distinguish soldiers deserving of praise and those deserving of shame and penance. The just war doctrine is the tool that enables the Church to know when to deny Christian participation in evil (unjust wars) and when to encourage participation in good (just wars). Penance provides a means of healing for those who participate in an unjust war or do evil in a just war. The relationships between penance, virtue, and just war show us why imperfectly just wars are still just and not necessary evils.

I. Penance For Soldiering: Who and Why

Roman, Anglo-Saxon, Irish, and French Penitentials until the 11th century all prescribed penances for soldiers who killed in battle. The seventh-century Penitential of Theodore recommended 40 days of penance for those who killed in war.[2] A more detailed list of penances for those returning from battle can be found in the penances imposed upon those who fought with William in the Battle of Hastings in 1066:

1. Anyone who knows that he killed a man in the great battle must do penance for one year for each man that he killed.

2. Anyone who wounded a man, and does not know whether he killed him or not, must do penance for forty days for each man he thus struck (if he can remember the number), either continuously or at intervals.

3. Anyone who does not know the number of those he wounded or killed must, at the discretion of the bishop, do penance for one day in each week for the remainder of his life; or, if he can, let him redeem his sin by a perpetual alms, either by building or by endowing a church.

4. The clerks who fought, or who were armed for fighting, must do penance as if they had committed these sins in

5.   their own country, for they are forbidden by the canons to do battle.

5.   Those who fought merely for gain are to know that they owe penance as for homicide [i.e., seven years].

6.   Those who fought as in a public war [i.e., out of a concern for justice] have been allotted a penance of three years by their bishops out of mercy.

7.   The archers who killed some and wounded others, but are necessarily ignorant as to how many, must do penance as for three Lents.[3]

What we notice here is that penance was imposed even on those who fought justly in a just war. This seems strange to us. Why should soldiers who fought well in a just cause be made to do penance? Does this mean that those who wrote the manuals of penance regarded all wars as evil (though some may be necessary), and thus all who participate in them de facto guilty of sin? Bernard Verkamp offers an answer. First, the idea of imposing penance on those who shed blood "was probably just a carry-over from ancient pagan and Jewish worlds."[4] According to this argument, ancient Hebrews shared with other ancient cultures a *horror sanguinis* that made one who shed blood ceremoniously unclean. The Old Testament book of Numbers records, for example, that those who killed in battle (a battle ordered by God) had to go through a ceremonial cleansing process (31:19). Early Christians seemed to believe much the same thing as evidenced in the apostolic command to abstain from blood (Acts 15:20,29).

There can be no doubt that the shedding of blood did make one unfit for certain ecclesial practices in early and medieval Christianity. The great third-century Alexandrian theologian Origen, in fact, used this argument against Celsus, who accused Christians of not being good citizens because (among other things) they did not serve in the military. Origen countered that Christians should be considered as priests in the eyes of the Romans, and thus as people who should abstain from blood just as the Roman cultic priests did

(*Contra Celsum* VIII.73). Although the majority of the tradition did not follow Origen on this (and held instead that Christian laymen could serve in the military), the tradition did agree overwhelmingly that clerics should not participate in battle. The reasons why are amply summarized by St. Thomas, who argued that the shedding of blood simply did not "fit" with giving the Eucharist. Bishops and clerics cannot soldier because the occupations of soldiering and ministering cannot "be fittingly exercised at the same time" (*convenienter simul exerceri non possint*) (*ST* II-II.40.2). St. Thomas offers two reasons why: First, warlike pursuits are incompatible with being a Bishop or cleric because it keeps them from their proper duties. Second, it is "unbecoming" (*non competit*) for those who give the Eucharist to shed blood. Thus, those Bishops and clerics that do shed blood, even if it is without sin (e.g., in a just war), become "irregular" (*irregulares*). As we have seen in the list of penances for the Battle of Hastings, "irregular" Bishops and clerics had to do their own penance for shedding blood.

Bishops and clerics cannot fight in just wars. Why this is so is clear; thus why they must do penance if they fight is also clear. But it is still not so clear why soldiers who fight justly must do penance. The ambiguity of St Basil's three-year penance (discussed in Chapter 3 above) demonstrates the lack of clarity on the issue. Disordered passions cannot be the reason. St. Augustine, for example, argues that Paul's warning not to render evil for evil is, in fact, a warning against giving into the passion of revenge, but that such a passion does not exist in those who fight justly in a just war (*Epistle* 138.9–15). Instead of fighting with a lust for domination, just warriors, "cherish the spirit of a peace-maker, that, by conquering those whom you attack, you may lead them back to the advantage of peace" (*Epistle* 139.4).

Furthermore, in St. Augustine's *On Free Will*, he makes this famous argument for why Christians ought not defend themselves against bodily attacks:

197

> Augustine: For me the point to be considered is whether an on-rushing enemy, or an assassin lying in wait may be killed with no wrong-headed desire [for the saving] of one's life, or for liberty or for purity.
>
> Evodius: How can I possibly think that men are void of inordinate desire who fight for things which they can lose against their will? If they cannot lose them, what need is there to go so far as to kill a man on their account?
>
> Augustine: Therefore the law is not just which grants the power to a wayfarer to kill a highway robber, so that he may not be killed [by the robber]; or which grants to any one, man or woman, to slay an assailant attacking, if he can, before he or she is harmed. The soldier also is commanded by law to slay the enemy, for which slaying, if he objects, he will pay the penalty by imperial order. Shall we then dare to say that these laws are unjust, or more, that they are not laws? For to me a law that is not just appears to be no law. ...
>
> Evodius: The soldier in slaying the enemy is the agent of the law, wherefore he does his duty easily with no wrong aim or purpose ... That law therefore, which is for the protection of the citizens ... can be obeyed without wrong desire. (I.5)

Here we find St. Augustine arguing that it is both lawful and just for soldiers to kill for the sake of justice *precisely because* no disordered desire existed in soldiers, who, by necessity of the case, use force out of a sense of duty and not out of disordered desire. So, for those following St. Augustine on this matter, no penance should be imposed on soldiers returning from battle simply because soldiers kill in battle. There has to be something more to the story than the simple fact that a soldier did what a soldier is supposed to do: kill enemy soldiers. That "something more" may rest in the idea of not what makes a soldier a soldier but in the idea of what makes a knight a knight.

The knightly virtues represent an ideal character that could in reality only be approximated, and shame results from the failure to realize the ideal. Penance is that ritual necessary to restore the knight to the community. Piety and virtue are the very essence of the knight's life. Romance legends abound in knights that strove to transform their love of women and battle into pious forms: Platonic affairs and blessed swords used for pious purposes. In the 10th-century the blessing of the knight's sword was an important part of "dubbing" knights.[5] The blessing of the sword, which took place when the knight placed the sword on the altar and thus "gave it up to God's purposes," meant that the knight was pledged to use his sword in restricted ways. John of Salisbury explains: the knight with the consecrated sword was to use his weapon only:

> ... to protect the Church, to fight against treachery, to reverence the priesthood, to ward off injuries from the poor, to ensure peace throughout the provinces, and (as taught by a true understanding of the Sacrament) to shed blood and, if need be, to lay down his life for his brethren.[6]

This ideal is constitutive of knighthood. These are the practices of knighthood that makes it what it is; in other words, to fail to carry out these practices is to fail to be a knight. But few could live up to these ideals. As Verkamp points out, the blessings and the oaths "did not keep them from behaving in battle as soldiers have always behaved."[7]

The knightly ideal was necessary to make knights the sort of people they were: soldiers who strove to fight in ways pleasing to God. But this is hard work and can only be approximated according to the virtue attained by each knight. Because no knight can be perfect in virtue and thus perfect in battle, no knight ever fought in a perfectly just fashion, and thus every knight had something to be sorry for after the battle was over. However, exactly what the knight had to be sorry for changed over time. The reason for the change rests with the very justification for war in Christendom: charity. As far back as St. Ambrose, Christian justification for war was found in love of God and neighbor. In the hands of St. Ambrose, charity not only allowed for Christian participation in war but also actually demanded it. Nevertheless, the full implications of the idea did not come to bear until St. Thomas, who treated war as a part of the virtue of charity.

Verkamp points out that shame usually calls for acts of charity. In other words, when you do something that brings shame, you have to do acts of charity to remove that shame and thus to be reconciled to the community. The thinking behind the older Penitentials reveals that shedding blood in itself is something shameful that requires charitable acts to be remove. But, beginning with St. Ambrose and finding full fruition with St. Thomas, just war is an act of charity; thus fighting justly in a just war is one thing you could do to remove shame and to be reconciled to the community. So, if Verkamp is right that the tradition once required soldiers who fought honorably to do penance, then there seems to be a definite change by the time we get to St. Thomas. However, Verkamp may not be right and, in fact, we have good reasons for claiming that the tradition is not as homogenous as he implies. After the Battle of Fontenay in 841, for example, penance was imposed only on those who had done anything "from wrath or hatred or vainglory or any passion."[8] Also, Otto of Freising reports that, in 1158, Frederick Barbarossa addressed his troops with the admonition that "It is not lust for domination that drives us into battle [a direct reply to the Augustinian notion of *libido domini*], but a fierce rebellion ... Milan has given us a just cause for war, since it stands revealed as rebellious against lawful authority ... Since the war is just ... let us act now to secure the highest praise of knighthood."[9] In so far as they fought justly, such knights had no need to do penance.

The 12th-century debate between the two schools of thought (penance for all or only some soldiers) is captured quite neatly in opposing arguments of Allan of Lille and Hugh of St. Cher. Alain of Lille cited a canon that enjoined penance for killing even on command of princely authority, but Hugh of Saint Cher countered that soldiers could exercise their office without sin when they did so with right intention and out of necessity. For Hugh of Saint Cher, only those who killed for vainglory or other vicious desires were guilty of sin, and thus in need of doing penance.[10] In this matter, Hugh of Saint Cher was simply following a strand of Christian thought that can be traced back at least as far as Eusebios of Caesarea, who argued that both the soldier and the cleric played a role in sacred history. According to Eusebios, the Christian should and must fight for the emperor. Nevertheless, clerics and Bishops must remain separated from bloodshed to some degree; so they must pray rather than fight for the emperor, just as Origen had insisted was the duty of all Christians. The key passage (which we have had occasion to refer to in Chapter 3 above) occurs in the *Demonstration of the Gospel*:

> Two ways of life were thus given by the law of Christ to His Church. The one is above nature and beyond common human living, it admits not [earthly matters] ... it devotes itself to the service of God alone ... And the other is more humble, more human, permits men ... to undertake government, to give orders to soldiers fighting for the right ... A kind of secondary piety is attributed to them ... so that all men, whether Greeks or barbarians, have their part in the coming salvation, and profit by the teaching of the Gospel. (I.8)

For Eusebios the Christian layman fulfills sacred history in his own way by fighting for the emperor. The just war represents the standards to which we hold Christians when they fight. This is the strand of the tradition we see extended in St. Thomas as well, which does not view the shedding of blood as something that necessarily brought shame on the soldier.

Nevertheless, we cannot escape the fact that pious battle behavior is something to be approximated, and because there are no perfectly virtuous soldiers, there will be no perfectly fought battles. Evil will be done, and when evil is done, penance is required. Penance was the rite that both acknowledged the sin and reconciled the knight to the community of believers. Acknowledging the fault and reconciling the offender are important parts of Church discipline, but before we say more about Church discipline, we need to say something about the measuring rod that enables the Church to judge who is in need of penance when it comes to warfare.

II. The Role of the Just War Doctrine in Penance

The Christian just war doctrine serves a very useful purpose: it provides Christians with the conceptual tools that enable them to decide if they can make a nation-state war their own war. As we have seen, the Western Christian just war doctrine, originating with St. Ambrose of Milan, began, in fact, as a way to figure out if Christians could make the wars of the Roman Empire their wars. St. Ambrose did not formulate a full-blown just war doctrine. Instead, he both provided the theological justification for such an enterprise and then laid the groundwork for what the enterprise would look like once it was built. The theological justification is, simply put, the demands of charity. For St. Ambrose, love of God and neighbor impels Christians to do all that they can—including acts of force—to protect their neighbors from evil-doers. St. Augustine and (especially) St. Thomas greatly expand upon St. Ambrose to give us a full-fledged Christian just war doctrine, but always from an "Ambrosian" base: warfare for the love of God and neighbor. Thus every Christian knew why he had to support wars if they were just wars: virtue demands it.

St. Ambrose did not say much about what was soon to be called the *jus ad bellum*: those criteria that enable us to figure out if the proposed war is, in fact, a just war. St. Ambrose was faced with a situation of invading barbarians against Roman forces. The reasons for war were clear and just for St. Ambrose: protection of the

202

Roman citizenry, which included Christians, from an unjust invading force. Thus St. Ambrose had no need to expound *ad bellum* criteria. But such criteria are necessary if Christians are going to be able to decide if they can make a nation-state war their war. St. Thomas, as we have seen, mentions three *ad bellum* criteria: right authority, just cause, and right intention (*ST* II-II.40.1). Theologians would later add to the list, and the criteria vary slightly from list to list, but a definitive list includes the three given by St. Thomas and adds the following: the war should be the only reasonable means of righting the wrong done, and there must be a reasonable hope of success. With these five criteria in hand, Christians ought to be able to see if there are good reasons for them to support a proposed war.

Deciding if you can make a nation-state war your war is not the only job for Christians; they also must ask themselves if the war is likely to be fought in a just manner, and, once the war begins, whether in fact the war is being fought in a just manner. Thus, what just war theorists call the *jus in bello* serves two purposes: it helps Christians decide if their nation is the sort of nation that fights justly (and hence if their nation should be supported in their war-fighting efforts), and it serves as a constant guide that enables Christians to know when war is being waged unjustly. We can summarize the *in bello* criteria by saying simply that a just people will employ just means when they wage war. Just means in war are usually reducible to two: discrimination and proportion. The first tells us that only those who deserve to be attacked ought to be targeted intentionally, and the second tell us that all acts of force must be those by which we estimate that more good than evil will come from them.

The Task of the Church in War

The Church's task is to make the just war criteria clear to its people. Christians must understand how to use the tools put at their disposal. Karl Barth's argument that the Church's main task is to act as a delaying movement misses the mark on two counts.[11] First, there are times when delay could debilitate success. Besides, how long should the Church delay? Barth seems to imply that the Church ought to delay until war is actually declared, but why should the Church delay a war that is clearly just and is clearly the only way to right a wrong? Of course, one might say in defense of Barth that the delaying movement of the Church is one that ensures our leaders have thought about the alternatives and consequences. This certainly has merit, for we do not want to rush into a war impatiently and imprudently. However, the image of nation-state leaders worried about whether a severely fractured body of Christ is calling for delay is not very credible. Put more bluntly: the Church as it is presently constituted simply does not carry that much weight with secular authorities, which brings us to the second point. The Church would be better off forgetting about an imaginary effective delay and concentrating on educating its members to be able to decide if the proposed war, if entered into, is a just war and is likely to be fought justly and what will count as just fighting once it begins.

The Church needs to educate its flock, but what sort of weight will this education have? In other words, what moral authority ought the Church's teaching have with its members? There seems to be two, broad possible responses. The Church may respond that it decides for its members. This does not mean that the Church will simply pronounce its findings and be done with it. No, it means that the Church will certainly pronounce its finding but will also make the reasoning behind those findings public so that its members can better understand and support their Church's teachings. Nevertheless, in this scenario, the decision on whether a particular war is just and what counts as justice in this particular war is something made by the ecclesiastical authorities. The other scenario is that the Church simply allows its members to make up their own minds about a proposed war. But even here, the Church cannot give up completely its duty to guide. The causes, justifications, and means of fighting a proposed war are often confusing to the trained mind—how much more so for an untrained laity? The laity, it should be pointed out, will not be untrained completely, for they will, at the very least, have been exposed to the propaganda that exists whenever a nation proposes a war. No nation prepares its people for a war by informing them that the proposed conflict is an unjust war and that it will be fought as viciously as possible. The Church must offer its guidance, for Christians will be shaped by something, and if not by the Church, then by the world.

Oliver O'Donovan surely gets it right when he argues that the Church may command "with the sanction of discipline in matters where a theological argument alone seems to require a certain conclusion."[12] His example is euthanasia, which is unconditionally inconsistent with biblical ethics, even though it is not explicitly condemned in the biblical text. In such cases, the argument is to be kept open to public examination and discussion in order to prevent it from looking like mere ecclesiastical decree. However, in arguments that are not simply theological but involve critical judgments of facts, the Church can give counsel and encourage others to understand the arguments and be able to distinguish those disagreements that are matters of disobedience to the word of God and those not. Thus, we can say that the Church counsels when it is unsure and commands when it is. The person who deliberately and willfully acts against what the Church commands is the person whom the Church disciplines.

Church Discipline: Roman Catholic and Reformed

What is the point of Church discipline and how does it work? The Roman Catholic and Reformed traditions share many basic assumptions that give us a unified answer to these questions. We find it so perhaps because there is very little that separates St. Thomas and Calvin on this issue. According to St. Thomas, Church discipline depends upon the two keys of the Church (*Summa Contra Gentiles* IV.72.10). Calvin agrees with St. Thomas and adds that

205

"discipline is like a bridle to restrain and tame those who rage against the doctrine of the Church" (*Institutes* IV:12.1). The Roman Catholic Church followed St. Thomas closely on this just as the Reformed tradition followed Calvin closely.[13]

Broadly speaking, the Church disciplines for three reasons: to reconcile the sinner to the body of Christ, to check the spread of similar sin, and to protect the purity of the Church and the honor of Christ. When the Church punishes it is, according to Calvin, "the best support of health, foundation of order, and bond of unity" (*Institutes* IV.12.2). Thus, when someone sins, they place themselves outside the community and they need to be restored. In this respect, Church discipline is for the purpose of persuading the person "to meet expressions of repentance" as Richard Baxter says (*Reformed Pastor* 87), in order to receive them back into the body of Christ. Checking the spread of sin is equally important. Should the Church fail to discipline one who has violated the moral order, further violations may result. This is especially true in warfare, which is brutal enough as it is and very susceptible to progressive immorality. The Church has to be the Church, so its members cannot live viciously. There can be no true witness to the world if the Church's members support or seem indifferent to injustice or immorality of any sort. Thus the goal in the third purpose of discipline is to make sure that the vicious cannot be called "Christian" and thus dishonor the Church and Christ.

We now turn to how the Church disciplines. Generally, there are two ways: restriction from participating in the Eucharist and acts of penance. St. Thomas argues that "Holy Communion ought not be given to open sinners when they ask for it" (*ST* III.80.6). Calvin, too, is adamant that the "Lord's Supper" is not to be profaned by clerics giving the Eucharist to vicious persons. By seeing that the vicious are not able to partake of the Lord's Supper, the good are not influenced by the bad. Moreover, the sinner is moved to repent when he knows that he cannot participate in the Lord's Supper.

For St. Thomas, penance is a virtue (a species of justice), for it includes a right choice on the part of the will. Moreover, penance is a special virtue because it destroys past sin as well as shaping the offender to be the sort of person who offends no more (*ST* III.85.1–3). The virtue lost through sin is restored through penance because grace is infused in the offender through penance and the virtues enter through that same infusion of grace (*ST* III.89.1). Nevertheless, sin leaves its mark in one aspect: the sinner rises again to less virtue than he had before he sinned (*ST* III.89.2). Because penance is a virtue, it can preserve the sinner from future sins (*ST* III.84.8). Penance, therefore, makes the communicant fit for communion. This is especially important since those unfit may die from receiving the Eucharist. Thus, as Calvin argues, the sinner should be "deprived of the communion of the Supper until he gives assurance of his repentance" (*Institutes* IV.12.6), and this typically means doing penance.

Discipline is to be carried out in the following way. Calvin counsels that the first stage should always be private admonition for those who have not committed public sins (*Institutes* IV.12.2). St. Thomas held that some sins required "solemn or public penance" because public sins need public remedy. Grave crimes deserve the "greatest confusion in this life," in order to deter others, and to serve as an example to others who have committed grievous sins that they too can be forgiven and reconciled to the Church (*ST* III.sup.28.1). This does not mean that a person is cut off completely from Christ until penance is carried out, for that much reconciliation takes place immediately upon confession. Rather it means that the Church has to show that it takes seriously violations of the moral order (in which the just war criteria have place) and that our acts have human ramifications that cannot be put right simply by saying, "I'm sorry."

St. Thomas insists that solemn or public penance should be done only once because frequency of this type of penance brings contempt upon the Church. Hence those who fall after they have done public penance should be given private penance (*ST* III.sup.28.20). Calvin discusses with approval the practice of the "ancient and better church" (he refers to Cyprian in particular) that employed solemn rites as marks of repentance that have to be performed to the satisfaction of the Church, and when completed, "the penitent was received into grace with the laying on of hands" (*Institutes* IV.12.6). As the great Puritan theologian Richard Baxter argues, heinous sins require more than sudden professions to count as evidence of repentance. There must be evidence of contrition and this is not done in a moment. If people should "hear of a man's murder, perjury, or adultery today, and hear that he is absolved tomorrow, they will think that the Church consisteth of such, or that it make very light of sin" (*Christian Directory* III.Q.94). Thus Baxter goes on to speak approvingly of the ancient Church's practice of delayed reconciliation and imposed penances in order to avoid scandal.

John Paul II's 1994 Catechism of the Catholic Church states that, in making satisfaction, the sinner must try to repair harm he has done as much as possible (par. 1459). Absolution does not remedy all the disorder caused by sin. Simple justice is also required. Nevertheless, the Church should be careful not to go too far in its discipline. Calvin argues that severity with gentleness befits the Church and warns that the early Church's practice of severe penance was positively harmful to the soul of the offender (*Institutes* IV.12.8). That is why Calvin is for immediate reinstatement to the Eucharist for confessing sinners and he quotes St. Cyprian, St. John Chrysostom, and St. Augustine in his favor (*Institutes* IV.12.8). But even after the offender is allowed to return to the Lord's Supper, penance may still be required. Calvin argues that the Law, Prophets, and Apostles agree that the practice of penance is necessary to reconcile the offender to the believing community. In practice, this usually means fasting, solemn applications, or "other acts of humility, repentance, and faith" (*Institutes* IV.12.14). Because these

208

are not specified in scripture, it is left to the judgment of the Church to decide.[14]

Of course, the penance must fit the crime. St. Thomas argues that penance should last for a fixed time according to "the measure of the sin" (*ST* III.84.8). The Catholic Catechism concurs, stating that "the penance must fit the offence" (par. 1460). The Westminster Confession (the 1646 creed of all Reformed Churches) states that the Church is to admonish, suspend from the Lord's Supper for a season, or excommunicate according to the "nature of the crime and the demerit of the person" (Church Censures, section 4). St. Thomas employs an analogy with physical health and argues that, just as a doctor applies different methods of healing in accordance to what is wrong with the patient, and what sort of person the patient is, so too in order to be healed from the bad effects of spiritual sickness, the spiritual doctor (in this case, the Church) must take into account exactly what the offender has done and how to put him right. The Catholic Catechism reinforces this point, stating that the confessor must take into account the penitent's "personal station and must seek his spiritual good" (par. 1460).

Nation-state leaders who violate the *jus ad bellum*, and thus plunge their nation into an unjust war, and those soldiers who violate the *jus in bello*, and thus combat viciously, and their military leaders who either overlook, countenance, or actively support vicious combat behavior, are those who go astray and cut themselves off from the body of Christ. Public discipline must occur when a violation is publicly known or outwardly evident. Again, the Church must be seen to be the Church. Just as it is important for an earthly political regime that justice not only be done but seen to be done, so too must the Church be seen to dispense discipline in publicly known just war violations. Christ must be honored and the Church must prevent its people from imitating vice, and public discipline is how this is done when just war violations are publicly known. Calvin argues that the great are to be disciplined along with the lowly, and he uses St. Ambrose's dealings with the Emperor Theodosius as the model for how the Church should treat the powerful (*Institutes* IV.12.7). Should the Church have to excommunicate the great, it should remember that it does not do so to flaunt ecclesial power but to get the offender "to turn to a more virtuous life" (*Institutes* IV.12.10).

III. Discipline in Practice: Contemporary Wars

Let us take the late wars in Afghanistan and Iraq as test cases. In the war in Afghanistan, President Bush and Secretary of State Colin Powell both declared that the U.S. was engaged in warfare against terrorists hiding in Afghanistan, and, furthermore, that the U.S. was de facto in a war against Afghanistan because the sovereign rulers of Afghanistan refused to hand over the terrorists. Afghanistan was, in fact, a terrorist-controlled state. Right authority and just cause for the war are clearly met. Right intention seems to be met as well, since the clearly stated goals of the war are to secure peace and punish evil-doers. In a hearing before the Committee on Armed Services, General Tommy Franks outlined the goals of the conflict: "The very purpose was to build and maintain pressure inside Afghanistan with the objective of the destruction of the al Qaeda terrorist network and the government of the Taliban."[15] But was it the only possible means of righting the wrong? This is a call for patience, but as a virtue, patience is what the virtuous do to check them from doing what is rash. Therefore, we can ask, was it rash to go into this war against terrorists in Afghanistan? Clearly not. There were no immediate reprisals for the attacks on "Nine-Eleven"—an extremely good sign that patience did rule the day—and plans were carefully made for exactly how the U.S. would respond. As to the last criterion—reasonable hope of success—we had every reason to believe that we would succeed. Thus, the war against Afghanistan was a war to which Christians could have and should have said "yes."

210

There really is no question about how the war was fought in Afghanistan. On October 7, 2002, al Qaeda and Taliban forces controlled more than 80% of the country. By December 22 of that same year, a new governing administration had been established. This astonishingly quick victory was achieved with an even more astonishing lack of collateral damage. Enhanced command, control, communication, and computer capabilities made for unprecedented situation awareness and ensured real-time command and control. Liberal use of precision-guided weapons (out of the 18,000 munitions delivered to Afghanistan, more than 10,000 were precision-guided) also facilitated the armed forces' ability to keep damage centered upon legitimate target areas. This enabled the armed forces to reduce civilian casualties to an absolute minimum. When one adds to the sterling record on collateral damage the humanitarian aid provided to the area (including 500,000 metric tons of food; 320,000 blankets; and 5,000 radios), there can be no serious doubts as to the armed forces meeting the requirements of proper combat behavior.

The war in Iraq is more complex but certainly not beyond our moral grasp. President Bush and Secretary of State Colin Powell both urged war with Iraq for two main reasons: because of Saddam Hussein's continuing support of terrorist organizations who pose an imminent threat to U.S. citizens and because of Hussein's continuing program of developing weapons of mass destruction. Humanitarian concerns also figured into the moral equation. Iraq's ruling regime was one of the most oppressive fascist ruling powers the world has seen since Hitler. True (and thankfully true), Hussein's Iraqi Republican Guard can hardly be mentioned in the same breath as the military might at Hitler's disposal, namely the *Wehrmacht*, Luftwaffe, and SS, but the humanitarian abuses within each ruler's sphere of power is comparable in evil. Just cause and right intention are surely met, but, again, we may ask: was it rash to invade Iraq when we did? Again, we may answer in the negative. In fact, a

211

good case may be made that Iraq should have been invaded during the Clinton Administration. Hussein began breaking his agreements with the U.N. (made at the conclusion of the Persian Gulf War) before the ink was dry. Technically, the U.S. would have been justified in invading Iraq in a matter of months after the conclusion of the Persian Gulf War.[16] As to reasonable hope for success, there was never any reason to assume that we could fail to remove Hussein from power, destroy a major terrorist source of finance and arms supply, and end the program of weapons of mass destruction.

As far as just conduct goes, we have every reason to believe that the sterling record set in Afghanistan was actually improved upon in Iraq. A maximum use of precision-guided munitions by the U.S. forces (over 90% of the missiles fired were precision guided) stands in stark contrast to Saddam Hussein's use of unwilling human shields around important military targets. U.S.-led armed forces painstakingly evaluated targets with the goal of minimizing civilian casualties.[17] Depending on the military target in question, a specific sort of missile was used. Also, if a given target was located in an area where many civilians were present at a certain time of day, care was taken to choose the time of day when civilians were less likely to be in the area. To take just one example, a military target that Hussein placed near a school (quite deliberately) was targeted for a mission when the school was empty.

Let us pause here to make a murky situation clear. When an evil enemy deliberately places his own innocent people in areas where proper military targets exist, that evil enemy—and he alone—is responsible for the collateral damage. So, if the U.S. armed forces had wished, they would have been guilty of no breach in the just war tradition by targeting a legitimate military target that had been situated deliberately in a residential area. Nevertheless, the U.S. went the extra moral mile and made all efforts to hit such targets when as few as civilians as possible were in the area.

212

We must also add that, here again, humanitarian aid was forthcoming from the very beginning of the campaign. Millions of meals, medical supplies, and other supplies for the Iraqi people were ready to go even before the campaign began. Lastly, since the cessation of major conflict, the provisional Governing Council has moved speedily to make Iraq a sovereign state once again. The U.S. and British governments have made it clear that they wish to see a constitutional convention for Iraq, the resulting constitution submitted to the Iraqi people for approval in a referendum, and free elections to produce a fully sovereign Iraqi government.[18] Surely more good than evil has resulted from this war, which does not say that no evil was done, but as long as the evil done was neither systematic or great, the justice of the war is not in doubt.

Unfortunately, the U.S. has not always fought justly in just wars. In World War II, for example, the U.S. had right authority, a good cause, and good intentions. But the U.S. did not always fight honorably, and, in fact, its dishonorable fighting became systematic. We are thinking particularly of the practice of saturation bombing and the use of atomic weapons on Japan (a practical extension of the purposes behind saturation bombing). One of the chief reasons why the U.S. employed the tactic of saturation bombing was to terrorize innocent civilians and thus demoralize enemy countries. The atomic bombs were dropped on Japan for much the same reasons. Much the same thing can be said about the My Lai massacre in which U.S. soldiers slaughtered a village of noncombatants with little or no military value (and so violated both discrimination and proportion). These were unjust acts by the measure of Christian just war doctrine. Even if some good was attained (a quicker end to the war), one of the basic assumptions of the Christian just war doctrine is that we can never do evil that good may come. Slaughtering intentionally thousands of innocent people is a moral evil that requires repentance and penance.

Soldiers who fail to abide by the *jus in bello* criteria of discrimination and proportion cut themselves off from the body of Christ. They have done moral evil and are outside the community of the Church. Ministers need to discipline these soldiers so that they can be reconciled to the Church. Exactly how to go about this rests with the prudence of ecclesiastical authorities, but the Christian tradition agrees on a rough guideline: if the sins are not notorious or a matter of public record, private admonition is recommended. If other members of the body are unaware of the immorality committed, they cannot be led astray by such "secret" sin. Also, the purity of the Church and the honor of Christ are not seen to be threatened when such sins are dealt with in a private manner. Notorious or public sins are another matter. Everyone, for example, who took part in the saturation bombing practices or in ventures such as the My Lai massacre are subject to public discipline. Should the Church not make discipline public in these cases, other members of the Church may think that the Church does not put much weight on what is done in war. Also, the failure to publicly discipline notorious soldiers is also a failure to protect the purity of the Church and the honor of Christ, since the world will see that the Church does not take immorality in war seriously. Put differently, if the Church does not discipline publicly soldiers who take part in infamous acts of combat, the Church will fail to make itself distinguishable from the world.

When ecclesiastical authorities are aware or suspect that some soldiers in their flock took part in immoral combat, they have an obligation to discuss the matter with the soldier before they allow him to partake of the Eucharist or the Lord's Supper. Again, the purity of the Church and the honor of Christ are at stake. The Church cannot be seen allowing infamous people to take part in Holy Communion. But this is not the only reason. The soldier's own life may be at stake, since participation in Holy Communion could harm the soldier if, indeed, he has committed unconfessed unjust acts in

214

war. Moreover, the soldier may be led to repent if Holy Communion is withheld from him.

Some, especially Protestants, may wonder why penance is needed once confession is made. After all, God promises to cleanse us from our sins as soon as we confess our evil acts. St. Thomas and Calvin (and the Eastern Orthodox fathers and canonists) agree that God does cleanse us from our sins immediately upon confession. Nevertheless, all call for penance. Why? Because penance is a virtue that destroys past sin and starts building a new, restored character—a character that is better able not repeat its mistakes. In other words, penance, by leading the repentant sinner to act in ways that are contrary to evil and promoting of good, shape the repentant sinner's character so that he or she is in a better position to avoid evil and do good in the future. Since soldiers are the sorts of people who are likely to return to duty and thus be in positions where they will face the same sorts of temptations, a re-tooling of character is necessary. But there is more to be said for penance. Penance is what enables us to be sure that we have really repented. Too often we are merely sorry that we are found out as opposed to being sorry for committing some evil act. Acts of penance suggest a real repentance that goes beyond superficial confessions. Also, we must admit that "I'm sorry" does not always suffice. When we have, for example, unjustly killed innocent people, the evil we have committed has terrible ramifications. Plain justice demands that we right the wrongs that we commit to the best of our ability. Of course, there is no way to right the wrong of murder, but something must be done. Here again the prudence of the ecclesiastical authorities is important. The penance should fit the crime. We are dealing with a very vague area, but one would think that reparations should be made as much as the offender is able.

215

Conclusion

Christian soldiers participate in war partly to show that we do not have to rely on viciousness to win. Thus the tradition of St. Ambrose, St. Augustine, St. Thomas, and Calvin in the Christian West and the Eastern Orthodox justifiable war trajectory serve together to counter to all forms of political "realism" that insist that we must act just as "dirty" as the enemy in order to bring justice (of a sort). The Christian just war doctrine represents a firm "no" to all acts that bring dishonor to the soldier. When soldiers kill intentionally innocent people or commit acts in which they know more evil than good will come, they bring dishonor to themselves. They need God's forgiveness and reconciliation with God's people.

We began this chapter by noting that Christians did not follow the practice of some ancient peoples of rewarding or punishing returning soldiers according to the number of people they did or did not kill. The Christian Church—East and West—has often demanded penance, especially and particularly from those who either fought in an unjust war or fought dishonorably in war. The just war criteria enable us to distinguish honorable from dishonorable war. Thus the just war criteria is that measuring rod for the Church by which its members are judged to be in need of penance or not. Penance both protects the integrity of the Church and restores the soldier to the body of Christ. While it is generally true that early Christian soldiers who fought in a battle had to do penance regardless of how they fought, and this probably because of ceremonial concerns of shedding blood, this was not always the case; by the time we get to St. Thomas, we see that those who fight honorably are in no need of penance. Nevertheless, fighting honorably is hard work and it requires a great deal of virtue to be able to return from a battle without a troubled conscience. Penance therefore is how the Church goes about restoring such people to the body of Christ. The virtue of war requires nothing less from its virtuous warriors.

NOTES

Chapter 1

[1] Text available online:
http://www.whitehouse.gov/news/releases/2001/09/20010914-2.html

[2] T.S. Eliot, *The Wasteland* (75th Anniversary Ed.; New York: Harcourt Brace, 1997), 22f (section V, lines 367–377).

[3] Michael Walzer, *Just and Unjust Wars: A Moral Argument With Historical Illustrations* (New York: Basic Books, 1977), 177.

[4] Jean Bethke Elshtain, *Just War Against Terror: The Burden of American Power in a Violent World* (New York: Basic Books, 2003), 69.

[5] Much in the next few pages appeared originally in Alexander F.C. Webster, "Between Western Crusades and Islamic 'Crescades,' " in Jack Figel (ed.), *Byzantine Christianity and Islam* (Fairfax, Virginia: Eastern Christian Publications, 2001), 159–66.

[6] Charles A. Kimball, "Roots of Rancor: Examining Islamic Militancy," *The Christian Century* 118:29 (Oct. 24–31, 2001): 22.

[7] Clifford Geertz, *Islam Observed: Religious Development in Morocco and Indonesia* (Chicago: Univ. Chicago, 1968).

[8] "Text of Al-Qaida's Statement," Associated Press wire story (Oct. 9, 2001).

[9] Diana West, "Islam is in the Dark Ages," *The Washington Times* (Oct. 26, 2001), A21.

[10] Walter E. Kaegi, *Byzantium and the Early Islamic Conquests* (Cambridge: Cambridge Univ., 1995), 8, 18.

[11] Hilmi M. Zawati, *Is Jihad a Just War: War, Peace, and Human Rights Under Islamic and Public International Law* (Lewiston, NY: Edwin Mellen, 2001), 107. His view reflects "the majority of contemporary Muslim jurists," according to Richard C. Martin, "The Religious Foundations of War, Peace, and Statecraft in Islam," in John Kelsay and James Turner Johnson (eds.), *Just War and Jihad: Historical and Theological Perspectives on War and Peace in Western and Islamic Traditions* (New York: Greenwood, 1991), 108.

[12] John Kelsay, *Islam and War: A Study in Comparative Ethics* (Louisville: Westminster/John Knox, 1993), 95, 35.

[13] Quoted in Elshtain, *Just War Against Terror*, 131.

[14] Quoted in Elshtain, *Just War Against Terror*, 132.

[15] Samuel P. Huntington, *The Clash of Civilizations and the Remaking of World Order* (New York: Simon & Schuster, 1996), 256.

[16] Ivo Andric, *The Bridge on the Drina*, Lovett F. Edwards (trans.) (Chicago: Univ. Chicago, 1977).

[17] *The Lives of the Pillars of Orthodoxy* (Buena Vista, CO: Holy Apostles Convent and Dormition Skete, 1990), 352f.

[18] See, for example, the succinct explanation in Kelsay, *Islam and War*, 34.

[19] All quotations from the Qur'an are taken from *The Koran*, N.J. Dawood (trans.) (9th rev. ed.; New York: Penguin, 1997).

[20] Edward LeRoy Long, Jr., *War and Conscience in America* (Philadelphia: Westminster, 1968), 22–47. See also LeRoy Walters, "The Just War and the Crusade: Antitheses or Analogies?" *Monist* 57 (Oct. 1973): 584–94, 593.

[21] Majid Khadduri, *The Islamic Law of Nations: Shaybani's Siyar* (Baltimore, MD: Johns Hopkins Univ., 1966), 15.

[22] For examples of such irregular "holy wars" in Eastern Orthodox history and the argument against holy war as a normative moral position in Orthodoxy, see Webster, "Between Western Crusades and Islamic 'Crescades,' " 151–56, and Alexander F.C. Webster, *The Pacifist Option: The Moral Argument Against War in Eastern Orthodox Theology* [Lanham, MD: International Scholars (imprint of Rowman & Littlefield), 1999], 84–87.

[23] That is not to dismiss the moral complexities of the resort to war, in the first place, in Afghanistan and Iraq. In neither country, at this writing, is a reasonably stable political regime in place, and guerilla violence by terrorist, Taliban, or Ba'athist hold-outs continues to exact a heavy price among the U.S., NATO, and United Nations forces engaged in the "nation-building" phases of those operations. In the final chapter of the present volume, Professor Darrell Cole will consider how the classic Western Christian tradition of the just war, particularly the practice of penance, may be applied to the current war against terrorism in both Afghanistan and Iraq.

[24] Elshtain, *Just War Against Terror*, 67f.

[25] Text available online:
http://www.cnn.com/2003/US/05/01/bush.transcript/index.html

218

Chapter 2

[1] Substantial portions of this section of the present chapter are adapted from Alexander F.C. Webster, "Beyond Byzantium: Eastern Orthodoxy in the American Public Square," *St. Vladimir's Theological Quarterly* 41:4 (1997): 337–49.

[2] Richard John Neuhaus, *The Naked Public Square: Religion and Democracy in America* (Grand Rapids, MI: William B. Eerdmans, 1984), 21.

[3] Neuhaus, *The Naked Public Square*, 263.

[4] This paragraph is adapted from a previous one in Alexander F.C. Webster, *The Price of Prophecy: Orthodox Churches on Peace, Freedom, and Security* (2nd rev. ed.; Grand Rapids, MI, and Washington, D.C.: William B. Eerdmans and Ethics and Public Policy Center, 1995), 11f.

[5] Deno Geanakoplos put this issue to rest in his essay, "Church and State in the Byzantine Empire: A Reconsideration of the Problem of Caesaropapism," in *Byzantine East and Latin West* (New York: Shoe String, 1976), 57–83.

[6] Nicolae Iorga, *Byzance après Byzance: continuation de l'"Histoire de la vie byzantine"* (Bucarest: l'Institut d'etudes byzantines, 1935).

[7] H. Richard Niebuhr, *Christ and Culture* (New York: Harper & Row, 1951), Chapter 6.

[8] Stanley S. Harakas, "The Natural Law Teaching in the Ante-Nicene Fathers and in Modern Greek Orthodox Theology" (Unpublished Th.D. dissertation, Boston Univ. School of Theology, 1965), 329.

[9] In the predominantly Orthodox chapters in this volume, we follow the important nuance in Paul Ramsey, *War and the Christian Conscience: How Shall Modern War Be Conducted Justly?* (Durham, NC: Duke Univ., 1962), 24f. The great Princeton theologian substituted "justifiable" for "just" in his assessment of St. Augustine of Hippo's moral doctrine of war, since the Latin Church father declared that victory in war, as a good from God, goes to the side with the "juster" cause and not an absolute claim to justice. St. Augustine also refrained from undue glorification of the Christian Roman Empire, which also pointed to a relativizing of justice in political entities and in war.

[10] For an explanation of the concept of trajectory, see Webster, *The Pacifist Option*, 59–62. The third moral position, which has figured prominently in the

Christian West at least until the 17th century and remains a moral imperative in the Qur'an (as we saw in Chapter 1 above), is "holy war," or the crusade / "crescade." For an argument against including "holy war" as a morally legitimate third option for Orthodox Christians, see Webster, *The Pacifist Option*, 83–87.

[11] These chapters are adapted and expanded from previous versions of the text: Alexander F.C. Webster, "Justifiable War as a 'Lesser Good' in Eastern Orthodox Moral Tradition," *St. Vladimir's Theological Quarterly* 47:1 (2003): 3–57, and Webster, "Justifiable War in Eastern Orthodox Christianity," in Paul Robinson (ed.), *Just War in Comparative Perspective* (Aldershot, UK: Ashgate, 2003), 40–61.

[12] Earlier versions of these three criteria may be found in Webster, *The Price of Prophecy*, 22f, and Alexander F.C. Webster, "Just War and Holy War: Two Case Studies in Comparative Christian Ethics," *Christian Scholar's Review* 15:4 (1986): 358–61.

[13] One of the marks of contemporary traditional Protestants is a "rediscovery" of the early church fathers and St. Thomas Aquinas. Witness, for example, the Protestant-led project of the Ancient Christian Commentaries series, with a Protestant Evangelical publisher (Inter Varsity), headed by a Methodist theologian (Thomas Oden) and with a Lutheran Pastor (Joel Elowsky) as the on-site director. In regards to Aquinas, even the prolific popular theologian R.C. Sproul, a hard-line Calvinist if there ever was one, finds much of use in Aquinas for Calvinists!

[14] The remark occurred in a colloquium at The Center for the Study of Values in Public Life at Harvard Divinity School and was published in *Religion and Values in Public Life*, vol.3, no.4, (Summer 1995): 8.

[15] Oliver O'Donovan, *The Desire of the Nations: Rediscovering the Roots of Political Theology* (Cambridge: Cambridge Univ., 1996), 217.

[16] It should be apparent that what we have called an "Augustinian withdrawal" differs to some degree from the pacifist-influenced withdrawal ethics of Stanley Hauerwas or John Yoder. The Christendom-informed citizen withdraws not gladly; not entirely; and hopefully, not permanently. As we make clear, even the Christian who withdraws has a duty to witness against the current system that requires seriously religious people to withdraw. The goal of that witness is to make future Christian participation in the public realm possible. And this (we believe) is the crucial difference between the position we are defending and that espoused by Hauerwas and Yoder.

[17] John Rawls, *Political Liberalism* (New York: Columbia Univ., 1993), 215.

[18] Robert Audi and Nicholas Wolterstorff, *Religion in the Public Square* (New York: Rowman & Littlefield, 1997), 24.

[19] William Lee Miller, *The First Liberty: Religion and the American Public* (New York: Alfred A. Knopf, 1986), 331–353.

[20] Alasdair MacIntyre, *Whose Justice? Which Rationality?* (Notre Dame: Univ. Notre Dame, 1988) 345–346.

[21] Duncan B. Forrester, *Beliefs, Values and Policies: Conviction Politics in a Secular Age* (Oxford: Clarendon, 1989), 95–6.

[22] While it is true that the traditional Orthodox understanding of the limits of the Church does not include the Protestant denominations or even the Roman Catholic Church since the Great Schism in 1054 (while making no final conclusions as to who may be saved), and thus no Orthodox theologian who wants to escape the heretic label can agree fully with this statement, it is also true that in matters of morality, an Orthodox theologian can recognize how traditional Catholics and Protestants, as opposed to those who have made their deal with contemporary liberal culture, behave in ways consonant with what it means to be Christian.

[23] Jeffrey Stout defends liberalism as the right move at the time: "What can be granted without hesitation is that liberal principles were the right ones to adopt when competing religious beliefs and divergent conceptions of the good embroiled Europe in the religious wars." See Stout's *The Flight From Authority: Religion, Morality, and the Quest for Autonomy* (Notre Dame: Univ. Notre Dame, 1981), 241. Perhaps, but as Sandel has questioned, "is it possible that we have learned that lesson too well?" [in "Political Liberalism: Religion and Public Reason." *Religion & Values in Public Life*, vol. 3, no. 4 (Summer, 1995), 8]. In other words, even if liberalism was the right path to take during the religious wars of the Reformation, it is now time to loosen the stranglehold liberalism has had on the airing of religious views in the public realm. I should point out that the liberal interpretation of history is coming under well-deserved and long-overdue scrutiny. William T. Cavanaugh has argued that the European wars of religion in the 16th and 17th centuries were symptoms rather than causes of the emergence of modern nation-states. Thus it is wrong to refer to these wars as "Wars of Religion." Central to Cavanaugh's thesis is the argument that the so-called "Wars of Religion" involved the construction of "private religion," which allowed the state to gain absolute sovereignty in the public realm. See Cavanaugh's "A Fire Strong Enough to Consume the House" in *Modern Theology*, vol. 11, no. 4 (Oct. 1995): 397–424.

---

[24] Michael Howard, *War and the Liberal Conscience* (New Brunswick, N.J.: Rutgers Univ., 1978), 11. Liberals vary on how much stock they place in human moral progress, so it is important to distinguish the belief in the inevitability of human moral progress and the simple hope for such progress. Kant provides a clear example of the former in his essay, "On the Common Saying: 'This may be true in theory but it does not apply in practice,' " in which he is so confident of the human race's moral progress, a progress that he believes is so obvious, that he claims that the burden of proof is on those who would oppose the idea. Kant's political essays are collected in the volume *Political Writings 1784–1797*, Hans Reiss (ed.). (New York: Cambridge Univ., 1970). Rawls's project of political liberalism is a good example of the latter.

[25] Kant is clear about this in his essay, "An Answer to the Question 'What is Enlightenment?' " In the essay, Kant defines enlightenment as "man's emergence from his self-incurred immaturity" (Kant, 54) and exhorts the reader to "Have courage to use your own understanding!" Only laziness and cowardice keeps people from being enlightened. People would rather rely on dogmas and formulas than use their own understanding. All enlightenment requires, then, besides courage, is public freedom to exercise reason (Kant recognizes the importance of obedience in the role of a public office or service). To restrict public reason would be a "crime against human nature, whose original destiny lies precisely in such progress" (Kant, 57). Religious dogma is the prime target of the enlightenment not only because the rulers use religion over their subjects, but also because religious immaturity is "the most pernicious and dishonourable variety of all" (Kant, 59).

[26] Charles Curran, *Politics, Medicine, and Christian Ethics: A Dialogue with Paul Ramsey* (Philadelphia: Fortress, 1973), 77.

[27] Ramsey, *War and the Christian Conscience* (Durham, N.C.: Duke Univ., 1961), 138.

[28] Ramsey, *War and the Christian Conscience*, 151.

[29] Alasdair MacIntyre, "The Wrong Questions to Ask About War," *Hastings Center Report*, 10: 40–41.

[30] Edmund Pincoffs, "Quandry Ethics," in *Revisions*, Stanley Hauerwas and Alasdair MacIntyre (eds.) (Notre Dame: Univ. Notre Dame, 1983), 93.

[31] Stanley Hauerwas, *Dispatches From the Front: Theological Engagements with the Secular* (Durham, NC: Duke Univ., 1994) 138.

Chapter 3

[1] The best recent study of the older holy war tradition and the emergent justifiable war in the Hebrew version of the Old Testament is Susan Niditch, *War in the Hebrew Bible: A Study in the Ethics of Violence* (New York: Oxford Univ., 1993). For useful summaries of the various types of "ban," see especially pp. 28, 35, 77. Eastern Orthodoxy, however, has rejected the possibility of the "holy war" or "crusade" as intrinsically immoral. See Webster, *The Pacifist Option*, 83–87, and, more recently, Webster, "Between Western Crusades and Islamic 'Crescades,' " 149–66.

[2] All quotations from Holy Scripture, unless otherwise indicated, are taken from the Revised Standard Version (RSV) of the Bible.

[3] Niditch, *War in the Hebrew Bible*, 103–104.

[4] Niditch, *War in the Hebrew Bible*, 105.

[5] Darrell Cole, *When God Says War is Right: The Christian's Perspective on When and How to Fight* (Colorado Springs: Waterbrook, 2002), 19.

[6] Webster, *The Pacifist Option*, 133–42.

[7] Ignio Giordani, *The Social Message of Jesus*, Alba I. Zizzamia (trans.) (Boston: Daughters of St. Paul, 1977), 340–41.

[8] Edward A. Ryan, "The Rejection of Military Service by the Early Christians," *Theological Studies* 13 (1952): 4–5.

[9] John T. O'Rourke, "The Military in the NT," *Catholic Biblical Quarterly* 32 (1970): 236. O'Rourke's conclusion exceeds, however, the limitations of the texts, when he adds that "this effort was directed with no view of the military having to abandon their careers."

[10] Homily 21.4. English translation: *A Select Library of Nicene and Post-Nicene Fathers of the Christian Church*, Vol. 12, Philip Schaff (ed.) (1st series; New York: The Christian Literature Company, 1889), 120. Hereafter this collection cited as *NPNF* with volume and page numbers.

[11] Saint Cyril of Alexandria, *Commentary on the Gospel of Saint Luke*, R. Payne Smith (trans.) (n.p.: Studion, 1983), 73.

[12] *Epistle* 138:2.15. ET: *NPNF* 1:486.

[13] Cole, *When God Says War Is Right*, 41.

[14] The secondary literature about St. Augustine's perspectives on the morality of war is quite extensive. The best attempt by a modern ethicist to evaluate his contribution remains the second chapter of Paul Ramsey, *War and the Christian Conscience: How Shall Modern War Be Conducted Justly* (Durham, NC: Duke Univ., 1961). For a briefer analysis also see Webster, "Just War and Holy War: Two Case Studies in Comparative Christian Ethics," 347–50, 364–66. An analysis of St. Augustine's contribution to the Western Christian just war tradition appears below in Chapter 6.

[15] George W. Forell, *History of Christian Ethics*, I (Minneapolis: Augusburg, 1979), 162.

[16] *Contra Faustum* 22:78. ET: *NPNF* 4:303.

[17] *De Civitate Dei* 19:7. Hereafter cited as *DCD*. ET: Augustine, *Concerning the City of God Against the Pagans*, Henry Bettenson (trans.) (Baltimore, MD: Penguin, 1976), 862.

[18] *DCD* 15.4 (ET: 600).

[19] *Epistle* 138. ET: St. Augustine, *Letters*, III, Sr. Wilfrid Parsons (trans.) (New York: Fathers of the Church, Inc., 1951), 46.

[20] Stanley Windass, *Christianity Versus Violence: A Social and Historical Study of War and Christianity* (London: Sheed and Ward, 1964), 24–25.

[21] *Epistle* 138.

[22] *Contra Faustum* 22.74 (*NPNF* 4:301); *DCD* 19.12, 15 (ET: 866, 875).

[23] Richard Shelby Hartigan, "Saint Augustine on War and Killing: The Problem of the Innocent," *Journal of the History of Ideas* 27 (1966): 196–97.

[24] 1 *Clement* 37.3. ET: Cyril C. Richardson (ed. and trans.), *Early Christian Fathers* (New York: Macmillan, 1970), 60, 61.

[25] *Paidagogos* 3.12.91. ET: Clement of Alexandria, *Christ the Educator*, Simon P. Wood (trans.) (New York: Fathers of the Church, Inc., 1954), 268.

[26] *Exhortation to the Heathen* 10:100.2. ET in Alexander Roberts and James Donaldson (eds.), *The Ante-Nicene Fathers*, II (American Reprint of the Edinburgh Edition; Grand Rapids, MI: William B. Eerdmans, 1975 reprint), 200. Hereafter this volume cited as *ANF*. The passage does, however, retain some ambiguity insofar as Clement may have preferred that soldier converts abandon their previous obedience for a higher variety: to the "commander" who is Christ.

[27] *Stromata* 1.24. ET in *ANF* 2:337.

[28] *Stromata* 4.8.61. ET in *ANF* 2:420.

[29] *Paidagogos* 1.12.99 (ET: 87–88).

[30] *Epistle* 106. ET: *NPNF* 8:186.

[31] *The Homilies of Photios, Patriarch of Constantinople*, Cyril Mangos (trans.) (Dumbarton Oaks Studies, no. 3; Cambridge: Harvard Univ., 1955); quote of Theophylactos in Joseph A. Munitz, S.J., "War and Peace Reflected in Some Byzantine Mirrors of Princes," in Timothy S. Miller and John Nesbitt (eds.), *Peace and War in Byzantium: Essays in Honor of George T. Dennis, S.J.* (Washington, D.C.: Catholic Univ., 1995), 53.

[32] ET of the original Syriac text of Aphrahat's *Demonstrations* may be found in *NPNF* 13:352–62. All quotations in the following paragraphs are taken from section 5 of that translation.

[33] Eusebios of Caesarea, *Demonstration of the Gospel* 1.8. ET in *The Proof of the Gospel Being the Demonstratio Evangelica of Eusebius of Caesarea*, Vol. 1, W.J. Ferrar (trans.) (London: S.P.C.K., 1920), 48–50.

[33] These canons (or theological, moral, or administrative guidelines) number several hundred and include those produced by the bishops assembled at the seven Ecumenical Councils of the ancient Church between 325 and 787, in addition to those approved at a subsequent council in the imperial capital of Constantinople in 861 (the so-called First & Second Constantinople Council) and those canons of earlier regional councils and from the writings of various esteemed Church fathers that were ratified at a special council that convened in 690 in Constantinople. The original Greek texts may be found in G.A. Ralles and M. Potles (eds.), *Syntagma Ton Theion kai Ieron Kanonon* ("The Order of the Divine and Holy Canons"), 6 vols. (Athens, 1852). This collection also intersperses among the texts the invaluable commentaries of three highly influential canon lawyers in 12th-century Byzantium: John Zonaras, Alexis Aristenos, and Theodore Balsamon. Also useful is the widely-used ET known as *The Rudder* [*Pedalion* in Greek], which contains valuable interpretations of each canon by St. Nikodemos of the Holy Mountain, an 18th-century Greek Orthodox monk: Agapius and Nicodemus (eds. and comps.), *The Rudder*, D. Cummings (trans.) (Chicago: The Orthodox Christian Educational Society, 1957). The canons that restrict the participation of the clergy in worldly or military affairs are analyzed in detail in Webster, *The Pacifist Option*, 165–81.

[34] The remainder of this section is an abridgement and updating of Alexander F.C. Webster, "The Canonical Validity of Military Service by Orthodox Christians," *Greek Orthodox Theological Review* 23:3 & 4 (Fall/Winter 1978): 271–76.

[35] The ET is Fr. Alexander's own based on the Greek original in Ralles and Potles, *Syntagma* 4.69.

[36] *Rudder*, 762.

[37] St. Maximos the Confessor, *The Four Centuries of Charity*, Polycarp Sherwood (trans.) ("Ancient Christian Writers," 21; Westminster, MD: 1955), 173–74. [The quotation is from part 3, section 4, in the Greek original.]

[38] St Maximos, *Four Centuries* 2.36–37 (ET: 160).

[39] The ET is Fr. Alexander's own based on the Greek original in Ralles and Potles, *Syntagma* 4.131.

[40] Ralles and Potles, *Syntagma* 4.132–133.

[41] *Rudder*, 801.

[42] Ralles and Potles, *Syntagma* 4.131–132.

[43] Ralles and Potles, *Syntagma* 4.132–133.

[44] *Rudder*, 801–802.

[45] Ralles and Potles, *Syntagma* 4.131.

[46] For an excellent analysis of Blastares's dissident interpretation of the canon, see Patrick Viscuso, "Christian Participation in Warfare: A Byzantine View," in Miller and Nesbitt, *Peace and War in Byzantium*, 33–40. The ET of Blastares's comments is Viscuso's. The original Greek texts may be found in Ralles and Potles, *Syntagma* 6.489–490. Another episode wherein St. Basil's "advice" was promulgated literally and boldly occurred during the reign of Emperor Phokas (A.D. 963–969). For more details, see Webster, "Canonical Validity," 276.

Chapter 4

[1] Webster, *The Pacifist Option*, 183–95. The remainder of this section on hagiography is a revision and expansion of portions of Alexander F.C. Webster, "Varieties of Christian Military Saints: From Martyrs Under Caesar to Warrior Princes," *St. Vladimir's Theological Quarterly* 24:1 (1980): 3–35.

[2] A standard legendary version of his *vita* may be found in an ET of a Russian *menologion* (collection of *vitae* arranged by month of celebration): *The Passion and Miracles of the Great Martyr and Victorious Wonderworker Saint George* (Jordanville, NY: Holy Trinity Monastery, 1976), esp. 2–4.

[3] *The Passions and the Miracles of the Great Martyr and Victorious Wonderworker Saint George*, 26.

[4] ET of text in *For the Glory of the Father, Son and Holy Spirit: History of Eastern Orthodox Saints*, Michael James Fochios (trans.) (Baltimore, MD: Phanari), 147–48.

[5] ET of text in Fochios, *For the Glory*, 17–19.

[6] Often depicted in icons in full Roman armor and bearing swords or lances are St. Michael the Archangel as the "captain of the heavenly host" in the war against Satan and his minions (according to Revelation 12:7–9) and protector of Christians (as he was of ancient Israel, according to Daniel 12:1); the Old Testament prophet and military commander, Joshua; and numerous other ancient soldier-martyrs and warrior princes of Russia, Serbia, and Romania.

[7] Quoted in *The Life and Works of Our Holy Father, St. Daniel the Stylite*, 56. ET in *Three Byzantine Saints*, Elizabeth Dawes and Norman H. Baynes (trans.) (Oxford: Basil Blackwell, 1948), 40.

[8] Quoted in *The Life of St. Theodore of Sykeon*, 120. ET in *Three Byzantine Saints*, 169.

[9] Quoted in *Commemoration and Life of Our Blessed Father and Teacher Methodius, Archbishop of Moravia*, 11.5 (unpublished ET by Prof. Igor Sevcenko of Harvard Univ., 21).

[10] ET in Serge A. Zenkovsky (ed. and trans.) *Medieval Russia's Epics, Chronicles, and Tales* (2nd ed.; New York: E.P. Dutton, 1974), 284.

[11] G.P. Fedotov, *The Russian Religious Mind*-Vol. 2: *Collected Works* (Cambridge: Harvard Univ., 1966), 175.

[12] *The Life of the Saint and Most Blessed Martyr, Tsar Lazar, Ruler of the Serbian Land*, in Yoyeslav Yanich and C. Patrick Hankey, *Lives of the Serbian Saints* (London: S.P.C.K., 1921), 74.

[13] Zenkovsky, *Medieval Russia's Epics, Chronicles, and Tales*, 224–25. An ET of the text itself appears in 225–36.

[14] Zenkovsky, *Medieval Russia's Epics, Chronicles, and Tales*, 233.

[15] Quoted in Zenkovsky, *Medieval Russia's Epics, Chronicles, and Tales*, 228.

[16] Zenkovsky, *Medieval Russia's Epics, Chronicles, and Tales*, 227.

[17] Steven Runciman, *The Fall of Constantinople 1453* (Cambridge, UK: Cambridge Univ., 1965), 145

[18] Runciman, *The Fall of Constantinople*, 146.

[19] Runciman, *The Fall of Constantinople*, 147.

[20] Runciman, *The Fall of Constantinople*, 148.

[21] Archbishop Chrysostomos of Etna, *Constantine the Ethnomartyr: Last Emperor of Byzantium* (Monographic Supplement Series, No. 30; Etna, CA: Center for Traditionalist Orthodox Studies, 1998), 29, 31.

[22] For example, the popular *St. Herman Calendar* of the Russian Orthodox Church Outside Russia, based on a Russian *menologion* (i.e., list of saints for each month), commemorates Constantine XI as a saint on May 29. Archbishop Chrysostomos, *Contantine the Ethnomartyr*, 16n32, cites another Russian source dating from 1880: I. Kosolapov, *Mesyatsoslov Pravoslavnoy Katholicheskoy Tserkvy*.

[23] For a useful summary of the various primary sources for the fall of Byzantium and the role of Emperor Constantine XI, see the annotated bibliography in Chedomil Mijatovich, *Constantine Palaeologous, Last Emperor of the Greeks 1448–1453: The Conquest of Constantinople by the Turks* (Chicago: Argonaut, 1892), 231–37. For a critical assessment of the biases and reliability of the major chroniclers, see Archbishop Chrysostomos, *Contantine the Ethnomartyr*, 8–10.

[24] Donald M. Nicol, *The Immortal Emperor: The Life and Legend of Constantine Palaiologos, Last Emperor of the Romans* (Cambridge, UK: Cambridge Univ., 1992), 67.

[25] Quoted in Nicol, *The Immortal Emperor*, 67f.

[26] As reproduced, serendipitously, in the excellent 1997 television documentary by John Romer on The Learning Channel: "Byzantium: The Lost Empire".

[27] As noted above in Chapter 2, it has become commonplace for Orthodox Christians to define "Orthodox" etymologically as a compound of two ancient Greek words: the adjective *orthos* ("correct") and either the noun *doxa* ("glory" or

"worship") or the infinitive *dokein* ("to think")—hence "correct worship" or "correct thinking."

[28] *Service Books of the Orthodox Church*, Vol. 2 (South Canaan, PA: St. Tikhon's Seminary, 1984), 58.

[29] Text in *The Festal Menaion*, Mother Mary and Archimandrite Kallistos Ware (trans.) (London: Faber & Faber, 1977), 133. Hereafter cited as *FM*. The biblical event is narrated in Exodus 17:10–14.

[30] Text in *FM*, 142. The biblical event is narrated in Joshua 10:12–13.

[31] Text in *FM*, 145.

[32] Text in *FM*, 148.

[33] Text in *The Lenten Triodion*, Mother Mary and Archimandrite Kallistos Ware (trans.) (London: Faber & Faber, 1984), 334. Hereafter cited as *LT*.

[34] Text in *LT*, 335.

[35] Text in *LT*, 336.

[36] Text in *FM*, 453–54.

[37] "Akathistos Hymn," in Alexander P. Kazhdan (ed.), *Oxford Dictionary of Byzantium*, Vol. 1 (New York: Oxford Univ., 1991), 44.

[38] Lev Tolstoi, *War and Peace*, Vol. 3, Nathan Haskell Dole (trans.) (New York: Thomas Y. Crowell, 1889), 210, 211.

[39] See the excellent black-and-white photo in Spiro K. Kostof, *The Orthodox Baptistery of Ravenna* (New Haven: Yale Univ., 1965), figure 133.

[40] Text in *The Great Book of Needs (Expanded and Supplemented)*, Vol. 4: *Services of Supplication (Moliebens)* (South Canaan, PA: St. Tikhon's Seminary, 1999), 130–50, esp. 132, 135, 140, 145, 149. This collection is called *Euchologion* in Greek and *Trebnik* in Slavonic.

[41] Texts in Isabel Florence Hapgood (comp. and trans.) *Service Book of the Holy Orthodox-Catholic Apostolic Church* (5th rev. ed.; Englewood Cliffs, NJ: Antiochian Orthodox Christian Archdiocese of New York and All North America, 1975), 439, 449, 450, 452.

[42] Hildo Bos and Jim Forest (eds.), *"For the Peace From Above": An Orthodox Resource Book on War, Peace and Nationalism* (Bialystok, Poland: Syndesmos, the World Fellowship of Orthodox Youth, 1999), 120–21. In the Byzantine era,

according to Kazhdan, *Oxford Dictionary of Byzantium*, 2:1373, "the blessing of standards and weapons" was one of the "prebattle rituals," together with mutual forgiveness, fasting, holy confession, and partaking of the holy mysteries of the Body and Blood of Christ.

[43] ET of text in Dmitrii Pozdneev, *Archbishop Nicholas of Japan: Reminiscences and Characteristics*, Rev. John Bartholomew (trans.) (Unpublished manuscript), excerpted in *Divine Ascent: A Journal of Orthodox Faith* 6 (2000): 46f.

[44] ET of text in *Divine Ascent: A Journal of Orthodox Faith* 6 (2000): 46.

[45] From the February 11, 1904, encyclical. ET of text in *Divine Ascent: A Journal of Orthodox Faith* 6 (2000): 47.

[46] ET of text in Bos and Forest (eds.), *"For the Peace From Above,"* 67.

[47] Nikolai Velimirovich, *The Serbian People as a Servant of God*, Vol. 1: *A Treasury of Serbian Orthodox Spirituality*, Theodore Micka and Steven Scott (trans.) (Grayslake, IL: The Free Serbian Orthodox Diocese of America and Canada, 1988), 36, 37.

[48] Velimirovich, *The Serbian People as a Servant of God*, 40. His disquieting use of the old polemical term "infidel" to refer to Muslim Turks was, unfortunately, not an aberration. St. Nikolai, like many Serbian intellectuals, was quite fond of the dramatic poem by Bishop Petar Petrovic Njegos entitled *The Mountain Wreath*. Published in 1847 by that archbishop of Cetinje, Montenegro, who was simultaneously the head of state in that principality, the poem seems to exult in the forced conversions of Muslims and the bloody massacres of those who resisted in the modern history of the Serbian nation.

[49] Vladimir Soloviev, *War and Christianity from the Russian Point of View: Three Conversations* (London: Constable, 1915), 9.

[50] ET of text in Bos and Forest (eds.), *"For the Peace From Above,"* 66.

[51] ET of texts in Bos and Forest (eds.), *"For the Peace From Above,"* 203, 202.

[52] Aleksandr I. Solzhenitsyn, *Letter to the Soviet Leaders*, Hilary Sternberg (trans.) (New York: Harper and Row, 1975), 46.

[53] Alexander Solzhenitsyn, *et al.*, *From Under the Rubble*, Michael Scammell (trans.) (New York: Bantam, 1975), 142, 112.

[54] Alexander Solzhenitsyn, *August 1914*, Michael Glenny (trans.) (New York: Bantam, 1972), 10–11.

55 Alexander Schmemann, "A Lucid Love," in John B. Dunlop, Richard Haugh, and Alexis Klimoff (eds.), *Aleksandr Solzhenitsyn: Critical Essays and Documentary Materials* (2nd rev. ed.; New York: Collier, 1975), 389.

56 Schmemann, "A Lucid Love," 390.

57 This identity of author and character is suggested in Patricia Blake, "Solzhenitsyn and the Theme of War," in Kathryn Feuer (ed.), *Solzhenitsyn: A Collection of Critical Essays* (Englewood Cliffs, N.J.: Prentice-Hall, 1976), 87.

Chapter 5

1 John Finnis, *Fundamentals of Ethics* (Washington, D.C.: Georgetown Univ., 1983), 109.

2 See, for example, the brilliant section on the moral analysis of an act in St. Thomas Aquinas, *Summa Theologiae*, 1a–2ae.6–17.

3 In light of the evidence presented in this book, the senior author now disavows his own use of the "lesser evil" concept (instead of the "lesser good" approach adopted herein) in several previous works beginning with Webster, "Just War and Holy War: Two Case Studies," 360.

4 Paul Ramsey, *War and the Christian Conscience*, xxviii, made a strong case for the primacy of "the norm of Christian love, and not natural justice only" in the Western just war tradition since St. Augustine. But the textual sources of the Eastern Orthodox justifiable war trajectory, aside from Latin Church fathers such as St. Augustine, focus primarily on justice or "righteousness," the preferred term (*dikaiosyne* in Greek) in the New Testament. The virtues of love (whether *agape* in the New Testament era or *philanthropia* in the patristic era after the second century) and mercy govern those texts which constitute the absolute pacifist trajectory in Eastern Orthodox moral tradition. See, for example, the conclusions on this dichotomy in Webster, *The Pacifist Option*, 256–59, and summarized in Chapter 2 above.

5 George Dragas, "Justice and Peace in the Orthodox Tradition," in Gennadios Limouris (ed.), *Justice, Peace and the Integrity of Creation: Insights From Orthodoxy* (Geneva: WCC Publications, 1990), 42. Hereafter this volume abbreviated as *JPIC*.

6 Vassilios Giultsis, "An Ethical Approach to Justice and Peace," in *JPIC*, 63, 38.

7 "Orthodox Perspectives on Justice and Peace," in *JPIC*, 17–18.

[8] Complete text in *The Orthodox Church* (monthly newspaper of the OCA) 27:5–6 (May-June 1991): 4.

[9] These texts are currently archived on the official OCA website online: http://www.oca.org/pages/ocaadmin/documents/Official/NYCTrag/petitions.pdf. Hard copies of the originals downloaded from the official OCA website are available from the author.

[10] "The Basis of the Church's Social Concept" (Jubilee Bishops' Council of the Russian Orthodox Church, August 13–16, 2000, Moscow), II.2, VIII.2, VIII.4. ET by St. Innocent / Firebird Videos, Audios & Books (available online:

http://www.incommunion.org/resources/orthodox_church_and_society.asp). There is, to be sure, a surprising precedent for this statement. In a little but influential pamphlet published in the middle of the First World War titled, *The Christian Faith in War* [(Reprint edition; Jordanville, N.Y.: Holy Trinity Monastery, 1973), 11, 12], Metropolitan Antony (Khrapovitsky) of Kiev and Galich also conceded, "War is an evil, but in the given case, and in the majority of Russian wars, a lesser evil than declining war and surrendering to the power of the barbarians either our holy homeland or the other Orthodox nations who are our brothers…" That bishop's fundamental moral perspective was, however, uncharacteristically at once utilitarian and parochial: "[I]n such situations the following question must be asked: which choice will produce the least harm and the greatest good for the Orthodox faith and one's native people?"

[11] Stanley S. Harakas, "The Morality of War," in Joseph J. Allen (ed.), *Orthodox Synthesis: The Unity of Theological Thought* (Crestwood, N.Y.: St. Vladimir's Seminary, 1981), 75.

[12] Reprinted in Stanley S. Harakas, *Wholeness of Faith and Life: Orthodox Christian Ethics: Part One—Patristic Ethics* (Brookline, MA: Holy Cross Orthodox, 1999), 154, 157, 155.

[13] Stanley S. Harakas, "Thinking About Peace and War as Orthodox Christians," *Praxis* (Quarterly Journal of the Department of Religious Education, Greek Orthodox Archdiocese of America) 3:1 (January, 2002): 28–29.

[14] Text online: http://www.oca.org/pages/news_printable.asp?ID=335.

[15] Text online: http://www.oca.org/pages/news_printable.asp?ID=340.

The implication that the U.S. was engaged in "terror" in Iraq is particularly troubling and stands in stark contrast to the encyclical of the Greek Orthodox Archdiocese of America on March 20, 2003. Those bishops, taking a cue from

James 4:1 in the New Testament, declare that "war, terrorism, hatred, and intolerance are the tragic results of sin and evil in a suffering world." But this statement does not equate war with sin. Further, the Greek bishops also generously "pray for the courageous men and women who serve in our armed forces and who face uncertain dangers and the threat of death. May God grant them and their families assurance and strength." Text online:

http://www.goarch.org/en/news/NewsDetail.asp?printit=yes&id=865.

[16] Text online on The Orthodox News website:

http://www.orthodoxnews.netfirms.com/Ecumenical%20Patriarchate%20Urges.htm. Two other Orthodox patriarchs appear to agree. In a *Novosti* (Russia) wire story reported on January 21, 2003, Patriarch Alexis II of Moscow is quoted in agreement with Patriarch Ignatius IV of Antioch: "I share the opinion of His Beatitude that war is evil." Text online on The Orthodox News website:

http://www.orthodoxnews.com/doodad.fcgi?tcode=98&story=RIA1222003040510.shtml.

[17] Text still available online on the OPF website:

http://www.incommunion.org/resource/iraq.asp.

[18] In private conversations with the senior author of the present volume, more than a dozen signatories admitted that they either had not read the statement, did not agree with all of its points, or reluctantly affixed their names, since the "Plea" was the only public instrument of ostensibly Orthodox opposition to the prospective war in Iraq.

[19] Frank Schaeffer, "Stripped of Spiritual Comfort," *The Washington Post* (April 6, 2003), B7.

[20] ET of text in George Dennis, S.J. (ed.), *Three Byzantine Military Treatises* (Dumbarton Oaks Texts, no. 9; Washington, D.C.: Dumbarton Oaks, 1985), 21.

[21] However, another major Protestant reformer, Jean Calvin, managed to maintain the classic virtue-based tradition on war and peace. See Chapter 7 below. To be sure, Luther's moral evaluation of the Christian soldier and his work was, however, more complex and difficult to fathom, much of it hinging on a sharp distinction between the office and the personal agent. For example, in his 1520 treatise *On Secular Authority*, Luther tried to dissuade Christians from feeling hypocritical or sinful when taking up the sword in obedience to secular rulers as long as the cause was not subversive of the gospel of Jesus Christ. The command of Christ in Matthew 5:39 ("Resist not evil") Luther applied to self-defense by a Christian, a la St. Augustine; but Luther also insisted that "for others, however, he may and

should seek vengeance, justice, protection and help, and do what he can toward this." ET of text in John Dillenberger (ed.), *Martin Luther: Selections from His Writings* (Garden City, N.Y.: Anchor, 1961), 379. The teleological problem is another one that vexes Luther scholars. The extent to which a good intention renders an otherwise naturally evil act morally acceptable or even imperative is often an open question. In his 1526 essay, *Whether Soldiers, Too, Can be Saved*, Luther referred approvingly to the ancient "virtue, or wisdom, which can and must guide and moderate the sovereignty of law according to cases and which judges the same deed to be good or evil according to the difference of the motives and intentions of the heart." ET in Helmut T. Lehman (general ed.), *Luther's Works*, Vol. 46 (Philadelphia: Muhlenberg, 1967), 102.

[22] Darrell Cole, "Virtuous Warfare and the Just War: A Christian Approach" (Unpublished Ph.D. Dissertation, Univ. Virginia, 2001). See also a briefer presentation of this thesis in Darrell Cole, "Good Wars," *First Things* 116 (October 2001): 27–31.

[23] Cole, "Virtuous Warfare," 104, 112.

[24] Paul Robinson, "The Justification of War in Russian History and Philosophy," in Paul Robinson (ed.), *Just War in Comparative Perspective* (Aldershot, UK: Ashgate, 2003), 71–72.

Chapter 6

[1] A major influential work that exemplifies this sort of thinking is Roland Bainton's *Christian Attitudes to War and Peace: A Historical Survey and Critical Re-evaluation* (New York: Abingdon, 1960).

[2] Two works that cover this material admirably are Louis J. Swift, *The Early Fathers on War and Military Service* (Wilmington: Michael Glazier, 1983) and David G. Hunter's essay "A Decade of Research on Early Christians and Military Service," *Religious Studies Review* 18.2 (April 1992): 87–94.

[3] Translations from St. Ambrose's *On the Duties of the Clergy, On the Christian Faith*, and *On Widows* are by H. De Romenstin in *Nicene and Post-Nicene Fathers of the Christian Church*, vol.10., Philip Schaff (ed.) (New York: Charles Scribner's Sons, 1909).

[4] Saint Ambrose, *Epistles*, Sister Mary Melichior Beyenka (trans.) (New York: Fathers of the Church, 1954).

234

⁵ Neil B. McLynn, *St. Ambrose of Milan: Church and Court in a Christian Capital* (Berkeley: Univ. California, 1994), 329.

⁶ S.L. Greenslade [*Early Latin Theology* (Philadelphia: Westminster, 1956), 227] finds it troubling that St. Ambrose shows an apparent disregard for public order in the affair of the Jewish synagogue, but we must remember that, for St. Ambrose, public order is from God, and hence is conceived as being partly determined by the Church. In short, where the Church is allowed to be attacked or injured, there is no proper maintenance of public order.

⁷ For more on the subject, see, again, David G. Hunter's essay, previously cited.

⁸ Angelo Paredi, *Saint Ambrose: His Life and Times*, M. Joseph Costelloe, S.J., (trans.) (Notre Dame: Univ. Notre Dame, 1964) 318.

⁹ See St. Augustine's *On Free Will* (Book I, Chp.5), and Luther's *Secular Authority: To What Extent It Should Be Obeyed* (Ch. 6).

¹⁰ The modern distinctions between the judicial and military functions of a soldier (or a commander) simply do not apply in antiquity as concretely as they do in modern times. Soldiers in the ancient world fought wars, policed cities, acted as government officials in annexed and conquered lands, and guarded and executed criminals. A Roman soldier, seen with modern eyes, could be a member of the military, a governing official (depending on rank and personal distinction), a policeman, or a civil servant (e.g., prison guards and executioners).

¹¹ In a striking passage in *On Joseph*, St. Ambrose offers Joseph as a sterling example of the virtuous man who "shows compassion when harmed and forgiveness when attacked," who does not retaliate when force is used against him, and whose conduct "we all have learned after the Gospel yet cannot observe"(1.3). That "yet cannot observe" is what leaps out at the reader. Has St. Ambrose anticipated Reinhold Niebuhr by being the first to claim that the rule of the Gospel cannot be followed by a politically responsible people? Or is he merely claiming that our sinful nature hinders us from following the command of Jesus to forswear retaliation for personal injury? The answer is clear from our discussion. The rule of the Gospel—the Christian's duty to follow Jesus—still applies. There is no Niebuhrian split between the Gospel and the politically responsible citizen, because the rule of the Gospel is binding on Christian civilians: do not use force in self-defense. We can say with some confidence, therefore, that the "yet cannot observe" is a reflection of our defective human wills that makes abstinence from self-defense, a basic instinct in fallen human nature, very hard to achieve.

---

[12] St. Augustine makes this quite clear in his discussion on suicide (*City of God* 1.27) where he argues that one cannot commit suicide even if one's motive is the avoidance of a greater sin.

[13] Portions of this section appeared in an earlier form in Darrell Cole's essay, "Thomas Aquinas on Virtuous War," *Journal of Religious Ethics*, vol. 27, no. 1, (Spring 1999), 57–80.

[14] St. Thomas does not deny that Christians ought to love everyone equally, but the "equally" here means that "all men ought to be loved equally insofar as we ought to wish for all of them the same good, viz., eternal life" (*On Charity* Q.8, reply to objection 8).

[15] Stanley Hauerwas, *Dispatches From the Front: Theological Engagements with the Secular* (Durham, N.C.: Duke Univ. 1994), 139–40.

[16] St. Thomas was not unique in emphasizing the importance of virtue for soldiers and commanders. The chivalric tradition emphasized the virtuous nature of the combatants and sought to keep those without proper excellence away from battle. A nice account of the chivalric tradition can be found in James Turner Johnson's *Ideology, Reason, and the Limitation of War: Religious and Secular Conceptions: 1200–1740* (Princeton: Princeton Univ., 1975), 64–75.

[17] None of this is to deny the developmental capacity of a practice. Just as baseball remains baseball after the introduction of the designated batter, so just war remains just war after the criterion of last resort is introduced. Both additions are meant to make the practice a better practice in some way. Whether they succeed or not is a hot topic among sports enthusiasts and just war advocates.

[18] Johnson, *Ideology, Reason*, 8–21.

[19] But, again, lying is the exception here. As lying is a species of injustice, it is forbidden to lie to the enemy or to break a promise given to the enemy (*ST* II-II 40.3).

[20] When St. Thomas discusses sedition, he says that a tyrant can be overthrown if the "consequent disturbance" does not outweigh the good sought. Yet this is not a seditious act properly speaking, for in such cases, it is the tyrant who is seditious (*ST* II-II 42.2). It is probably best not to view such acts as acts of a just war, since just warfare, properly speaking, usually comprises those acts of force that occur between sovereign powers. Nevertheless, the just war model is apt for rebellious conduct insofar as that conduct, when just, is a controlled and orderly plan of forceful action with the overthrow of a tyrant as its goal. We say "controlled and orderly" because we cannot see how the proportion criterion St. Thomas puts on such plans of action

236

can be accommodated any other way. The question of who the "lawful authority" may be in a rebellion is an interesting one, but this is not the place to take it up.

[21] But we should not apply double-effect to soldiers killing soldiers. Hauerwas, for example, uses Paul Ramsey's formulation of double-effect (culled from St. Thomas) to argue that just warriors "can never kill gladly;" moreover, "the Christian soldier should not intend to kill the enemy but rather seek only to incapacitate him so as to prevent him from achieving his purpose." Two things need to be said here. First, St. Thomas's formulation of double-effect is meant to distinguish killing in self-defense from murder. St. Thomas never used double-effect in discussing warfare, but his use of intention in double-effect is ripe for such possibilities. Second, one of those possibilities is to use double-effect to show how *innocent* people may be killed unintentionally in war without doing damage to the justice of that war. It is a mistake by Hauerwas (and Ramsey) to extend the principle of double-effect to show how soldiers should fight *each other* in combat. In short, double-effect is misapplied when it is used to cover soldier-on-soldier fighting. See Stanley Hauerwas, *Dispatches*, 152.

[22] Aristotle says that regret shows that someone has acted in ignorance, and hence involuntarily; an act that accrues no guilt (*Nic. Ethics* 1110b 20–25). The difference here is that the soldier is not acting in ignorance but regrets what he knows is likely to be one of the unintended consequences of his act.

Chapter 7

[1] Here Calvin draws on St. Augustine's *Reply to Faustus the Manichaean*, a very apt work to draw from, for St. Augustine, like Calvin, was arguing against opponents at pains to separate Christian morality from the morality evident in the Old Testament.

[2] Vigen Guroian, *Incarnate Love* (Notre Dame: Univ. Notre Dame, 1989), 22; cf. 47.

[3] Calvin was very aware of the reputation Swiss soldiers had for being good fighters. Swiss mercenaries were a commodity prized by all European armies. But soldiering loses its Christian function and bearing when it becomes a commodity. Calvin realized this and argued against such practices vehemently.

[4] Hans Frei, *The Identity of Jesus Christ: The Hermeneutical Basis of Dogmatic Theology* (Philadelphia: Fortress, 1975), 80.

[5] We are indebted to Gene Outka for these points. See his "Following at a Distance: Ethics and the Identity of Jesus Christ," in *Scriptural Authority and Narrative Interpretation*, Garrett Green (ed.) (Philadelphia: Fortress, 1987), 144–160.

[6] John Howard Yoder, *When War is Unjust: Being Honest in Just War Thinking* (Minneapolis: Augsburg, 1994), 204–5.

Chapter 8

[1] Robin Lovin, *Reinhold Niebuhr and Christian Realism*. (New York: Cambridge Univ., 1994), 4. This section of the present chapter advances the briefer argument presented by Fr. Alexander in Chapter 5 above.

[2] Reinhold Niebuhr, "Walter Rausenbusch in Historical Perspective," *Faith and Politics*, Ronald H. Stone (ed.) (New York: George Braziller, 1968), 33–45.

[3] Reinhold Niebuhr, *Love and Justice: Selections From the Shorter Writings of Reinhold Niebuhr*, D.B. Robertson (ed.) (Louisville: Westminster/John Knox, 1957), 29–39.

[4] Reinhold Niebuhr, "The Problem of a Protestant Social Ethic," *Union Seminary Quarterly Review*, 15.1 (November 1959), 2.

[5] Niebuhr, *Love and Justice*, 46–54.

[6] Reinhold Niebuhr, *Christian Realism and Political Problems* (New York: Charles Scribner's Sons, 1953), 171–172.

[7] Reinhold Niebuhr, *The Nature and Destiny of Man*, 2 vols. (New York: Charles Scribner's Sons, 1943), 2:68–69.

[8] Niebuhr, *Love and Justice*, 25.

[9] Reinhold Niebuhr, *An Interpretation of Christian Ethics* (New York: Harper and Row, 1935), 121.

[10] Niebuhr, *The Nature and Destiny of Man*, 1:283.

[11] This was not Niebuhr's early view. While not an absolute Christian pacifist, the early Niebuhr possessed, to use Harries words, a "positive evaluation of the techniques of non-violent resistance." Richard Harries, "Reinhold Niebuhr's Critique of Pacifism and His Pacifist Critics," *Reinhold Niebuhr and the Issues of Our Time* (Oxford: A.R. Mowbray, 1986), 105.

[12] Niebuhr, *The Nature and Destiny of Man*, 1:284.

[13] John Howard Yoder, *When War is Unjust: Being Honest in Just War Thinking* (Minneapolis: Augsburg, 1984), 82.

[14] Niebuhr, *Love and Justice*, 222.

[15] The question of whether we did especially vicious things in World War II because we were already engaged in self-confessed "dirty hands" practices (a sort of progressive decay in morality) or whether we did not see ourselves as doing anything vicious in going to war, or even in doing things like obliteration and saturation bombing, is, admittedly, an open one. We have two reasons for preferring the former answer. First, the popular reasoning that what we did in Japan with atomic weapons we had already been doing in Germany in the way of obliteration and saturation bombing is a perfect example of "dirty hands" moral regression. The reasoning goes like this: "we were already doing something morally evil when we saturated German cities with bombs, so there is nothing wrong with committing more evil in order to get the job done as quickly as possible." We suggest that noncombatant immunity is an important moral threshold, and once crossed, it is hard to go back, but very easy to keep going forward.

The second reason is that obliteration bombing was, in the words of John Ford, a "regression toward barbarism," a regression that was probably psychologically impossible for the war leaders to deny. For anyone to deny that one intention of obliteration bombing is to harm innocent people is very nearly a psychological impossibility, since the very thrust of the reasoning behind the strategy is to terrorize citizens. We should also note here the disgust that some war leaders expressed over the tactic, exemplified by General George Patton—not exactly the most merciful leader in modern war—who called saturation bombing "barbaric and sadistic." Our war leaders seemed to realize, even if only very vaguely, that they were doing something new and evil. Churchill even openly criticized the Nazis for the practice of saturation bombing in the early days of the war. Ford argued that the war leaders' consciences were not "sufficiently delicate," to trouble them. We suggest that one important reason why their consciences were not "sufficiently delicate" is "dirty hands" moral regression. The overwhelming desire to shorten the war *at any cost* may be evidence of this. Churchill may have been in a desperate situation in the early days of the war, and may have wrestled mightily with his conscience when he first approved of obliteration bombing practices. But Churchill continued to support the practice even when it became obvious that Britain was not in a supreme emergency. He even encouraged the use of the atomic bombs on Japan. Again, we suggest that Churchill crossed a threshold when he approved of obliteration and saturation bombing tactics, a threshold that not only could he not get back over, but one from which he continued to slip further away. Obviously we do not limit such criticisms to Churchill and the British war leaders, for as even Rawls points out, "in the case of Hiroshima many involved in higher reaches of government recognized the questionable character of the bombing *and that limits were being crossed.*" See John Ford, "The Morality of Obliteration Bombing," *War in the Twentieth Century*, Richard B. Miller (ed.) (Louisville: Westminster/John Knox, 1992), 162; George S. Patton, *War As I Knew It*, reprinted edition with a new introduction by Rick Atkinson (New York: Houghton Mifflin, 1995), 288; and John Rawls, *Collected Papers* (Cambridge: Harvard Univ., 1999), 569, (emphasis added).

[16] Timothy Jackson, "Christian Love and Political Violence," *The Love Commandments: Essays in Christian Ethics and Moral Philosophy*, Edmund N. Santurri and William Werpehowski (eds.) (Washington, D.C.: Georgetown Univ, 1992), 191.

[17] This position is scattered throughout Hauerwas's work, but we are thinking especially of the various constructions of the argument found in Hauerwas, *A Community of Character: Toward a Constructive Christian Social Ethic* (Notre Dame: Univ. Notre Dame, 1981). Even here the position is worded differently from essay to essay, but the gist of it is presented on page 10: "The fact that the first task of the church is to be itself is not a rejection of the world or a withdrawal ethic, but a reminder that Christians must serve the world on their own terms; otherwise the world would have no means to know itself as the world." Nevertheless, Hauerwas's strong opposition to the nation-state as a political entity may be construed as a withdrawal from it, and since we live, at present anyway, in a world divided largely among nation-states, it would seem that Hauerwas's position would drive us to withdraw from the world as it is presently constituted.

[18] All citations in the text refer to the paragraph number of the letter.

[19] Though pacifism has been a traditional option in the Roman Catholic Church by way of vocation (for example, certain orders of monks), only recently has pacifist thinking been rearing its head in Roman Catholic social thought. Gordon Zahn has pointed out that "the pacifism that once earned The [Catholic] Worker a reputation for being 'extreme' or even 'heretical' is now accorded almost equal status with the just war theory." Nevertheless, officially at any rate, just war theory still holds primacy of place in the Roman Catholic Church. See Gordon Zahn, "Pacifism and the Just War," in *Catholics and Nuclear War*, Philip J. Murnion (ed.) (New York:

Crossroads, 1983), 120. However, Fr. Alexander Webster shows how Eastern Orthodoxy offers a full-fledged absolute pacifist "trajectory" alongside the more familiar justifiable war "trajectory" in his *The Pacifist Option: The Moral Argument Against War in Eastern Orthodox Theology* (Lanham, MD: International Scholars [imprint of Rowan & Littlefield], 1999).

[20] Finn also chides the bishops for being too selective about their sources. The bishops, for example, maintained that they drew heavily on Vatican II and the Popes of the nuclear age, from Pius XII to John Paul II. But the bishops failed to note that it was Pius XII, the first "nuclear Pope," who "disallowed pacifism as an acceptable choice for Catholic citizens." See James Finn, "Pacifism and Just War: Either or Neither," *Catholics and Nuclear War*, 133.

[21] Donald Kagan, *On the Origins of War and the Preservation of Peace* (New York: Doubleday, 1995), 8.

[22] One need not rely upon an evolutionary theory of religion in order to reconcile the picture of God found in the Old Testament and Jesus Christ. As Hauerwas has argued, it is as if the bishops "admitted that war is seen as a valid mode of God's way with Israel, but fortunately we have the New Testament to balance the emphasis" [See Stanley Hauerwas, *Against the Nations: War and Survival in a Liberal Society* (Notre Dame: Univ. Notre Dame, 1992), 200, nt.7]. Hauerwas believes that the bishops would have done well to read Millard Lind's *Yahweh Is a Warrior: The Theology of Warfare in Ancient Israel* (Scottsdale: Herald, 1980), for then "they would have been able to see a much stronger continuity between Israel and Jesus on the question of war." Perhaps, but perhaps not. Lind's book is entirely unconvincing to one unimpressed with Radical Reformation theology, and it is unlikely that anyone who is not already a pacifist of, say, the Mennonite community, would interpret Scripture the way Lind does. To be sure, Fr. Alexander Webster makes a case for a pacifist "trajectory" in the Old Testament in his book, *The Pacifist Option*, but, unlike Lind, he does not insist on its exclusive moral value. Lind's main argument is that Yahweh fought for his people by miracle and not "by sword and spear" (Lind, 23). For Lind, this means that Israel had to rely upon God rather than human soldiers and weapons for victory in battle. On this account, the human agent is more a prophet than a warrior in the work of war, which is God's work. Such an argument makes it much easier for the pacifist to explain how Jesus's alleged rejection of all violence reflects God's continuing concern to take the burden of violence off the human agent. First, it must be pointed out that Lind relies on what he calls the "Primary History" (Genesis through 2 Kings), thus leaving out those portions of Scripture (especially 1 and 2

241

Chronicles and Ezra-Nehemiah) that pose problems for his thesis. Second, we might ask, given his thesis, why did the Israelites fight at all? And since they did indeed fight, what do we make of this, theologically speaking? Do we view God as a sort of judge who condemns Israel's enemies to death and who sometimes (most of the time, in fact) delivers Israel's enemies over to the Israelites for execution? This view would characterize the role of the human agent as more an executioner/prophet than a soldier, but executioners still execute. Third, Lind is even selective within the "Primary History." To take one notable example, he makes nothing of the story in Joshua (chapter 10) where God holds the sun so that Israel can continue to fight and win. In the end, Lind admits that "Human fighting is freely acknowledged in all the materials [through the book of Joshua]" (Lind, 87). So, Lind must concede that even if downgraded in relevance to how the wars were won, human agents did fight by the command of and approval of God. A much more convincing treatment of warfare in the Old Testament is T.R. Hobbs's *A Time For War: A Study of Warfare in the Old Testament,* (Wilmington: Michael Glazier, 1989), which argues that "there is no evidence to suggest that warfare *per se* is regarded as even a necessary evil," and that *contra* Lind, there is no theology of warfare in the Old Testament, but only "shared and sometimes conflicting attitudes to the social institution of warfare" (Hobbs, 17 and 211). According to Hobbs, Lind's thesis suffers from the "teleological fallacy," which reads back into the past the concerns of the present; in Lind's case, Radical Reformation pacifism. True, the prophets sometimes criticized the wars of the monarchy, but there is no evidence to suggest that the prophets objected to war *per se*, but to warfare as a tool of imperial expansion. The problem here is one of the misuse of power and not of war. Also, to say that Yahweh fought miraculously for Israel is not to condemn all war but to talk about a certain kind of warfare (Hobbs, 213). The story of Gideon, for example, shows us the relative unimportance of human strength and numbers to carry out God's plans for destroying an enemy of Israel, but Gideon and a small number of men did fight and kill. So, the story of Gideon does not frown upon the use of violence but gives us an example of a God-directed "limited, but real use of violence" (Hobbs, 222).

[23] Charles Curran, *Directions in Catholic Social Ethics* (Notre Dame: Univ. Notre Dame, 1985), 79.

[24] For example, see James Childress, *Moral Responsibility in Conflicts: Essays on Nonviolence, War, and Conscience* (Baton Rouge: Louisiana State Univ., 1982), 63–94. The main goal of Childress's essay is to show that the "just war criteria can be illuminated by the language of prima facie obligations and the content of the

particular obligations not to injure or kill others that the justification of war must override" (67).

[25] Curran, *Directions in Catholic Social Ethics*, 179.

[26] G. Scott Davis, *Warcraft and the Fragility of Virtue* (Moscow, Idaho: Univ. Idaho, 1992), 73.

[27] Davis, *Warcraft*, 74.

[28] The bishops repeat the mistake of including the criteria of comparative justice in *The Harvest of Justice*). The bishops argue that the virtue of prudence is required when applying the just war criteria that constitute the just war tradition as a "way of moral reasoning to discern the ethical limits of action" (Sect. I.B). Interestingly, this way of looking at the just war tradition has more in common with Protestant theologian Karl Barth than St. Ambrose, St. Augustine, or St. Thomas, since the justice called for by the bishops is not discernable by prudence but by an admission of the lack of prudence.

[29] National Conference of Catholic Bishops, *The Harvest of Justice is Sown in Peace*, Nov. 17, 1993. The document can be located on the internet at the following address: http://www.ouccb.org.sdwp/harvest.htm. Citations from this document appear in the text.

Chapter 9

[1] Portions of this chapter by Professor Darrell Cole appeared in *Pro Ecclesia* 11:3 (Summer 2002): 313–328.

[2] J.J. Schmitz, *Die Bussbuecher und die Bussdisciplin der Kirche* (Graz, 1958), 528.

[3] David C. Douglas and G.W. Greenaway, *English Historical Documents 1042–1189* (New York: Oxford Univ., 1953), 606.

[4] Bernard Vekamp, "Moral Treatment of Returning Warriors in the Early Middle Ages," *The Journal of Religious Ethics* 16 (Fall 1988): 225.

[5] Marc Bloch, *Feudal Society* (Chicago: Univ. Chicago, 1971), 314–319.

[6] Douglas and Greenway, 785–786.

[7] Verkamp, 239.

[8] Bernard W. Scholz, *Carolingian Chronicles* (Ann Arbor, MI: Univ. Michigan, 1972), 156.

[9] Otto of Freising, *The Deeds of Frederick of Barbarossa* (New York: W.W. Norton, 1966), 205–6.

[10] Frederick H. Russell, *The Just War in the Middle Ages* (Cambridge: Cambridge Univ., 1975), 215–217.

[11] Karl Barth, *Church Dogmatics* III.4 (Edinburgh: T&T Clark LTD, 1961), 456–7.

[12] Oliver O'Donovan, *Resurrection and Moral Order: An Outline for Evangelical Ethics*. Second Edition. (Grand Rapids, MI: William B. Eerdman's, 1994), 175.

[13] Thomas Oden has shown that, even though the marks of the Church are different for Protestants and Catholics, they are in essential agreement, and this because where there is unity, holiness, catholicity, and apostolicity (Catholic), there must also be word, sacrament, and discipline (Protestant). See Oden's *Life in the Spirit: Systematic Theology: Volume Three* (Peabody, MA: Prince), 299.

[14] Calvin rejects any talk of this being an "external ceremony" that Protestants could do without. He maintains that the practice of penance is an "excellent aid for believers today (as it always was) and a profitable admonition" (*Institutes* IV.12.17).

[15] *Operation Enduring Freedom*, Hearing Before the Committee on Armed Services, Second Session, February 7 and July 31, 2002. (Washington, D.C.: U.S. Government Printing Office, 2002), 5.

[16] U.S. Senator Joseph Lieberman (D.-Conn.) has made similar claims. Thus one need not be a political conservative, or even a Republican supporter of President Bush, to hold this view.

[17] When this figure was reported by Professor Darrell Cole in a recent academic conference as a good indication of America's upright intention in the war, a respondent questioned the validity of the conclusion and offered instead the conclusion that President Bush merely wished to fatten the pockets of the munitions manufacturers and cut down on American casualties by using the more expensive precision-guided weapons as opposed to the older, less expensive weapons. This cynical interpretation of the military's preference for precision guided missiles is typical of a radical faction in contemporary academia that nonsensically attributes the worst motives to any political figure deemed out of

step with what that faction would like to see. The idiocy of such notions is apparent. If President Bush simply wished to fatten the pockets of armaments manufacturers while saving American lives at the expense of innocent Iraqis, then he could have ordered the Air Force to fly high altitude area-bombing missions using older style incendiary bombs. This would require roughly 10 times the amount of bombs used (that means 200,000 bombs instead of 20,000—big money in any language), American casualties would have been near nil, and the manufacturers could have really been fattened. It only requires a minute of real thinking to figure this out, but as Ludwig Wittgenstein once famously remarked somewhere, "thinking is hard, and a minute is a long time."

[18] See, for example, the Coalition Provisional Authority Operational Briefing for September 2, 2003. The reader can find it on the internet at the following site:

www.centcom.mil/CentcomNews/Transcripts/20030901.htm.